Beyond Evacuation

From the Himalayas to the Statue of Liberty

A Journey of Pain and Hope

Najib Azad

Beyond Evacuation
From the Himalayas to the Statue of Liberty

First Edition: 2022

ISBN: 9781524318017
ISBN eBook: 9781524328085

© of the text:
   Najib Azad

© Layout, design and production of this edition: 2022 EBL

Dedicated to All Refugees around the world

Table of contents

Author's Note

Less than a year ago, I was the leader of a major progressive party in my country and was the former spokesman for the President of Afghanistan. Five days before the fall of Kabul, my wife, a successful businesswoman who owned a fashion brand, had made a donation of thousands of dollars worth of clothing to internally displaced people (IDPs). When Kabul fell, the Taliban searched for me. They knew I had previously worked for the President of Afghanistan and was still a prominent media presence. I was a marked man, and everything was pointing to my death. Six days after the fall of Kabul, I stood in line at a military base in Qatar trying to get a used T-shirt for my two-year-old son.

I began writing this memoir on napkins and discarded cardboard until I received a laptop from a friend at a refugee camp in Germany. My family has been "settled" in the United States, and my notes are now this book: BEYOND EVACUATION, A Journey of Pain and Hope; From the Himalayas to the Statue of Liberty.

My target audience is anyone who reads the news and wonders about the people of Afghanistan, anyone who has suffered, and wondered what it is to be a refugee. This story will also interest scholars and historians, as I discuss the painful journey of four generations spending all their lives as refugees, starting with my grandfather, my father, me, and now my children.

All of us are travelers in this world. We spend our entire life striving to live a better life, get educated, get closer to God, bring up our children, make our country and so much more. Those of us who are refugees will arrive at an unexpected destination cut off from all our contacts and everything we know. Despite this, we spend our lives never complaining or getting frustrated, exhausted or disappointed because it is totally part of nature. When it comes to forced travel, that which goes totally against human nature, the pain feels as if it should be easily curable, if only you could talk to a doctor rather than simply wave from a distance. Then this travel becomes the bite of food stuck in the throat which you can neither swallow nor take out.

This memoir had to be written especially for those criticizing their governments for evacuating and accepting the Afghan refugees. I still don't know what made them oppose Afghan refugees, but they should know that no place is like home, no one ever leaves their home, family, relatives, friends and soil happily and easily, not like this.

Rare is the country that has upheld against such strong blows, and such troublesome blows, as has Afghanistan since its foundation as a modern, distinct political unit in 1747. Yet the country has managed to survive and to hold sovereignty and territorial integrity, despite wars and invasions, and swings between radical ideological miens, amplifying from the tribalist system to communism and Islamic medievalism. It is the only country in the world that has experienced military occupation or intervention by Great Britain (twice), the Soviet Union in 1980s and the United States of America and its allies (since 2001). It is the only country that has experienced a continuous proxy war of the big powers of the world for five decades. It is a country that has never experienced a stable ideological and political structure and insight for a single term of a ruler in the last century, yet it survives.

Afghanistan is a country with one of the richest and oldest civilizations on the earth. The Silk Road was once the world's intersection of civilization and commerce. The people were once famous for their music, arts, culture, knowledge, and education. This soil gave us scholars like Ibn-e-Sina also known as Avicenna, Abu Nasr Al-Farabi known as Alpharabius, Al-Biruni, Mulana Rumi, Sayed Jamal Ud-din Afghani, Imam Abu Hanifa, Rahman Baba, Khushal Khan Khattak, Ghani Khan and many more across diverse disciplines such as religious, Sufi, literature and science. Their works are taught in world's best universities. Afghanistan is one of the very few territories that had laws before states came to being and the concept of law and norms were introduced. 'Pashtunwali', still highly accepted and practiced as a complete set of laws, has a history of thousands of years. The art and poetry in the territory was there when paper had not yet been introduced to the citizens of the globe. For instance, 'Tapay' is one of the oldest types of folk poetry produced and sung by the local Afghan women thousands of years ago. Unfortunately, the peace and art loving soil was turned into a war zone by the world's powers for their own interests. From the cyclone operation to the war against terrorism was all big powers' game, which has caused four generations to have to continuously take refuge in other countries and live the lives as hostages. Neither the war nor the painful traveling nor necessary refuge was the Afghans' choice or decision.

Look at our tragedy!

We were born in terrible echoes of the AK47
Our childhood was welcomed by landmines' doorstep
We reached the threshold of youth by running after the Russian tanks,
And then the civil war began mocking faces,
The fear made us take self-imposed detention,

The apples began to rot in the gardens,
While the grapes smelled bad
Desolation began to waver in the fields,
The carts instead of fruits started loading bodies in bazaars.

When exterior walls of the house began to rust,
The broken doors were taken away by the reseller's dust,
And hunger began putting the plague's clothes on.

So, our parents stopped thinking,
They preferred to flow in the flow of time before eventually fleeing,
They tightened the migration with daughters' scarves and sons' belts,
To take a journey of pain.

Thus, paths became smoother by licking our purple lives,
But it did not end there,
When we arrived at the new frontiers, dressed as refugees,
The entrances of the cities kept kicking us back,
Yet we kept climbing the fence

And crossing the seas to reach alien homes
Where alienation greeted us like a stepmother,
We spent decades listening to her mockery and valediction.
While the religious monsters kept torturing and smashing the innocent souls back at home.
Yes, the days were deficit,
And the nights were deathly,
Which grew as long as the devil's gut.
There the new rays of the sun brought news one morning,
In the name of peace, iron birds are landing on our soil,
Now it was time to return home,
To keep goodwill in these nests,
With a hope that the nests are built on the top of Hyperion,
Where doves will keep singing and hunters arrows do not reach.
But,
Decades between peace and war,
We kept swinging in the polar night.
The same birds accepted the defeat,
The murmuration has returned,
The crunch has clawed my soil all over again,
And the question is still there,
We are travelers again
We are refugees again
We are still standing where we were,
Peace did not come, hope did not go.

"Beyond Evacuation" was given to me for a review, I read every sentence of the book with drops of tears from my eyes. All I could write for this masterpiece memoir is the poem "Look at our Tragedy."

Sincerely,

Sarwat Najib

The Echoes Of Fear

I believe excessive fatigue and three days of insomnia had made me faint. Indeed, I could not figure out how I really was feeling, but just felt my head in a warm and loving lap. I felt two small and soft, but cold hands trying to massage my forehead. A tear fell onto my eyelid and, opening my eyes I saw the most gorgeous face I had ever seen. The white shining teeth and the shivering red lips were like an innocent deer's blood spread on the Pamir's snow.

A thunderous rocket sound woke up a boy of nine. He had been sleeping under the northern window of the room built to face the rising sun. The screaming had already awoken the parents who ran into the room, not noticing that the broken glass cutting their feet.

The couple decided to flee from Chehalsatoon to Qala-e-Wakeel (airport area) where the civil war was not yet so intense. In September 1992, about an hour before the sun rose, the two doctors with their six children left the home they had built. Chehalsatoon was controlled mostly by Hizb-e-Islami Khalis (Haqqani's militants), it was a freezing cold day, 11-year-old Jana, the eldest daughter was holding five-year-old Pashtana's hand. Three-year-old Mallani was being cuddled by Agha Jan (dad) and the nine-month-old, Naqibullah, by Moraka (mom). I was holding two small bags of emergency food and some clothes, we started walking on a freezing muddy street towards the unpaved eastern road of the western gate of the Chehalsatoon garden.

Haji Ghuasuddin, the fifty plus man with three wives, was the most popular man in the area; he had owned almost the entire land of Chehalsatoon, but he had started selling off pieces, which provided an opportunity for Agha Jan to buy a piece.

Chehalsatoon was a piece of heaven. A child of my age had no clue about dirty politics. I didn't even know that one had to pay for the things he needs at home because Agha Jan had a coupon (food and goods stamp), and I thought we got all we needed and wanted for free.

All I did was get ready for school, go to school, return home, play with friends and do my homework. Haji Malem lived right between our house, the stream and the playground. Since the clean water stream had to pass through his house, I would always save a minute or two by sneaking through the short water tunnel in his house rather than taking the long route to the playground. There was a disused plot of around 20-hectares, and this became the cheering spot for the children of my age. I and many of my friends were noticing Zaki's (Ghaus-ud-din's youngest son from his third wife) clothing and tried to persuade our parents to somehow buy us the same. We did not know that he was the son of the richest man not only in the area but in the capital, and we, the children of the ordinary citizens had to be content with the coupon they were getting every month.

I always believed that life was what, and how, I was living, only natural, of course everyone at my age. At this age, my world didn't extend further than the street by the playground.

That terrible cold and dark morning could not make me lose all my beautiful memories before destiny had to ruin the dreams of millions of children in the country.

"Najib! Please help me!" I heard the scream while playing toop danda.

"What happened to Manjeet?" I asked.

Manjeet had badly injured his left leg; he was trying to catch the ball and fell on the hard ground. The beautiful orange and sometimes purple patka that Manjeet was wearing had always been a mystery for every one of us, we had never seen his hair, and he used to tell us that he never cut his hair out of respect for the perfection of God's creation.

I used to call Manjeet the ghondorai (snowball) because he was so cute with the knot of hair tied and covered by his turban. Manjeet used to come to our home on Thursday nights to watch movies with us, he would teach me basic Hindi. Manjeet and tens of thousands of other Afghan Sikhs and Hindus had been Afghans for hundreds of years, yet they still spoke typical Hindi Punjabi at home. The Afghan Sikhs and Hindus were the richest and most civilized citizens, we did not know what Pashtun, Tajik, Hazara, Sikh, Hindu and Uzbek were until the Mujahideen took over. I later understood that Hameed was a Tajik, Qurban a Hazara, Manjeet a Sikh, Tayep was Uzbek and I a Pashtun. We were all from different tribes and religions, but at that time all we knew was that we were neighbors, classmates and best friends.

The game was not finished yet, so when Aarati, Manjeet's elder sister, called him for lunch, Manjeet insisted that I join them.

Aprana aunty had made delicious aloo matar with tasty kheer as dessert. The beautiful dining room with agarbati's fragrance made the meal even tastier. Aprana aunty was very happy with the new sewing machine she had just bought.

"Najib! Will you please ask your moraka to let me know if she is available tomorrow, so I can bring the machine over, and we can together sew the dresses she was telling me about?" she asked me.

I had eaten enough and had to make it home because I knew that Jana would also be looking for me for our Friday family lunch. The old mud houses with the muddy streets were the most peaceful places to live. The black cloud had taken the transparent atmosphere into its control and made me run home, yet I couldn't reach home dry.

I was just about enter the main entrance gate when a terrifying sound made me sit where I was. I thought the sky had fallen down and taken everything I knew. I couldn't figure out what really happened, though, the country had been witnessing the war for a long time now. I experienced this frightening sound for the first time, I heard screaming from all over the street, I was not able to understand if something very bad had happened inside my home or anywhere close to me. I somehow made it inside the house where most of the windows of our two-story house were shattered. Agha Jan had just got out of the ground floor to make sure all of his children were okay.

"Agha Jan!" I ran towards him and hugged him so tightly. With his merciful hands checked my body within seconds to make sure all was all good, he then kissed me all over my head, face and hands.

I had never thought that I and Manjeet would ever say farewell this way. Moraka never saw Aprana aunty and the machine she was supposed to bring, and I portrayed my last meeting with Manjeet and Aarati on the ice and left it under the boiling sun. The rocket fired by the heirs of Islam had taken three innocent lives, so called infidels. Passing by the playground I acknowledged that I was leaving everything including my home, friends and of course my childhood.

It took us about fifteen minutes to reach to the main bazaar of Chehalsatoon where the main headquarters of Hizb-e-Islami Khalis (Haqqani militants) were patrolling with heavy guns, the militants with long beards and hair, their shalwar above their ankles, were wearing thick jackets, holding AK47s, rocket launchers and standing right in front of two Russian tanks and three jeeps. They stopped us, one with dark black kohled eyes that made him look even scarier, came forward. Agha Jan who was well shaved, with a black thick moustache was wearing a decent brown sweater made by Moraka was of course totally different for them.

The first word that came out of the mouth of the militant was, "hey-infidel, how dare you leave the area without notifying us?"

Agha Jan looked into my hazel eyes and then replied, "Do I really need to ask you where I have to live?"

With this, the angry militant started sneezing, and a harsh voice similar to dog barking silenced us. The next guy with a commando jacket and a pakol on his head was sitting on the tank's gun mantle observing the scenario. He suddenly jumped down, the sound of his feet hitting the ground broke the silence, "are you from Paktia?" he asked.

"Yes, I am," Agha Jan answered.

"Yes, your accent says it though," he said.

A guy with a matchstick in his mouth winked to the angry man and said, "let them go, they are our Paktiawal."

The first guy had already decided to kill us, at least Agha Jan, but we got lucky and were allowed to leave. Agha Jan looked at the chocolate-colored wooden door of a shop, and then kept his eyes on the board installed on the top of the door 'Dr. Mohammed Karim Halim, MD. Child and Medical Specialist', it said. I saw tears in his eyes for the first time in my life. I grabbed and kissed his hand with care, and we started our first immigration journey right from there. We kept walking without speaking a word to each other, we were all hearing our footsteps like a marathon horse running.

Suddenly Agha Jan broke the silence and said, "my children! Forget you have seen anything during the last weeks, a lion always retreats so he can attack with more power, we are just taking retreating. I am sure my children will come back with tons of potential energy and heads full of knowledge so no more children will experience what my children are experiencing today."

We were now closed to Agha Ali Sham's area where the death sun started breathing again, the golden rays crossing the pine trees were giving each of us a therapy heat, nine-month-old Naqiullah, who was sleeping on Moraka's shoulder started moving his angelic body and kept enjoying the little heat he was receiving from the peaks of Chehalsatoon mountains. We kept heading straight to our destiny, yes death is scary, but that fear did not allow any of us to feel tired or exhausted on our journey. Soon we arrived to Khushal Khan lacey (high school) where the same Russian tanks, jeeps and Kamaz trucks welcomed us. A man with Mongolian eyes, wearing a long brown shirt over another shirt, a turban without a shamla on his head, carrying AK47, shouted at us, "Oo – Afghan Khalqi! Kuja zanjeera ela dadee" (Hey Khalqi Pashtun, where have you broken the chain from?")

He stood up from his chair, took a small red and white packet with LM written on it from his pocket, and then a match from another pocket, lit a cigarette and blew the smoke in Agha Jan's face.

He pointed his finger at a small photo stuck on his jeep's windshield and asked, "do you know who this man is?"

"Yes, he is Dustum," Agha Jan answered.

"You Pashtun, you piece of shit, say His Excellency the great General Abdul Rashid Dustum!"

"His Excellency the great General Abdul Rashid Dustum," Agha Jan replied.

He did not try to stop us like the Haqani guys did, but his first look directly hit a SEIKO-5 watch on Agha Jan's wrist. His eyes asked for the silver shiny watch, which Agha Jan loved so much. It was the watch my uncle had brought for my grandpa from Kuwait, and grandpa gave it to his smart doctor son. I understood how hard it was for Agha Jan to give his most beloved watch gifted by his beloved father to a man with no dignity, no respect and a total unworthy, but he had no option if he wanted to save his family. The man took the watch, spat on the glass and the back and cleaned it with his long velvet shirt. He kissed the watch and put it on, but within seconds he took it off, saying if his colleagues came, they would want to share it, and put it back in his pocket. He then took the food and the dried fruit we had and asked us to leave and not look back.

Now our almost dead souls started breathing again and as we moved forward. It was about 9:00 am when we arrived at a place where I had my most beautiful memories. My maternal uncle, Shahwali, used to take me to this beautiful and historic garden every Friday (our weekend). The main gate of the garden opened to the west, giving a view over to the lap of the historic Balahesar mountain. The gate recalled all of my memories, I started hearing my own joyful voices and saw myself running through the gate, trying to play with the most beautiful, cheerful and happiest sparrows, canaries, pigeons and parrots that made the garden the great land of music. There was a marble pathway surrounded by apple, apricot and cherry trees running about 2km right to the upper swimming pole, where Shahwali uncle used to sit and watch me swim. I could still hear the seven-year-old boy's yells for help, 'Mama (maternal uncle) I am drowning,' and he used reply with a smile, 'my little champ is the best swimmer.'

After an hour of swimming, we would visit King Babar's tomb at the right corner of the swimming pool.

It was almost two years since the last time I visited Babar Garden. After swimming we were having lunch by the right wall of Babar's tomb, looking towards Balah-e-sar wall when a scary and massive voice made me drop my slice of Afghan Burger from my hand. Shahwali mama hugged me, and we tried to leave the area. Suddenly a woman of almost forty grabbed him and begged for help. She was crying and saying that her daughter died, and though I was scared and had put my head on Shahwali uncle's shoulder, I saw a girl of about four, her long curly golden hair had changed its color into dark brown. I noticed that she had lost her right hand, and I could clearly see a swimming pole of innocent blood from a beautiful soul. Uncle asked me if I could walk and follow him, I said yes. He picked up the girl and started running, her mother and I were following them. We got to the main gate very soon. Though, her hand was held tight by her mother's maroon scarf, her body was painted with blood, her inert body was laid beside her mother on the back seat, and I made it to the front with Shahwali uncle who drove full speed towards Ibn-e-Sina hospital not too far from the Babar Garden. The baby girl was taken to OPD right away and we left for home. At 7:00pm, we saw on national television (RTA) the news confirms that the rocket was fired by Hezb-e-Islami (Gulbadin Hekmatyar) and that it left ten dead including a four-year-old girl and seventeen injured.

I was feeling everything just like a déjà vu. Agha Jan saying, 'Agar Firdous bar roi zameen ast, hameen ast o hameen ast o hameen ast' (if there is a heaven on the earth, it's right here, right here and right here in 'Kabul'). "Don't worry son, Babar is resting, let him rest, but we are not, and we need to come back, since only dead bodies are silent. We need to move forward," brought me back to where we were.

"Bagh-e Babur is located on the slopes of Kuh-e Sher Darwaza, southwest of the old city of Kabul. The garden is around 11.5 ha large and arranged in fifteen terraces along a central axis in an east west direction. From the top terrace, the visitor has a magnificent vista over the garden and its perimeter wall, across the Kabul River towards the snow-covered mountains.

Created by the founder of the Mughal dynasty, Ziihir ad-Din Muhammad Babur (1483-1530), after his conquest of Kabul in 1504, Bagh-e Babur is one of the earliest surviving Mughal gardens. The king loved gardening and personally designed around ten gardens in the capital Kabul, which are described in Babur-Nama yet the origin of the historical name Baghe-e-Babur, is not known. Babur moved east and conquered northern India in 1526, where he died four years later. Babur always talked about his home country with love, thus he wished to be buried in Kabul, so his widow transferred his body to Bagh-e-Babur in 1544.

As the tomb garden of the founder of the Mughal dynasty, Bagh-e Babur became a place of veneration, a symbol, and hence gained superior importance among Babur's gardens: for nearly 150 years, his heirs, especially Jahangir (ruled 1605-1627) and Shah Jahan (ruled 1627-1658), paid their respects to his burial place and sponsored ambitious building programs to preserve and beautify the garden according to contemporary taste. However, beside the spiritual aspect there was also a political dimension through the representation of imperial presence. Amir Abdur Rahman, also known as the Iron King, implemented more building programs in Bagh-e-Babur. He constructed the haramsrai in the southeast corner and a pavilion in the central axes on the ninth terrace, and landscaped the terraces and water works. His structural interventions changed the 'face' and visual concept of the garden significantly: the formerly lofty tomb was enclosed by a wall; the pavilion blocked the view towards Shah Jahan's Mosque and Babur's tomb from the entrance in the lower west. In 1930, King Nadir Shah removed these structures apart from the pavilion and haramsrai, realigned the tomb terrace on one level, restored its airy appearance, and opened the park with tea houses and restaurants to the general public. He gave the garden a definite "European" touch." (UNESCO, 2019)

It might have taken us ten minutes to reach Pamir Cinema just after Ibn-e-Sina hospital. We were walking by the Kabul River, the same water that at its height with its all power and noise, took many souls with it but was dead this day. It was about two years ago, in last days of Dr. Najib's regime that I went with Moraka to Pol-e-Hassan Khan, the road connecting Chehalsatoon and Dar ul Aman. We were there to get the monthly fuel oil (khak) for the heater and other needs based on Agha Jan's coupon card. On our way back to home, tens of people were surrounding the river bridge in Pol-e-Hassan, where three people in a Russian Volga car had drowned. I could now see the Kabul River with the same level of water, which was of course affected by the environment. I believe that the water feels whether creatures around it are happy.

We were now by the Pamir cinema, Pari in her own world, was making towards Ghazi Stadium Road, while we had to make it left towards Taimur Shah's tomb where we were supposed to get on a bus for Qala-e-Wakeel (airport). Moraka pulled me back both from the Kabul River and my daydream. I had to call Pari and ask her to join us. She was near the bullet ridden power pole right in front of the Pamir Cinema, the second tallest building in the country in those days. I called her name and asked her to wait. The militants heard my words in Pashtu, and they immediately ran towards us, calling to their group that they had caught Pashtuns. The militants of Hezb-e-wahdat (Mazari/Hazaras) surrounded us with roughly twenty-five gunmen, this was when I noticed Agha Jan's eyes lost the last glimmer of hope, because he knew that Hazaras would not let us go alive, they had been killing every single Pashtun they caught. This was the height of their brutality. However, they did not ask us a single question, the only word they said was 'here' or 'there', which meant to kill us on the spot or take us to where they shot people. The answer was 'it's not a safe spot, we are under attack by Jamiat (Rabbani and Massoud), better take them there.' We were then escorted to the other side of the road; the eastern road goes towards Sar-e-Chowk. None of us was talking to each other, only Moraka was looking at me with her wet eyes, she wanted me to hug Naqibullah for the last time since I loved my only brother so much. We were taken to other side of the road where a three-story building had been mostly used for the shops on the ground floor and offices on the first and second floors before they were hit by rockets. Soon we were escorted to a totally burned-out building. We all had kept our eyes on a metal door covered by smoke. From here would we meet the one who would decide how we should be killed: by a direct shot, hanged, pulled by a truck or under a tank? These were the questions that every one of us were thinking. The sound of the metal door opening made us all flinch and a man wearing a cap with a red, black and white arch pattern and a small beard appeared. He kept looking at Agha Jan, after a while he asked if Agha Jan was Dr. Karim, and of course it was him. This was the group commander; he came forward and hugged Agha Jan; he told his guys that he owed Agha Jan his life. He, Commander Mehdi, was once a prisoner in Pol-e-Charkhi prison where there was a hospital and Agha Jan had been head of the hospital. The Commander had serious wounds after a fight with another Hazara commander and was admitted to the hospital where he was well cared for under Agha Jan's supervision. Though, it was purely professional medical ethics Agha Jan had performed, but he gained the reward now. Commander Mehdi, with respect, escorted us to other side of the road, indeed where they had taken us from, and said he was unable to escort us further ahead since the next area was under Jamiat Islami control.

We started walking again, the Shah-e-Do Shamshera mosque on the other side of the Kabul River took my attention, the beautiful amber and white painted Afghan-style mosque was built by King Amanullah Khan and used to be the place of gatherings, joys, tea and storytelling for everyone. The mosque shared the Kabul River railing, while on the opposite side, was the Spinzar Hotel, one of the top three hotels of Kabul in those days, in an area filled with old English style two story shops mostly used for optical services and antiques. The mosque's beauty was doubled by the thousands of pigeons and doves whose cooing used to make the area the most relaxing mental therapy. Feeding those birds was not only fun and joyous but we also believed it to be a sacred duty too. We believed that in return, God would increase one's income. But it wasn't the same mosque anymore, there were no humans around the mosque, which did not surprise me but what surprised me was that no cooing was heard: yes war, terrorism, panic, and fear even made birds take refuge. The only thing we felt was the blood-curdling stillness of surroundings and the dynamitic oxygen we were breathing. I understood for the first time that war doesn't only affect human beings, but every living thing, even the sky was mourning.

The Mosque of the King of Two Swords (name of the mosque is translated), is a two-story yellow building, also situated on the banks of the Kabul River. It was constructed in the 1920s during the reign of Amanullah Khan, whose rule was marked by dramatic political and social change of trying to modernize Afghanistan. The design of this mosque is quite unusual for Islamic religious architecture. Its Italian decorative stucco creates an interesting effect that some describe as 'Afghan Baroque'. Next to Sah-e-Do Shamshira Mosque is the burial place of an Arab commander who fell when the Arabs entered Kabul at the end of the 7th century. He fought heroically with a sword in each hand, and it is his name that is honoured by this mosque today.

I was still living in the joyful mosque that Taimur Shah Durani's tomb before Ayesha Durrani girls' college recalled my memories. The king was sleeping comfortably in his eternal residence while the Balah-e-Sar walls behind his tombs, once the guard towers for his palace, were now being hit by blind rockets. The Kabul River, cold and where once he used to come to drink and swim had changed its colour from blue to red: someone had just been killed by Hazara militants and his bleeding body was thrown to the calm river.

We kept going past the Ayesha Durrani girls' high school towards Pashtunistan roundabout, when suddenly a massive firing exchange began; the fight between Jamiat (Masoud's guys) and Hazaras had begun. The blue painted door and a board above the door of Ayesha Durrani high school had roughly more than two hundred AK47 bullet holes. As soon we reached the corner of the school where it connects the main and old Mandi bazaars, and the opposite bridge connects the south and north side of the Kabul River where the road goes to Pule Kashtee Mosque, we were confused. Agha Jan could not decide which way to go. He needed to find us a taxi or a local bus, and to protect us from the bullets that were making the sky cry for the fate of those living on this soil.

Ayesha Durrani was born into the powerful Barakzai family as the daughter of Ayub Ali Khan Barakzai in late 18th century in Kandahar, Afghanistan. She married Taimur Shah Durrani, Ahmad Shah Durrani's son and the second ruler of the Durrani Empire. Ayesha Durrani soon achieved fame as the most prominent Afghan female poet of the 18th century. She continued composing poetry into the 19th century. She wrote ghazals, qasidas and short lines verses in Pashtu and Arabic-She also wrote Persian literature and about Islamic law. She is known as the founder of the first girls' school in Afghanistan.

In the 19th century, during the rise of Barakzai-ruled Emirate of Afghanistan and the collapse of the Durrani Empire, Ayesha's poetry garnered renewed interest. Her many poems were compiled by an unnamed Afghan scribe into 336-page manuscript in 1882.

'Words by me' by Ayesha Durrani
Violated and repressed by twisted cultural toxicity
And stories misinterpreted to keep her in captivity
Hiding away the power of her enormous life force energy.

Backed by generations of women who did not have the luxury
Born to blaze in the expression of her sacred physicality
She will never, never, never be your property.

O fairy face for God's sake
Show me your complaint
I have been waiting for you for years
Nothing has come from you but anguish

Agha Jan was holding the orange pole of a street food cart, of course there was no street food, no shops and nobody except us, those bullets and the shooters. He took a deep breath and pointed towards the bridge. We all ran towards the bridge and crossed it like racehorses, we had to do it, or a bullet would have left its everlasting sign on any one of our bodies. Right after we crossed the bridge we tried to make it straight to the road between the Ministry of Communication, the tallest Afghan building, and Rabia Balkhi Maternity Hospital.

"Rabia, the daughter of the Emir of Balkh, is born. She is bathed in rose water, adorned in silk, and placed in a carriage made of gold. The day of her birth is celebrated by the people of Balkh, and they rejoice as they pray and read poetry on this auspicious day.

Rabia was raised in the palace where she was taught arts and literature, hunting and archery, until she reached the age of wisdom. She was enchanting, both in her beauty and her words. She moved and spoke with an eloquence that left her with many admirers. When Rabia recited her poetry, it would bewilder the poets and literati of her time. She captured not only the hearts of her mother and father, but the people of Balkh themselves nicknamed her Zain al-Arab (the beauty of the Arabs, or the most beautiful one of the Arabs), Iqbal (the auspicious), and Tela-ye Ka 'b (the gold of Ka 'b). Her youth and charm would illuminate the eyes of her aging father.

One day, a famous astrologer of Balkh named Atrosh tells her that although she is an irradiating star and will set the world aflame with her passion, she may fall into bad luck.

Rabia's mother passed away and this shattered her delicate being. The women of her court took Rabia to places of worship so that her soul was soothed by the sermons and verses of the great scholars and men of wisdom from Balkh.

Meanwhile, her brother Haris was jealous and envious of Rabia's skill, eloquence, and the admiration she received from her father and the people of Balkh. When their father was on his deathbed, he called them both to him. He told Haris that he will be his successor and advised him to be just and generous with all of God's creations, and to ensure that he will look after Rabia.

...

One day as Rabia stood on her balcony overlooking a garden, she caught sight of a beautiful man serving wine to Haris. Baktash, Haris's Turkish slave and a guard of the treasury, captured Rabia's heart. This moment marked the beginning of Rabia's love story and poetry, and her tragic fate.

Rabia would compose love letters to Baktash in verse, longing for him. These would be delivered by her loyal court maiden and friend, Ra 'na. Her love for Baktash was an affliction that no doctor of Balkh was able to cure.

Rabia wrote:
Oh the absent and present one where are you
If you are not with me then where are you
My eyes are illuminated by you
My heart is acquainted by you
Come and invite my eyes and soul
Otherwise take a sword and end my life
Baktash, in response, says:
I don't have the sight to see you
I don't have patience and rest without you
What am I going to do with you now
How can I carry this pain without you
Your hair has pierced my veil
With your face I have fallen in love
From your hair I have become under and over
Because from your hair my life has been destroyed
...

During this time, Asher al-din, the ruler of Kandahar, sought to attack Balkh and subject it to his rule. Haris, who had claimed his throne, was fearful and prepared to stand in opposition. With the consultation of his advisors, he knew that without the help of Baktash, he was unable to defeat his enemy.

Haris told Baktash that if he killed Asher al-din, he would reward him with whatever he desired. On the battlefield Baktash was victorious but at a dear price. As he nearly lost his life, a soldier with a covered face came galloping into the battlefield to save him and win the war. This soldier was none other than Rabia.

Balkh was the epicenter of literary events, but it was unmatched by Bukhara. Amir Nasr, the king of the Samanids, was a lover of poetry and organized grand literary events in Bukhara, the home of the great poet, Rudaki. One day, Haris was invited, together with the newly defeated Asher al-din of Kandahar, the ruler of Herat, and other notables, to witness Rudaki recite his poetry.

When Rudaki recited his poetry, he dazzled his audience. One of his poems was Rabia's, whom he would join in the Balkh court. After he recited her poem, he attributed it to her and said that although Rabia was a sacred woman, she fell in metaphorical love with her slave Baktash, the inspiration behind this poem. When Haris heard this, he coiled like an injured snake. The event came to an end and Haris returned to Balkh, thirsty for the blood of Rabia and Baktash who had brought shame to his name.

Upon his arrival in Balkh, Haris ordered that Rabia be thrown in the hammam and Baktash in a well. In the hammam, she slashed her wrists, and wrote the last few lines of poetry for Baktash in blood on the walls. After days of being in the well, Baktash was saved with the help of Ra 'na. He first took Haris's head and then went to the hammam, only to find Rabia's beautiful lifeless body on the ground covered with her blood and the walls of the hammam adorned with her last love poems for Baktash. He fell to the ground and took his own life next to his beloved.

> One of the poems that are on the wall reads:
> I wish my body was aware of my heart
> I wish my heart was aware of my body
> I wish I could escape from you in peace
> Where can I go regretfully." (Ebtikar, 2021)

Before we cross the road connecting the river and the Rabia Balkhi hospital, a militant with a commando jacket and a pakol on his head appeared from behind the red and white zebra painted traffic cabin at the corner of the bridge. He grabbed my hand, making me scream.

Agha Jan said, "relax, relax, he is a child."

From the photo of Ahmad Shah Massoud on his AK47's we understood who he was. He started interrogating Agha Jan in harsh language. He was forcing Agha Jan to confess that he was Hezb-e-Islami (Gullbudeni). Agha Jan tried to make him accept that he was a medical doctor who belonged to no jihadi groups, which he always called 'ashrar' (the evil doers). Though he could see how little we had from my dad's look, he still checked to see if we had expensive goods in our remaining bags. After this Dustomi militant found what he wanted, he pointed to the bag I was carrying with the bayonet of his AK47. He took the two bags and told us to leave. As we were about to go, he noticed the black loafers, vintage Japanese shoes, that Agha Jan was wearing. Those were the shoes I loved even more than Agha Jan liked them, I used to polish them every night so Agha Jan would put them on the next morning and look like my hero. I started crying and begging him not to take Agha Jan's shoes; he gave me a strong slap on the face. Agha Jan was almost broken but was not able to do anything, all he had was us. He took the shoes off and started walking ahead in his soft, white bare feet. We were now in front of the Rabia Balkhi Maternity Hospital and the hotel (now the Kabul Serena Hotel), when an old man of approximately sixty shouted to us from a 1980 model Carina taxi, 'do you guys want to be killed? Come and get into the car!'

This taxi and its driver were not less than angels for us, he did not even ask our destination but made it towards Pashtunistan roundabout and pushed the gas pedal on the ARG (Presidential

Palace) roads straight towards Aryana Square followed by the airport road.

The roads were totally empty except for us. It might have taken him only fifteen minutes to drop us in front of an almost twenty-year-old thick wooden gate, where Adey Moraka, my grandma (my mother's mom) was waiting anxiously, though she did not know we were coming. As the popular saying goes, "a mother's heart feels everything." We were warmly welcomed. Agha Jan did not have a single penny in his pocket, all he had was already taken by small colonial governments on our way from Chehalsatoon, so Adey Moraka brought some cash from the house and gave it to the taxi driver, he refused to take a single penny, instead asking her to pray for him and our countrymen.

The Chickpea, AK47 And The Jeep

We started living with our grandma's family including her two sons Shahwali and Shir Mohammad, their wives, a son and a daughter of nine months. Although we were provided housing and every support, Agha Jan, as an independent and self-sufficient man asked my uncles to find us a reasonable house nearby, since he did not want his family to be a burden. We moved to a nearby apartment on third floor of Block 12. The buildings were called Hawaee Blocks. They were actually given to pilots and air force officers by the then former government. We rented an apartment with two bedrooms, a kitchen and a bathroom, which was good enough for us. Our block was hardly 100 meters from my grandma's house, which had five shops in the front. The first two were rented to a pharmacy, the third one was for a doctor's clinic, the fourth one was a grocery store and the last one was a nanwaee (bakery). Mukhtar, who owned the Darwesh Pharmacy, offered my dad the opportunity to practice in his pharmacy as a medical doctor. Since the clinic was already empty, Agha Jan started practicing there. Although, the civil war was at its height, the Ministry of Education, led by the people from previous regime, kept all schools open, so Jana, Pari and I were admitted to the nearby middle school called Maktab Mutawestah Qala e Wakeel. Although, Chehalsatoon was only one hour away by taxi, the civil war had made it almost impossible for residents of one area to go to another, so our school transfer certificates were not brought. Instead, we took a merit examination and I made it one class ahead of my class from my previous school. I started going to grade five. Our class was on the second floor of the eastern corner of the school building. There were about thirty students in our class, and soon I made new and good friends. Our classroom was attached to the mosque where I had to go early in the morning for Islamic studies with Imam Masjid, a very soft and intellectual cleric. The mosque had the capacity for about 200 people to pray inside at one time. We children used to see our faces in the small pieces of mirrors installed on the edges of the Mehrab as decoration pieces. The soft, red carpet and the beautiful voice of the Haji Imam Saheb sometime gave us the mental therapy and we would fall asleep. This sleep would always be broken by the voice of Imam Sahib, a voice full of love and care. Hajib Imam Sahib with his pure white beard, a stick in his hands, dark grey turban on his head, a Mezari overcoat also known as Karzai coat now, with all seven colors and Russian shoes (Kalocha) was the most graceful old man in the area. He was the only Imam Masjib who never took a penny from anyone to teach them Qur'an, Hadith, Fiqh or for the Imamat.

One Friday, my grandma held Khatam-ul-Qur'an (Reciting the whole Qur'an) and of course Haji Imam Sahib with his students were invited to do the Khatam. Grandma's house was built in an old Italian architectural design; there was one main gate opening onto south-east street, it also had a garage for two cars, one dining room, two bedrooms and a kitchen to the left of the garage, and one dining room, two bedrooms and kitchen on the right side of the garage. Two blackberry trees, almost sixty years old, stood in front of each entrance. The external walls were built with golden rocks brought from Reeshkhur (an area connecting Kabul and Logar Provinces). The story goes that these rocks would turn to gold when touched by a human hand with love and care.

The large front terrace was made of white Chishti Onyx and Marble with dark red lines running through it, making it look like the dark red juice of Kandahari pomegranates flowing down the white neck of ones' beloved. The six bedrooms were connected by long hallways, making the villa a private house for a Mughal King. In the garden, of course between the garage and the villa, was an area that was fantastically farmed with tomatoes, green chili, okra and onions. This area was a great environment for the best green house. The three cherry trees on the eastern and two on the southern front provided shading to the terrace for the beautiful evening poetry, chess and chit chat.

The single gate from the one-story market was used to go directly to the back road and market that provided all our daily needs.

Haji Imam Sahib, sitting on the maroon mattresses in the upper portion of the dining room located left side the garage was making the house shiver with his awesome voice while reciting the Qur'an for the Khatam. After the Khatam-ul-Qur'an, we had to serve lunch to him, his fellows and invited guests. According to the Afghan culture, the guests and elders of the family get their hands washed in a mobile basin called dastshoi. This is often brought by the younger of the family, the guests and elders of the family wash their hands in water poured by the basin carrier.

It was the first time, I had ever seen such an aged and decent man refusing to wash his hands in this way, "I have hands, I eat for myself with these hands. Why would I need someone, especially a kid, to pour water for me?" Imam Sahib said.

After the Khatam-ul-Qur'an and lunch was finished, everyone, including me, went to the mosque for the Jummah prayers. After we were done with the Jummah prayers, Haji Imam Sahib explained and interpreted some Ayas of Surah-e-Baqara to the audience, which generally took about one hour. Barely thirty minutes after we left the mosque, we heard firing and people screaming. My grandma and Shahwali mama rushed out of the garage gate and onto the street. An innocent, handsome decent old face with his last smile on his face was badly bleeding, his white Kotsuton clothes were leaving the red print of the Karbala ground[1], people surrounding him were in deep shock. My grandma, who had suffered a lot in her life, was a strong woman. She shouted at everyone to get back to normal. Haji Imam Sahib had been brutely killed; the innocent soul was telling the story of how he left the mosque after us, saw three Panjeshiri militants sexually harassing an eight-year-old girl, and when he tried to stop them, in response the AK47 magazine was emptied into him.

Although, the whole country, in particular the capital Kabul, had been mourning for two years by then, that night, the sky started crying for Haji Imam Sahib. It doesn't normally rain in September in Kabul, but I remember that it rained the whole night. I was in a deep shock, recalling the great and kind words of the Imam Sahib just hours before. Yet, the next morning sun rose as usual, and people started their daily chores as normal. I too went to school, studied and played with my mates during break. At 12:00 pm, when the school day ended, all the students, as usual, formed

---

[1]   The Battle of Karbala (10 October 680 CE) was a small-scaled military engagement, fought near the river Euphrates, in modern-day Iraq, which saw the massacre of heavily outnumbered Alid troops under the command of Hussain ibn Ali (l. 626-680 CE and also given as Hussayn, the great son of Prophet Mohammed P.B.U and the son of Ali, the first cousin and son-in-law of Prophet Mohammed P.B.U and fourth Muslim Caliph) by the army of the Umayyad Dynasty, ruled by Yazid (661-750 CE). Yazid was son of Mu'awiya, the fifth Muslim Caliph and the founder of Umayyad Caliphate. Though the battle was one-sided and ended with a decisive Umayyad victory, the fallen soldiers of the Hussainid faction, including Hussain himself have ever since been venerated as martyrs of Islam. This battle also became one of the core reasons for opposition against the Umayyads, who were overthrown around 70 years later in a bloody rebellion. Even to this day, the battle remains one of the central defining elements of Islamic heritage and is commemorated annually through the Ashura festival by Muslims especially by Shia Muslims.

a mob at the school gate. A sudden blast made everyone run in all directions. Zakeria, the seven-year-old brother of my classmate had picked up a pen that had explosive installed inside. He lost four fingers on his right hand and his right eye. Zakeria's old blue school shirt changed its color to deep blood red. Shah Mahmood, his ten-year-old brother was crying for help, he had his younger brother in his lap, screaming towards the sky and asking God, 'Why...why...?'

Though the teachers and other staff were badly scared, they were all outside and helping us to reach home as soon as possible. Our home was about five-minute walk from school, I kept running, but as usual forgot to go to my home but entered my grandma's house. As soon as I pushed on the heavy thick wooden gate, a massive blast sounded, smoke and the gas took my senses away, only a long-lasting buzz kept my ears occupied. I was sitting in the garage and all I was thinking was that what if I had lost my uncles, my grandma, and my sister Jana who was generally with our grandma all the time? My voice was crushed inside me, and I could not even cry.

A sudden voice brought my senses back "Adey Morakey, Adey Morakey!!! It was Moraka, she had reached there in seconds, and then she started screaming, "it's the end of school, where is my son? Where is my soul?"

This voice of Moraka gave me another life, I surprisingly shouted "Morakey I am here, what happened?" Moraka, with dust on her face hugged me, she was crying and kissing me, checking my arms and legs if I was all okay. Soon we came to know that a rocket had landed on the lawn, most of the windows were broken but with the grace of God no one was injured.

This was how we were living every day.

It was never a single grieving moment that one would think had passed, but we were expecting one after another awful moment. As usual, Agha Jan was seeing his patients when a fat local Panjsheri militant commander entered the clinic. He was thoroughly seen by Agha Jan and prescribed the medicines which he could buy from anywhere, but he went to the next pharmacy which belonged to Mukhtar. Agha Jan was seeing another patient when that same commander, this time with two men, reentered the clinic and started beating Agha Jan with their guns. They kept abusing Agha Jan and asking why he did not write a note asking the pharmacy not to take any money from them, how dare the pharmacy ask a Mujahid for money. They pushed Agha Jan into their jeep, I ran, crying, after the jeep. They kicked Agha Jan from the moving jeep, he was bleeding and I tried to clean his bleeding nose with my shirt.

Life was becoming tougher every day. The country, especially the capital Kabul, became totally upside down: rockets and bullets that are very expensive and hard to find in other societies were plentiful and available for everyone, while food, the top priority and available for everyone in other countries, was expensive and unavailable for Afghans. Although Agha Jan was trying all his best to make money for his family, we were not able to buy some very basic food stuffs including bread and cooking oil. It was decided that I needed to work too. The Russian stroller Agha Jan had bought for Naqibullah became my mobile shop; we removed the upper portion and installed a wooden pallet over the wheels. Moraka had to boil peas, beans and baked popcorn during my school time, and as soon I got back from school, my mobile shop would be waiting for me. Most days I wouldn't have lunch but would take my trolly and visit every street calling, 'Shor Nakhud O Shor Meshing garm dagh,' (buy the hot peas) all the way to Macroryan Market, which was about five kilometers from our home. Since I was only nine, sometimes the teenagers and adults would take the peas and popcorn without payment. They would beat me up when I asked them to pay. Moraka used to collect all my weekly income and then buy the goods for the next week so she could boil and bake, and I could sell. But this time, since I had made good money during the month, she could save most of the money, and buy lentils at retail price from the main market. I had made about two million Afghanis, the equivalent of $40 USD in those days, which was good enough for our one month in our kitchen. Not only us but most people used to convert AFN into PKR, the AFN 2 million was equivalent to PKR 2000. Moraka had rolled up the money in a dastmal, or piece of cloth. Naqibullah, who had started crawling by this point, climbed up the balcony's concrete railing, and threw the dastmal down. It was almost three hours before Moraka found out that the money, made by sweat and tears, had gone. It is always said that the bad time is forgotten once your good time comes, but I won't ever be able to forget that night, the night our home witnessed the most grief. It wasn't only Moraka and us, but also the walls, doors, windows and every part of the home was crying with us. It wasn't only PKR 2000, but life.

The world was too big in those days; one had to travel days and nights to see loved ones living just few hundred miles away. No one in my country could ever have imagined today's fast communication technology.

Kabul was completely on fire. As Akhtar ul Rahman, a Pakistani Army General, said "Kabul must burn." Deaths and blood had become the daily routine, there wasn't a day that I personally did not see at least up to five killed or injured. One day, I believe around 4:00 pm, I was biking my Russian bicycle, the type that you pedal backwards to brake, and Shafa, Shahwali mama's seventeen-year-old brother-in-law, was riding his grey bicycle with the beautiful seven color diming lights in the wheels that were grabbing every boy's attention. We were supposed to make a round and buy notebooks, but he suddenly lost control and hit the fence installed around a small but beautifully managed planting garden in front of block 10, just 100 meters from our block. I jumped from my bicycle and ran towards him, I thought perhaps he had a problem with his blood pressure or was dizzy. As soon I tried to lift his head from the dust, he pointed at his belly so I thought he might have had an appendix attack, but as soon I touched his belly, I felt my hand in hot liquid and I realized that he had been shot. You could not know when and from what direction those tens of hundreds of stray bullets would come every day. I started yelling for help, and he was soon taken to Agha Jan's clinic where there were not enough tools, yet he with no tools and not a general surgeon, performed open surgery and took the bullet out from his intestine.

The next sunny morning, I went to enjoy the sun downstairs before calling 'Shor Nakuhd garm dagh'. I saw many of the community residents had brought their furniture out to sell. They were talking about migrating to Pakistan so they needed some cash that could help pay for their transportation. I was thinking what if everyone leaves and we remain here? We don't even have anything to sell and make it to Pakistan. I had always been hearing of Pakistan as the beast behind all the Afghan misfortunes. I was busy asking and answering myself but wasn't able to convince myself one way or other when two middle aged men in white Shalwar Kameez with ochre-colored turbans on their heads and black thick soled Peshawri Chapli on their feet started talking to the young guys sitting in front of the grocery shop. I noticed that they didn't understand each other's language, so I went to help,

"He speaks Pashtu," a young boy there pointed to me.

"Young man! Do you know Dr. Mohammed Karim Halim? He is from Paktia?" they asked.

"Yes, I know him, why are you asking for him?" I asked. I had to be careful, since they looked like those Mujahedeen guys, and I did not want to give them any information, unless I needed to.

"He is my brother; he has a son of your age named Najibullah. My name is Yar gul and this gentleman's name is Haji Mohammed Gul, he is his brother-in-law and we have come from Pakistan to take my brother and his family with us."

I had gotten all the answers to my earlier questions. My eyes filled with tears, and I hugged him telling them that I was Najibullah. Yar Gul kaka gave me a big bear hug, kissed me and thanked God.

He could not wait to see his brother, "what we are waiting here for, take me to my beloved brother."

They started following me and we all were walking fast, I could not figure out if I flew because within seconds, I was at the doorstep. I was sure that we wouldn't be killed now, God had made his way to save our lives.

"Agha Jana, Yar Gul kaka is here," I gave him the best ever news of those years.

I was so surprised. The two brothers gave each other big bear hugs and cried for almost fifteen minutes. They were not only meeting after fifteen years, but a brother had come to save another brother and his family's life. They did not even take enough rest and said we had to leave the next morning. Although Agha Jan and Moraka were not ready to leave within the next few hours, they had no other option, the civil war was raging. Mujahedeen were taking the ex-government high officials out of their homes and killing them on the spot. Meanwhile, we did not even have enough to eat; poverty and hunger would have killed us if not bullets. We picked our stuff, locked it in a tiny storeroom and handed the apartment over to Adey Moraka.

The Tractor

One's own soil is the most precious thing one leaves, but at my age at that time, it was my all-time love and best buddy, my Ring-Necked parakeet parrot who had lived with me for about one and a half years that I was devastated to leave. My talkative parakeet was very vocal and excellent at sharing his emotions through his beautiful sounds. He was my only motivation, we kept talking all night before we left the next morning. He understood that I was going to leave him, though, I wanted to take him with me, but Yar Gul Kaka told me that it would be a risk to the parakeet's life to take him with us, so better to leave him to Adey Moraka, which I did.

We left at 4:00 am, before the morning Adhan prayers. There were no taxis—the taxi owners were scared of the Mujahedeen since they used to take peoples' vehicles and kill them—so we started walking towards Kabul-Jalalabad Road. We kept walking under the fire exchanged between Hezb-e-Islami on Maranjan Hill and Jamiat-e-Islami on the other side of the old Macroryan. Since there was no electricity in the town, we could see the lightning bullets flying over us clearly, I still remember the 'shooo' sounds of the bullets. Many other families joined us at the Banaee T- junction, they were also on their way to Pakistan. After around ninety minutes, we reached Pul-e-Charkhi bazaar, where we were expecting to find transportation to Torkham (Durand Line Gate) or at least to Jalalabad, but we found no buses or other vehicle at all. The area was completely under Hezb-e-Islami control; they had started on road interrogation. We were lucky and were permitted to proceed since Yar Gul and Haji Mohammed Gul Kakas looked similar, but others were stopped. Our next good luck charm started shining when a Russian-made tractor with a trolly came by accepting passengers who could pay. It was an American Boeing Airline's business class for us at that moment. It was the first time I had ever seen a tractor and I did not know how it would make it on the road, but I remember the sound was terrible and so annoying, I still don't know how much Yar Gul Kaka paid but I am sure it was quite good money since no negotiation took place.

The sun's dying orange rays were kissing the peak of the Mahipar's tall mountains. The dark rocks of the mountains were also reciting the stories of those beasts in human guise who had eaten the flesh of innocent souls for decades, every rock had hundreds of untold stories to tell. The aggressive water of the Kabul River was hitting the rocks with all its power, the freezing morning breeze started leaving its punch on our faces; the angry Kabul River was asking us to whom we were leaving it?

The tractor made its way through the lap of the arrogant mountain on the right and the competitive river on the left. Naqibullah was still the luckiest one among us, he did not know what was happening and what had to come next, this most beautiful and innocent soul was taking his nap like a prince sleeping in his royal bed, I must say that no beauty is needed when a heart falls in love and no bed is needed when one falls asleep. The tractor had awakened me from the world of upsetting questions and answers by entering into the Mahipar tunnel, a sudden solar eclipse scenario scared me since I had never seen a tunnel before: of course, a tunnel with no light would look like a cave going to hell to a child who had never seen a tunnel. Passing the tunnel, Agha Jan asked me not to look down, we were hundreds of meters above the river and the road was circling down. Agha Jan wanted us not to get dizzy but yes it was a beautiful, landscaped Hollywood scene. It did not take too long to leave the asphalt road behind. Now our organs started fighting; it wasn't only the dust that began entering our lungs but tractor's ride itself and rocky road. We had all had a fair breakfast and Moraka had already taken an antiemetic drug, yet she was sure she was going to vomit.

We were unable to clearly see and hear each other because of the dust and noise the tractor was making. I thanked God for a sudden stop, which I assumed to be our final destination in Pakistan. I was wrong, it was three Mujahedeen, and we were in the small desert of Sorubi district of Kabul province. The militants belonged to Hizb-e-Islami, and I later found out that the same checkpoint was famous for keeping a human dog, though I didn't see him myself, but the stories about a man who used to bite people were famous. The militants, after talking to Yar Gul and Haji Mohammed Gul let us to go, of course they had taken good amount of money from them.

About an hour driving, we reached Sorubi Bazaar, where we stopped for a while to eat the lunch Moraka had cooked the previous night. The bazaar had about fifteen-twenty local shops on both sides of the road. There was a restaurant as well, a boy of almost my age, wearing a white Peshawri cap, was busy keeping the coal fire lit so the seekh-kabab could be baked and served to customers sitting on the wooden terrace made at the front of the restaurant. I can still feel the pleasant, sweet smell of that seekh kabab. The bazaar was quite calm, there were no clashes, no firing and no killing since it was completely under Hizb-e-Isami control and no other Jehadi group was there to fight with them. Once we'd had our meal, Haji Mohammed Gul Kaka took the thermos to buy some tea from the restaurant. In Surkhaken, along the Kabul-Jalalabad Road, a Russian made tank of the previous government had become a plaything for the kids of the area, they were playing hide and seek and acting just like in the film, 'The Beast'. The Kabul-Jalalabad highway was like a 2021 model Mercedes compared to driving on a rocky mountain's glacier. Despite the atmosphere of smoke, bullets, terror and fear, the Nangarhar University took my attention as we entered the city. The almost fifty-year-old tall pine trees looked as if they were kissing the clouds, and the beautiful white buildings behind those trees brought to mind a bride trying to hide her face with her green wedding veil. The sun was about to set, its yellow rays clearly saying that it can't help either the country or its population. Did we have to stay the night in Jalalabad or keep on moving towards Torkham? We were confused, Moraka's situation was of a fish lying on boiling hot desert sand, simply searching for moisture. Looking at Moraka's situation we knew we should stay the night in Jalalabad but thinking of the ongoing civil war in the country we could not take the risk, so we decided to keep moving forward.

It was about 6:00 in the morning when we arrived near the Torkham Gate. As soon as the tractor found a place to park, Yar Gul Kaka jumped up but asked us not to move. There was a flood of people pushing each other towards the gate; we were about five kilometers from the gate, women were screaming for their separated kids, an old man was yelling for help, but people could not help to pick him up, he was crying while the flood of people were stepping on him, this fallen old man, there wasn't an inch space between the people for anyone to stop and pick him up. This unbelievable situation scared us; we were not even able to get off the trolly. Yar Gul Kaka took a pack out of his pocket, lit a cigarette and started thinking how to manage in a crowd of thousands of people all rushing towards an unknown refugee future. He asked Haji Mohammed Gul to take care of us and he left to facilitate the next step of our journey. About three hours later a six-foot-tall man wearing a short brown waistcoat with three pockets on each side tightened at his waist with a maroon piece of cloth and a black cotton turban on his head was standing next to Yar Gul Kaka. He was rolling his long white mustache and looking at the seven bags on the trolley.

"Hurry up we don't have enough time!"

"What you are looking at, these are all you have to take to the other side," Yar Gul Kaka told him.

"PKR 2000," he said.

Yar Gull gave him an angry look, and told him "Are you a fool or you are trying to make me fool? I have told you that there are seven bags, and I won't pay you a penny more than PKR 800? Are you good with PKR 800 or shall I call the other guy?"

The guy who used to traffic human and goods on an illegal route agreed and called his two young helpers to take the luggage to his horses. He could have taken us too, but the route was not protected from the mines the Mujahideen and Pakistani militias had placed. He had already lost a horse the week before.

Yar Gul Kaka wanted to go with the luggage but he knew he couldn't leave Haji Mohammed Gul to take us through thousands of people, so he sent Haji Mohammed Gul with the luggage and stayed with us, waiting for the right time. Since the tractor was already stuck in the rush, the driver was in no hurry. Yar Gul Kaka once again left to see if he could find some way to take us to the gate through thousands of people. After around an hour, a middle-aged man with a fair brown beard, green eyes, a thin European nose, wearing black Peshawari Chaplis and carrying an AK47 on his shoulder, began shouting at people to get away.

"Komandan Sahib, Mr. Commander, please help me!" was the sentence said by everyone.

Mr. Commander was there to escort us to the gate, he was also a Hizb-e-Islami militant, Yar Gul Kaka had introduced himself as one of the Hezbi Mujahid, while also paying him. Yet, we were badly scared to cross thousands of people, it was a game to win only, there was not a chance to lose, since losing meant losing life. Mallani was carried by Yar Gul Kaka, Agha Jan had Pashtana on his shoulders, and I was enough strong to pick up Naqibullah. Moraka was holding Jana's and Pari's hands, and we all were following Komandan Sahib. It must have taken us about two to three hours to make it to the Torkham main gate right on the Durand line.

The big steel gate painted with the Pakistani flag was locked but there was a small door that was strongly controlled by the Pakistani militias, police and army. This was used to let selected people enter. There were such loud noises we couldn't hear even each other's words. Komandan tried to talk to the Pakistani forces, but the result was PKR 10,000, which was a big money in the 90s, especially for people like us and for every refugee. All those tens of thousands trying to immigrate to Pakistan had burned their chances behind, they could have only saved their lives, but they had no treasury with them. This flood of poor but totally dependent people had become cash cows for the Pakistani forces. Yar Gul Kaka started bargaining with the forces, and finally paid them PKR 4500, a saving of only PKR 2,000, one that could hardly take us to Haripur Hazara division via Peshawar.

The mutually agreed amount was for the family only, while Yar Gul Kaka was excluded, he said "don't worry, you guys cross the gate, I will make it for myself somehow."

We still had to wait for about one more hour, until the wave of mercy would shake the leaves of their hearts and open the gate for us. Finally, they opened the gate and provided a room that one person could hardly go through, the gate was tightened with a thick chain to keep it to a limited space, Moraka, Jana and Pari made it first, I holding Naqibullah and Mallani were after them, and Agha Jan with Pashtana were the last ones. As soon I tried to enter right after Moraka, I heard a pained cry from Naqibullah, he was badly hit with a hard stick on his head by a Pakistani police officer and the blood was all over him as well as my face.

His painful scream just brought my all senses back. I suddenly shouted Barlas Khan's name, I wanted the same warm but small lap, the two soft but cold hands, the cheetah shaped shiny green eyes, the dried red lips pulling me towards him.

The Tragedy

Wadan Khan kissed my forehead and said, "Baba (Dad)! Barlas Khan is all well, he is sleeping in Mor's (mom's) lap, you have gone to faint, thanks God you are okay, my hero baba."

I then realized that we were inside Camp Sullivan at the North gate of Hamid Karzai International Airport (HKIA), I pulled out my mobile phone from my pocket to see the time; it was 3:21am of August 21, 2021. I tried to move but could not. I understood that a spasm had completely taken my back in its control since I was wearing only a thin cotton shirt in 7° Celsius and had slept on a hard wooden pallet. I told Wadan Khan to keep my head straight on his knee and not to move, so I could try to move my frozen body, but I failed. I looked into his eyes, then at the sky and saw a C-17, US military plane flying over us.

It was 7:00 am on August 15, 2021. Attaullah Hairan said that breakfast was ready. Stanekzai and Hairan are my best friends and of course the core committee members of the Bawar Movement. I had been staying in my office for nine days by then. Although, I had remained in the office and stopped moving once the target killings in January reached their peak, people were being killed within 100 meters of the Presidential Palace, including five innocent souls of the Bawar Movement including Yousuf Rashid. The rumors even inside the Presidential Palace believed that most of the target killings were those who had offended the Afghan government, mostly the ex-first vice President Amrullah Saleh.

On January 04, 2021, Abdul Baqi Rashid, Yousuf Rashid's younger brother, told me, in my office, that Yousuf had been very scared before he was killed, "he told me that Amrullah Saleh's guys had threatened him with death twice that week, and I have other proof which shows that Yousuf was killed by Saleh," Abdul Baqi said.

By now, every civil activist and somewhat known politician had either left the capital or country or had limited their movements. It was only us, the Bawar Movement, who without notifying the Kabul Police protested against target killings. The ANDSF did their best to create obstacles, they even threatened us, but we protested against the government and then no target killings were carried out for twenty-two days not only in Kabul but across the country. Later I received nine notices from the NDS (National Directorate of Security, the Afghan intelligence Agency) in just nineteen days that I was on hit list according to their sources, so I flew to Dubai for a month and the target killings began all over again. Since I did not have enough money to stay longer, I had to come back after twenty-five days.

On August 05, 2021, Dawa Khan Menapal called and wanted me to see him. He came to my office at about 5:00 pm. Menapal was very scared and wanted me to arrange a UAE visa for him, because no visas were issued in those days due to COVID-19, and he knew that I had close friends in Dubai who could get him a visa. It was about 2:00 pm the next day that I got a call from Roh-ul-Amin, the former governor who wanted me to confirm if Menapal had been assassinated. I was shocked and did not believe it at all. Menapal and I had been friends since 2005, and then once we both were spokespersons to Ashraf Ghani the ex-president. Yes, he had been shot and killed right after he left the mosque after the Friday prayers. He was the GMIC (Government Media and Information Center) director those days. His assassination once again made me stay in the office and stop moving around outside. I called Spogmai

(Moon, my nickname for my wife) and told her not to expect me for few days.

I had taken shower, Mirza Khan our cook had already made his best omelets and milk tea. While sitting at the dining table, Hairan asked me if the Taliban could enter Kabul. Based on the information I had from the Palace, I knew that something bad could happen, but told him no, the international community in particular the United States would never let them to topple the regime they had spent more than two trillion USD, and thousands of their soldiers to uphold. A peaceful transition would take place, and the power would be transferred to a third party (neither the Republic government nor the Taliban), but I guess I was not so confident in my words.

"You have always been right, and your analysis and information are always authentic and accurate, but I don't know why my heart doesn't accept your words today," Hairan said.

We had taken our breakfast and had our cigarettes, and we were discussing the future of the country. I had eight interviews and hard talk shows scheduled for that day with Aljazeera, News Nation, TV9 Bharatvarsh, NDTV, Republic TV, ABP News Network, Zee News and VOA, I had also just received a WhatsApp text from Maj. Ryan Bamford, the air attaché at the U.S Embassy Kabul. It said, 'Brother, this is probably not a surprise, but due to the current situation, I will not be able to meet you today. I am sincerely sorry.' We were supposed to meet at 13:00, his message scared me that something very bad was going to happen. Suddenly, Agha Jan surprised me; I had not seen him for nine days, but here he was in my office to check if I was okay. I served him a cup of green tea, and he started talking with Stanekzai and Hairan. When I looked at him, his eyes told me the untold story that he was foreseeing, 'oh, don't tell me this Agha Jan,' I told myself. Agha Jan who doesn't smoke except when he is super tense, asked me for a cigarette, and I handed one over without reminding him he doesn't smoke. He hadn't finished when Khalil, my driver, breathlessly entered the room and said that the Taliban had entered the city. We looked at each other, and I told them, 'Don't panic, let's relax and let me confirm it.' I called everyone in authority including the Minister of Interior Mirzakwal and Abasin Baryal the deputy director of NDS, but got no responses. I told them, 'Yes the Taliban had entered Kabul but do what I ask you to do.' I suddenly noticed that Hairan had already left, I asked Stanekzai to give him a call over the phone, but the call did not go through.

I asked for the guards, who had already left, so I started collecting all the important and sensitive documents, my laptop and some other stuff. I asked Khalil to go and pick up Dr. Mallani from the hospital.

"She is already here," Khalil said.

I asked Khan to drive, Agha Jan sat at the front, Mallani, Stanekzai and I were in the back and bags were put in the back trunk of my 4runner truck. We left the office, but Kabul was totally jammed, so we turned back towards Rashid Dustom's house on the west, again the same terrifying traffic, men, women, children, vehicles, bikes and bicycles, everyone just trying to get home.

Agha Jan turned his head back and said, "it's finished."

"Yes, Agha Jan! We don't have time to think or talk about this now," I said.

We were also very worried about the possibility of running out of fuel. We could not afford to leave the truck on the road since we had the important items in the truck. The colorful and lively Kabul had gone to the 1990s once again. We could easily see grief, sorrow and fear on everyone's face. It was an unbelievable shock to everyone. I was receiving hundreds of

WhatsApp messages in a minute but did not have an answer for any of them, the grey truck we were riding had made it to the right of Dustom's house, towards the British cemetery and then to the recent asphalt ring road connecting Qala-e-Fatehullah and the airport road. It wasn't any better on this road either, the police had left their rangers, trucks and checkpoints, the high officials, including ministers, deputy ministers and MPs with black license plates on their armored vehicles were driving on one-way roads and hitting other vehicles with their gunmen guards shouting at people.

The truck turned right towards the Bibi Mahro Hill Street, connecting with the first K9 scanners and the police checkpoint at the Macroryan 4th intersection on the airport road. Traffic was badly jammed, the K9 scanner was left operational, and the security-trained dog was locked in its crate. The Kabul governor's armored vehicles were stuck in traffic trying to make it to the airport, his guards were shouting as usual but could not help their boss. Agha Jan, Stanekzai and I left Khan and Mallani in the truck and started to walk towards home, since our apartment in Macroryan 4th was about a five-minute walk from there. As soon we reached to the Macroryan 4th market, I noticed the fear on every face. Sharifullah, the money exchanger, always used to sit in his cabin beside the road very calm and relaxed, but he seemed very uncomfortable that day. When he saw me, he ran towards me. I could easily see tears in his eyes, I told him to relax, everything was going to be okay. The teenagers in their black clothes and white veils were running towards their homes from schools.

The most fear I noticed was in women's faces, every woman was out to pick up her children from school, while also trying to buy the food from the market, believing that stores might shut down for a while. I also turned to Mustafa Super Store to buy some cigarettes since you could not predict tomorrow. After I had picked up my cigarette packs and left the store to go home, a young man called me from behind. I turned back and saw it was Mohammed the grocery shop guy, he wanted to give me a carton of apples. He was poor but very hard worker and self-sufficient, he would open his small shop before sunrise and close it at about 11:00 pm after everyone had gone home.

"Mohammed, I don't have anything in my pocket to give you," I said.

With a beautiful smile of generosity, he replied, "Mashra (boss), I have never seen the Taliban, I was not even born during their era, all I know about them is that they are terrorists, they kill innocent souls, they destroy the country and our dignity. The little I have learned about life is to love everyone beyond their race, color, language and religion, and I have learned this best sacred religion called humanity from you, my leader. So, no one knows what will happen tomorrow, I live in a rented two room mud house, all I have is this cart shop. I don't want a Talib to eat a single apple from my shop, I am not able to take all the fruit home, so I am gifting these two unopened cartons to you. Maybe they will kill me tomorrow, and now you will always remember me whenever you see apples and oranges," and he turned to pick the cartons with a sweet smile.

"Mohammed, you know what? You are the richest person in the world, you might not have heard of TATA, he makes billions USD a year, and donates about sixty percent of his money to the poor and neediest, but he is not richer or more generous than you, since he keeps forty percent, but you donate your all without thinking of tomorrow, meanwhile you're the best manager and policy maker," I laughed, "Everyone around is badly scared, and isn't able to plan, while you donate your fruits based on the calculated plan that you don't know about the next morning, but making sure to do good with people, donate your shop instead of being robbed tomorrow and then you will make it home to stay there or move your family to your village. I am very sure, nothing bad will happen to you, since God always protects and keeps some people for great things to do, and yet you will do it."

I tried to pick up the cartons, but he did not let me, he carried the two heavy cartons and followed Agha Jan and me all the way to home. I gave him a big bear hug, kissed his forehead and wished him all the very best.

"I have only a two-bedroom house, but I have always respected and loved you like an elder brother, a father and a leader. I know my house might be not a comfortable place for you, but still I can keep you there for as long as you want, or I can take you to my village in Kunarr Province, I know they are not going to leave you, you have been a strong critic, and your anti-Taliban and Pakistan rallies have put you in trouble now, please either go with me or somewhere else, and also, please stop talking against them in the media," he said.

"Oh, Mohammed, it's so kind of you, thank you very much for your great words, you have become a great politician! You can carefully analyze things. Well, boy, it doesn't matter if I keep or stop talking against them, I have done enough that they can easily justify my murder. But don't worry, your Mashar has skipped all the other target killings by professional murderers, so I can manage this too," I told him.

I gave him my amethyst stone ring to remember me by; he gave me a tight hug and started to cry. I also got emotional, I wanted to see him again, but I knew it might not happen. He left with many untold words in his innocent heart, his dreams were all crushed, I could feel how hard it is when you accept that you have lost everything.

Spogmai and Moraka had heard us talking and the two doors were opened, they were surprised but shocked too, they were not expecting me home, especially during the day.

"What happened Azad? Is everything alright, you never come home at this time, especially when you go underground," they both kept asking me questions.

"All is well, let's move inside," I said.

I was covered by my four children's hugs who had not seen me for a few days. After drinking a glass of water, I set the camera, lighting and laptop for the scheduled interviews. The first interview was with Aljazeera and then other media outlets followed.

Since the Taliban had already made it to the city by the evening, I knew I was taking a great risk in talking to the international media outlets, but I didn't want to miss the chance to tell the world that what they did to us. I kept telling the world how Afghanistan and Afghans were left all alone in a war that did not belong to them but was being fought in the interest of big regional and international powers. Although I knew I wouldn't be able to bring about any change in my countrymen's fate with those interviews, I still did all my best to give moral courage to the Afghan security and defense forces and to the forty million innocent citizens of a war-torn country. I went exactly by the folk story Adey Morka had told me, 'A big forest caught alight, a sparrow who had lost her sweet home kept going to the nearby river bringing a drop of water in her beak and dropping it on the fire. Another sparrow laughed at her and asked if she had thought that she would be able to extinguish the fire with a drop of water in her small beak? 'I know the drop of water I try to extinguish the fire with doesn't even reach the fire, but one day when a historian writes about the forest and its fire, I want them to put my name in the list of the ones tried to extinguish the fire not those set the forest alight or those calmly watching as it burned.' I kept doing the same on the very last day of losing all hope.

There were many other international media outlets expecting me that night, but I was too tired of keep talking for seven hours, and also, I did not have enough time to stay at home. I knew the Taliban and of course ISI would trace me right after they entered Kabul. My tens of interviews in the previous week with international media outlets, in particular with the Indian channels, had made the Pakistani establishment particularly angry with me. I had two exclusive interviews with three Pakistani televisions, one as a guest with Dr. Moeed Yousuf, the Pakistani National Security Advisor, on Indus News on August 12, 2021, and then I started receiving threatening messages from unknown numbers.

Gul Mama (Shir Mohammed my maternal uncle) kept calling me but since I was busy in interviews with the media, he called Moraka. I called him back. He reminded me how when Dr. Najib's regime collapsed, the Mujahideen took people from their houses and killed them on the very first night of their entering Kabul. The Taliban did the same when they entered Kabul in 1995. Gul Mama told me how Jamiat-e-Islami militants took Sardar Khan, a young pilot, from his home in Qala-e-Chaman at about 11:00 pm the first night they took Kabul, no one knew where he was taken but his body was found two streets back. His fiancée hanged herself. Sardar had been the only provider for his three young sisters and old parents from Farah province.

It was 8:17 pm when I had to leave home. Spogmai and the kids were crying, they thought that they might not see me for a long time. I had to go underground not only to save my life but of course my family too. My life had never been mine but my family's, I knew if anything happened to me, my family would die right away. God forbid.

I didn't want to go in my truck, so I asked Khan to bring the keys for Dr. Omid Shah's car. Omid Shah my brother-in-law had already made it to Camp Eagle, since his team the OSF (Orgun Security Force the Special Strike Unit) were there. Omid Shah was one of the best general surgeons in Kabul, he had worked as general surgeon with OSF directly operating under the U.S. OGA and ODA for two years and had already a COM/SIV (Chief of Mission/Special Immigrants Visa) approved applicant with Pashtana, his wife, and Hamad Khan, their two-year-old son.

Moraka gave me a pakol and a chadar to wear, I removed my glasses and wore the mask. We sat in the 1996 golden Toyota corolla, the car's horn was broken, and the left front light was fused as well. Khan started the engine and Moraka who wanted to see her brother as well, sat in the back. The car had left the market behind and made it to the airport road, the police check point along with the K9 scanning truck was still there but with no police. I, for the first time missed those rude and illiterate policemen who used to bother people crossing their checkpoint, especially those wearing typical Pashtun clothes. The road that I had seen hours before with thousands of jammed vehicles was now an empty road. It did not take long to reach Gul Mama's house near HKIA. Khan had to go back. We did not press the doorbell but called Gul Mama over his phone to open the back gate for us and he did it accordingly.

We were on the third-floor balcony of the four-story house keeping an eye on the street. There was no one at home except Gul Mama, his family had gone to attend a wedding ceremony which was fixed a week ago. Nobody could even imagine that things would so dramatically change overnight. Gul Mama called Shiraz, his son to bring meal for us. Before they got home there was a massive shoot-out started near the main HKIA gate.

Gul Mama's house was about 200 meters from the main HKIA gate. We thought it was a clash between the U.S forces and the Taliban since the airport was controlled by the U.S. and other international forces. There was nonstop firing and since it was late night, we could clearly see the bullets in the air. We tried to find out what was going on, but no one knew until Gul Mama's wife, three sons, a daughter-in-law and two daughters arrived. His wife was shocked to see me late at night at their home, since I was generally very busy and could not even attend the family events. She asked about her son, Shirzad who was an Afghan Army officer posted in the foreign affairs department of the Ministry of Defense. She thought something bad might had happened to him when she saw us there. Once she was told the story of my presence, so she took a deep breath of thanksgiving to God.

Mami (maternal uncle's wife) asked us to go inside because of the continuous firing just 200 meters away. We had started to eat our dinner when Shirzad arrived home. He had got Indian visas on all his family's passports including his married sister, her husband and the two little daughters. They were not the first target but of course everyone was trying to leave the country. When he found out that I did not have a visa for any country, he started calling multiple embassies. Although, the Indian Embassy was still open for two more days, they denied him any assistance. Turkey, Kazakhstan, Tajikistan and China also came up with negative answers, while Iran gave him a green light, but I rejected going to Iran for two reasons. First, I had always had an anti-Iran ideology and kept motivating others to believe that Iran, like as Pakistan would never be our friend. Second, I had arranged and organized twenty-one protests and rallies against Iran early 2021, I preferred dying in Afghanistan to going to Iran or Pakistan. I knew Moraka was not happy with my decision, but

I tried to convince her by telling her that her prayers and love would protect me from all evils.

It was 01:00 am and everyone went to their bedrooms without little hope for a better sunrise the next morning. Moraka and I had our beds at the back of the dining hall, the room was decently decorated with red handmade Mezari rugs, purple mattress covers, and ochre Turkish sofas, the wall clock kept its tik-tik-tik, it did not care if the time for millions of humans on this part of the earth was changed but kept its own job. I kept my eyes on the clock and Moraka noticed me, she told me that she had been hearing since childhood that time is gold but the time for Afghans had never been even a simple metal except the metals used for knives, swords, bullets, rockets and bombs.

I had no answer for her but just said, "Chaos and disaster are always the mother of opportunities."

She smiled at me and said, "my philosopher son, I know you never smoke in front of me, but I can understand you need one right now, please don't leave the room, it's not safe, you can smoke here."

I gave her a tight hug and made it to the attached bathroom where I smoked my cigar. The night was too long, neither of us could fall asleep. Eventually she started massaging my head with her magic hands that sent me into deep sleep within minutes.

We could not sleep more than two hours because of the ongoing shooting, Moraka asked me to take a shower since I never start my day without taking a shower, but that day I just didn't want to. She understood and breakfast was served. I had already turned my phone off but thought to turn WhatsApp on to least to be in touch with close friends at the U.S. Embassy in Kabul. I received a text message from a Pakistani number saying "see you soon" right after I opened my WhatsApp. I received messages from tens of international media outlets asking me for interviews without even checking how I was. I understood how selfish the world is, everybody cares for their own interest, your death becomes a business for others in particular for the media, they need breaking news, doesn't matter if the news is genocide.

Moraka had to go home to see if things around the house were okay, I tried to call Khan to come and pick her up, but she preferred to walk since she didn't want anyone seeing Khan coming here. Gul Mama had already told his family not to tell anyone about my whereabouts and Mami's big family of around 200 people including her dad's uncles, aunts and cousins' families were living on the back street.

At about 9:00 am, I and Gul Mama went to sit on the fourth floor's balcony to drink some tea and for me to smoke a cigar; now we found out what the unceasing firing was for. There were few thousand people starting from our street to HKIA, trying to enter the airport, every one of them were shopkeepers, taxi drivers, regular people who were not wanted dead by any regime. A local barber living on the same street as us was carrying a black plastic shopping bag followed by his wife in a blue burqa (chadari) and his numerous children were trying to make it to the airport gate. I never saw if they made it. Mami 's two neighbors were working as sweepers in part of the airport, they called their families and successfully made it to Doha the same day. Her other next door neighbor who had a street food cart selling Bolani (boiled potatoes inside the fried bread) on the airport road with his eleven member-family was in Doha the same evening. So, all the shooting was the warning shelling by the U.S and Special Strike Unit forces to split and push back the crowds at the airport gate. I noticed a U.S C-17 escorted by two helicopters trying to land but even after almost three hours it had not succeeded and left. I understood that the runway was totally occupied by crowds.

At 3:00 pm I received a WhatsApp call from Naqibullah, my younger brother telling me that two Taliban vehicles stopped by my office, four Taliban with Helmandi Pashtu accents entered the office and asked for me, they then checked every room in the office and left a message for me to see them as soon as possible. I asked him not to move outside the office because they could trace him. Gul Mama and I also planned an emergency exit to the western neighbor's house, in case the Taliban showed up at our home. We spent all day on the balcony and were supposed to take our dinner there but the window of the room next to where we were sitting shattered into pieces. I told Gul Mama that it was a bullet, so we all left the balcony and made it to the back room on the west of the third floor.

The Marriage And A Tearful Farewell

It was about 11:00 pm that Shirzad got a call, he went out and came back with surprising news, he was told by his boss the director of the foreign affairs in Ministry of Defense (MoD), that the director with his family and Shirzad with his fiancée were called by the Office of the Defense attaché of the U.S. Embassy to make it to the north gate of HKIA by 6:00 am the next morning: they were going to be evacuated. Everyone was surprised and did not know what to do, Shirzad was not yet married. I asked him to call his father-in-law and tell him the story and that Gul Mama would ask him to bring his daughter (Shirzad's fiancée) at 5:00 in the morning so they could marry before departing for the airport, they did exactly that.

I left the family to their packing and went to the room I was sleeping in. I started smoking my few last cigars and I received a text message from a former high NDS official telling me that non-Afghan Taliban had entered the NDS directorate trying to trace phone numbers and had got a list of those wanted by them and that my name was on the top. I shared the issue with the office of the defense attaché at the U.S Embassy and with Maj. Ryan Bamford the air attaché. They told me to change my location, but they weren't able to help me right away and couldn't evacuate me. I kept smoking for hours and went to bed around 4:00 in the morning, I had not slept even an hour when Mami woke me up telling me that Shirzad's fiancée, father and mother-in-law were there.

Marriages are always the events and moments of happiness not only for the couple but also for both families involved. This was the first marriage that looked like a coffin was being taken out of a home; everyone was crying, the couple and the families had dreams and had planned differently but time had decided something else for them. The breakfast table was full, but no one was eating anything, they didn't have enough time. They married with a short Surah of Al-Quran. The couple were hugged and departed amidst crying. Although, I had slept only for three in forty-eight hours, yet I didn't feel sleepy, I lit my cigar and asked Hina (Gul Mama's) daughter-in-law for a strong coffee. During those two days, Nasir Khan a good friend of mine who used to be a senior advisor in good governance for IDLG (Independent Directorate of Local Governance) kept calling but could not reach me out since my phone was turned off. He contacted Naqibullah to ask me to get in touch with him as soon as possible, I called him from a different number, and he told me that commander Arsalan, head of peace committee of the Taliban, was from the same tribe and village as Nasir Khan, had contacted and told him that I was on the hit list, so I should soon contact him to get the Peace Badge they were providing to those in danger. This card would protect me. I knew the Taliban and my case, there was no government, no responsible body and no accountability, the Taliban themselves did not know the whereabouts of their different groups under different commands. I thanked Nasir Khan and told him I would contact them.

I did not.

Kabul had already been experiencing load shedding issue because the electricity pylons that bring imported power into Afghanistan were being damaged every second day. We neither had power nor Wi-Fi in Gul Mama's home and I badly needed to send some important emails to embassies especially the Defense Attaché office of the U.S. Embassy. The only place where I could have power and fast internet was my office, since we had solar energy power. Gul Mama did not let me go to the office and told me that his youngest son's in-laws who lived nearby had solar energy and also Wi-Fi. I called Khan to make it somehow with my laptop to Gul Mama's home; he brought the laptop and two packs of cigars for me. I rethought and decided that I was not in position to take the risk by going to a stranger's home: I had always been a media face that every second person would recognize. I convinced Gul Mama and promised that I would come back within a few hours. As soon we left Gul Mama's home, a young boy from Wardak province who was Gul Mama's son's best friend and neighbor saw me, I hadn't liked this guy since the day Shirsha, Mama's eldest son brought him to my office when I was the secretary general for Ashraf Ghani's presidential elections campaign. He asked me for job, after a short discussion I found him doubtful with bad intentions, so I rejected him and never let him come again to my official and private offices.

I told Khan that this guy had seen us, and I was sure that he would create problems for us right away since I believed he had links with the Taliban. The bad luck began when I noticed that I had forgotten my loaded pistol at Gul Mama's home. I asked Khan to make it through the local streets and then turn back to Bibi Mahro Hill, and then go straight to Sehat Tefal/Indira Gandhi Children Hospital instead of going to the office. He did as I asked and ten minutes later, we were at a busy checkpoint with a K9 scanning machine controlled by two Taliban wearing black long Afghan dress (Kameez), black cotton turbans, waistcoats and plastic sandals. Both were around thirty and had clearly never shaved their beards. Their AK47s were hanging the wrong way on their shoulders, they were confused by all the vehicles and smartly dressed people. After crossing the checkpoint, there were another four at the gates of the Supreme Court and Ministry of Tribal and Border affairs. At the south-east gate of the Indira Gandhi Hospital, we had to talk to the Taliban for the first time. I told them that I was a doctor and needed to go to the hospital, although they seemed very confused and did not know whether to let us go in or not, I asked Khan to go ahead before they thought to ask their commanders. There were only few vehicles, including ambulances that belonged to the hospital and looked like they had been parked a few days ago. The hospital was not empty but not busy as usual. We spent time walking in the corridors and gardens where there was no Taliban to ask us anything.

We left the hospital, but I told Khan it was too early to go to the office and asked him to make it to Gul Faroshi Street (Flower Street), a popular street for weddings and functions. It also had the main office and boutique of the fashion brand run by Spogmai, my wife, and Khan, my youngest brother. We parked our car inside the entrance of the market and opened the back door of the boutique. Entering brought tears to my eyes, I recalled how day and night Spogmai and Khan worked hard to make this the top Afghan brand. I well-remembered that Spogmai a patient of fibromyalgia and anxiety who took a drip every other day was working so hard to show the world this beautiful picture of Afghanistan. I supported them as much as I could, but as soon they started their business, COVID-19 changed everything; Kabul went into quarantine for months, all businesses went down, and many didn't survive. The surprising part was that the government locked down all the business but carried on collecting the complete rent without delay from those rented government owned lands. The brand's head office and boutique were built by us on land owned by the Ministry of Defense and rented to us. I could not keep supporting them, but they did not give up and took loan from a bank to keep their brand rocking. Spogmai introduced the first brand beyond typical tailoring Afghan copy paste dresses, she started creating eastern and western designs with international coloring and with fashionable patterns.

The brand had been at the forefront of the Afghan and international modified fashion since it was founded in August 2019 and was acclaimed as Afghanistan's leading fashion house for traditional, partywear, fancy, casual and special occasion wear. It proudly launched the first Afghan fashion designs, and offered exclusive, original and feminine styles for the fashion-conscious woman of today. The brand was not just a brand but a reflection of Afghanistan's 5,000-year history and a tribute to skilled Afghan women. Each garment is an everlasting story of the colorful Afghan culture that sends a message of peace and friendship to the whole world. In fact, the brand is the identity of Afghanistan made of threads of love.

The only street that always sang the song of life and beauty was nastily wounded that day. I am sure if it had a tongue, it would tell the story of an innocent deer torn by a starving wolf and it would write her last poem with its blood on the page of the blind history that always see things and passes to next generations but does nothing. The fresh flowers in front of the flower shops were taking their last breaths; they were badly missing those hands that kept them alive not only with water but feelings as well. These flowers were waiting to be held by a beautiful bride:

> Keep ambling my dearest love!
> I sacrifice for you, you my affectionate love
> You've got dark black eyes, that draw one in
> Oh, your long black hair
> For the sake of your own beauty
> Do amble and mooch while,

Your eyes can catch mine.
By keeping looking back while walking
My love is rubbing salt into my wounded heart
Do amble and mooch you my day and night!
"song by Dr. Sadiq Fitrat Nashnas, that is played when
a bride is waved off on her way to her new home"

And then they go with the bride to make her wedding night even more memorable. The flower would love to be spread in the bed to protect the beautiful soft velvet skin from any rash the mattress sheet would give. The same family of roses would perform the guardian's job by hanging around the bed and happily dancing with every move made in the bed. The flowers imprisoned in the bunch carried by the bride would take the breath of freedom after the bride's white gown is removed, the freed petals would further produce perfume and hide the scratch marks on her back while not only the two bodies but also the souls become one. The flowers would happily hand their lives over to these souls under the golden rays of the sun trying to enlighten the lustful yet shy and innocent eyes of last night.

I understood that since the flowers in front of the stores could not die happily in this heavenly bed, they preferred to commit suicide rather than be put on one's grave.

Sitting on an off-white couch and looking at the recently made Mermaid Fisheries Dress by Spogmai, for a collection named Oxygen - to raise awareness of the need to save water and protect the aquatic animals and climate. The dress reminded me of my birthday on February 14, of course I was born on Valentine's Day. Spogmai, Moraka, Eliana and everyone could not wait to see me home earlier than usual on my birthday. Of course, for Spogmai it had always been both my birthday and her valentine.

But unfortunately, this particular birthday I was stuck in meetings as usual and it took me until 8:00 pm to leave the office with Moin Stanekzai and Nangyalai Yousufzai, two great friends of mine. We walked from my office, which was right behind the Ministry of Women's Affairs and a popular shopping mall called Majeed Mall, to the flower street. Normally this would be a five-minute walk but that night it took us about fifteen minutes since the flower street was at its peak of joy. The beautiful and happy couples made the street a come to life. We asked the sales boy to order Chupan Kababs for all of us including himself right after we entered the boutique. I sat on the off-white couch and checked unread messages on my WhatsApp, of which I would receive more than 1000 a day. Stanekzai and Yousufzai were busy checking out the dresses.

Suddenly a couple that had just entered caught my eye: her beautiful big blue eyes, long thick dark hair falling all the way to her hips, decently tweezed eyebrows, a gorgeous young woman was trying to explain to the sales boy what she wanted. Her fiancé bought her the dress, another copy was right before my eyes.

Taliban And The Shopping Mall

We had spent enough time reminiscing in the boutique and then left for the office at 1:30. I had not yet made it to my office when Mokhlis, my secretary, told me that group of Taliban had just left the office thirty minutes ago. they had spent about one and half hours in the office to see if I would come or not. I looked at Khan, winked and told him, see I knew it, that's why we cruised all around to make them wait but leave disappointedly. I asked for a coffee and entered my office, which had become like the first dating girlfriend. The beautiful white painted walls with the three historic painting of wounded Dr. William Brydon on the southern wall of the office made me stand for a while and thinking if the historian exaggerated and lied to us.

William Brydon CB (10 October 1811 – 20 March 1873) was an assistant surgeon in the British East India Company Army during the First Anglo-Afghan War, he was famous for being the only member of an army of 4,500 men, plus 12,000 accompanying civilians, to reach Jalalabad alive.

In 1841 William Brydon was posted to Afghanistan as the assistant surgeon of Shah Shuja's Contingent - a British officered infantry force recruited in India to provide protection for the British-backed ruler in Kabul. This mercenary unit of a joint English and Indian armed force occupied the city in August 1839. In fact, subsequent to ruling over India, the British attempted to occupy Afghanistan also, which was obviously completely different than not only India, but every place British had invaded so far.

In January 1842, following the killing of the two British representatives there, the British understood that invading Afghanistan and ruling Afghans was impossible, so they decided to withdraw the British force in Kabul. Jalalabad, 90 miles (140 km) from Kabul was hosting the nearest British garrison, which had to accept the army coming from Kabul and then they would leave for British India. But the British, based on their divide and rule policy tried to breach the agreement, which in result, under the command of Major-General William George Keith Elphinstone, 4,500 British and Indian soldiers plus 12,000 civilian camp followers, only Dr. William Brydon was purposely left alive, Afghanistan wanted him to tell the story to Delhi and London of the war against Afghans.

Kabul Balah-e-Sar's painting was hanging on the wall right opposite my desk to always remind me of Afghanistan's greatness. Bala Hissar is an ancient fortress located in the city of Kabul. The estimated date of construction is around the 5th century A.D.

Bala-e-Hissar is built to the south of the capital Kabul at the tail end of the Koh-e-Sherdarwaza (Lion Door) mountain, which is right behind the fort. The walls of Bala-e-Hissar are 20 feet in height and 12 feet thick begins from the fortress and follows the mountain ridge in a sweeping curve down to the Kabul River. The walls support a set of entry gates to the fortress.

Bala-e-Hissar was the site of many bloodiest battles in Afghanistan especially during the 19th century when the country came into conflict with the invasion of British during the First Anglo-Afghan WAR (1838-1842) and the Second Anglo-Afghan War (1878-1880).

The British envoy to Kabul, Sir Pierre Louis Napoleon Cavagnari, was killed inside the fort in September 1879 triggering a general uprising and the second phase of the Second Anglo-Afghan War. From 1839 onwards the British used it on and off as their barracks until the massacre of the British Mission by mutinous Afghan troops in 1879.

The fort was badly damaged during the Second Anglo-Afghan War when Afghan forces burned down the British Residency. Although, General Frederick Roberts had wanted to destroy and level the fortress completely, but the British were defeated and made to leave the country before he could level the fort.

The Malalai of Maiwand's painting was hanging on the southern wall, to catch everyone's eye when they entered the room. "Malalai of Maiwand is a national folk hero of Afghanistan who rallied, encouraged and motivated the local Pashtun fighters in Kandahar against the British troops at the 1880 Battle of Maiwand. She fought under the command of Ayub Khan and was titled the victorious for the Afghan victory at the Battle of Maiwand on 27 July 1880, during the Second Anglo-Afghan War. Malalai is also known as "The Afghan Molly Pitcher" and as "The Afghan Jeanne D'Arc" to the Western world. There are many hospitals, schools and other institutions named after her in Afghanistan. Malalai's story is told in the Afghan school textbooks.

Malalai was born in 1861 in a small village called "Khig", about three miles southwest of Maiwand in the southern Kandahar province of Afghanistan. In late 1880s, when British tried to occupy Afghanistan for the second time, hoping to colonize the area and annex it with what was then British India (India and Pakistan). The British army had located their main garrison in Kandahar city which was quite close to Maiwand district. The Afghan military was commanded by Commander Ayub Khan, son of the Afghan Emir Sher Ali Khan. Malalai the daughter of a local shepherd and fiancée of a young Afghan who had joined Ayub Khan's army, came under the British-Indian forces attack in July 1880. Malalai like many other Afghan women was there to provide water, spare weapons and tend the wounds. It is worth mentioning that this was also supposed to be Malalai's wedding day, which unfortunately never happened.

When Malalai noticed that the Afghan army was about to lose since they were fewer in number compared to the British-Indian army, Malalai then took the Afghan flag and shouted:

"Hey My Love! If you do not get martyred in the battle of Maiwand,
By God, God is saving you as a symbol of shame!"

This encouraged and inspired the Afghan fighters to redouble their emotions and efforts. Malalai used her veil as the flag when the leading flag-bearer was killed, and he fell down along with the flag. Malalai with the veil flag in her hand sang a landai:

"With a drop of my sweetheart's blood,
Shed in defense of the Motherland,
Will I put a beauty spot on my forehead,
Such as would put to shame the rose in the garden!"

Malalai did not only keep giving strength to the Afghan fighters but also fought, and she was herself stuck down and killed. However, her words and poems had already spurred on her countrymen to victory. After the victory, Malalai was honored for her efforts, buried in her village along with other martyrs of the battle and named the heroine and victorious of the Battle of Maiwand. She was only 17 at her death.

There was a bathroom on the right side of my tight-grained walnut colored carved desk, hand made in Kunarr province; the bathroom had an emergency exit behind the tall mirror door, where I kept a 24/7 loaded gun in case of an emergency. Without wasting a second, I logged into my laptop and drafted two emails with required documents attached to the U.S. and Indian Embassies in Kabul requesting to evacuate my family and me. I was also in touch with Maj. Ryan Bamford, the air attaché in the office of the Defense attaché at the U.S Embassy and Mr. Vasudev Ravi the previous political attaché at the Indian Embassy over the phone. Since the U.S. Embassy was totally moved to HKIA and was very busy evacuating tens of thousands of people every day with the crowds around the airport making their job even tougher, they told me to wait, that they would take care of me but advised me to keep changing my location every four to five hours. I only asked for a single visa from the Indian Embassy, I did not ask them for any evacuation or to get me at the airport, but unfortunately the contact did not even reply to any of the messages after I asked for an E-visa. I then felt sorry for India, I wasn't an unknown or low-profile person, and also, I didn't only have personal friendship with the contact, but the two countries had been so called strategic partners. Yes, I felt sorry for their behavior. Afghanistan had always been blamed by Pakistan for having close ties with India, and we paid the unexpected price for the rivalry and proxy war between India and Pakistan. It reminded me of their partnership with the Ex-President Dr. Mohammed Najibullah, who was not given political asylum by the Indian Embassy in Kabul, which resulted in his brutal execution.

Mohammed Najibullah Ahmedzai was the president of Afghanistan between 1987 and 1992. The Taliban captured Kabul, in September 1996, executed him and brutalized his body under full international glare. The United Nations, India and various Afghan forces at that time paved the road towards Najibullah's killing.

The only chance for him to flee the country failed. Najibullah had already sent his wife and daughter to India some two weeks before Kabul completely collapsed, he had planned a secret flight to India with Benon Sevan, the UN envoy to Afghanistan. Sevan had already taken Nawaz Sharif the Pakistani Prime Minister into confidence before requesting India to give the Afghan president political asylum, so any Pak-India bilateral relations would be prevented from worsening over Najibullah. It only took one hour for Narasimha Rao, the Indian Prime Minister, to communicate that India would host Najibullah as state guest in New Delhi.

A renowned Indian writer Paliwal Avinash in his research paper published by Quartz India in 2017 wrote:

On that fateful morning, however, driving with his armed bodyguard and a team of UN officers, Najibullah's convoy was refused entry into the Kabul airport. The password he used throughout the journey from home to the airport did not work at the penultimate checkpoint. The airport was under the control of Abdul Rashid Dostum, an Afghan of Uzbek heritage, who led a local militia against the Mujahideen in the northern province of Jowzjan, and had been receiving political, financial, and military patronage from Najibullah. In a total "wild card," as the then Indian ambassador to Kabul Vijay K Nambiar terms it, Dostum turned hostile towards his patron, and shut down the airport for the next 24 hours. On the airport's runway stood a plane, and in the plane awaited Sevan. Dostum's men had decided not to storm the plane, and Sevan had decided not to disembark.

After a furious exchange of abuses with and impotent threats to Dostum's men, Najibullah turned his convoy around. But he would not return home. He feared that the people who sabotaged his escape would not let him live. His minister of state security, General Ghulam Faruq Yaqubi, was found dead in his house. While some allege that he committed suicide, Nambiar, who was in touch with Najibullah and his UN handlers, does not rule out assassination. Either way, Najibullah was escorted to the UN compound instead of the presidential palace.

Still, on being pressed by the UN officers, Nambiar agreed to look into giving Najibullah asylum at the Indian embassy complex on the condition that the UN would make an official request for the same. Using a "ham radio" that was available to him at the time (only the UN had an INMARSAT phone), Nambiar contacted New Delhi to report the developments and sought official clearance for hosting Najibullah in his residential compound. However, protecting Najibullah and his family in Delhi was one thing, but giving him protection in the Indian embassy compound in Kabul, quite another. At 5.15am, India refused to grant Najibullah asylum in its embassy.

JN Dixit, who was India's foreign secretary (1991–94), and who championed Najibullah in the early 1980s, was concerned that offering him protection in the embassy would further complicate the situation politically. India may never be able to build strong relations with the Mujahideen on a fresh note. Dixit could not voice this dilemma openly. There were many in India who wanted to give Najibullah asylum on the grounds that he was just 44 years old with political constituencies among Pashtun communities and argued that giving up on him would imply capitulating to the Mujahideen.

The ignominious end to the Najibullah affair underlined the limits of influence and capacity of both India and the UN in shaping events on the ground. The end of Soviet influence in Afghanistan, and India's economic strains in the early 1990s severely limited New Delhi's policy options in Kabul. As a R&AW officer recollected years later, "Dixit and gang had the guilt of not saving Najibullah. We sent the plane [in which Sevan was waiting for Najibullah, but which was not actually an Indian plane] to Kabul thinking that the Mujahideen would let him go. We told the world that we are taking Najib out but had no understanding with Dostum. We should not have waited that long to take him out."

Had New Delhi paid adequate bribes? Najibullah might have been a free man. Even if one agrees that the Indian leadership felt guilty for giving up on Najibullah, Dostum's argument that India had the capacity to bribe Dostum's men into letting Najibullah escape in those circumstances, fails to convince. Apart from keeping its promise of supporting Najibullah's family in Delhi, India did nothing more."

However, my Indian friends not in the government did their best to get me out of the Kabul, but they failed, because they had to get me a visa, which of course had to be issued by the Indian Embassy.

Hide And Seek

I was done with my emails and had to leave before finishing my coffee. I asked Khan to take the car out and come around from the Emergency Hospital side. I would leave the office from the back door and would meet him in front of the Majid Mall. Since I used to spend a lot of time in the office, I always had spare clothes there. I changed my clothes and made it to the Majid Mall before he did. I saw three young Taliban in Majid Mall's parking lot keeping their eyes on the five-story building.

They were shocked by how this tall building was built, "How could the infidels make it stand?"

I got into the car and asked Khan to head to Khair Khana. There was a huge traffic jam at the Shaheed Y-Junction: we were stuck there for about an hour and then made it via Lessa Maryam Road to Qasaba Road, but Qasaba Road was even more terrible, hundreds of vehicles were stuck, we had no idea where all these thousands of people were going to. Finally, at a snail's pace we reached to a friend's house in the Khwaja Rawash blocks. Thousands of men, women and children were trying to climb the security walls of the airport but were being prevented by the international and Strike Force Units (Units 0s) forces. My friend's mother was surprised to see me at her door for the first time since she moved there three years prior. My presence at her home was not normal and she knew it. She asked her daughter to bring me tea and kept asking if everything was okay. I told her to relax, all was well, but that I had to spend the night there for a good reason. Though she was very poor and had a meagre income from her and her daughter's handicrafts, the room was beautifully decorated and furnished. I received Spogmai's call over WhatsApp telling me that my kids were crying for me, I asked Khan to go and bring them to me, but he had to go to Gul Mama's home first to pick up my pistol and bring it to me. Aunty got busy in the kitchen and was cooking the best she had at home for us. I made some important calls to some close friends including Mirwais Afghan, the founder and the chief editor of Khabarial.com in London and Rohulamin the previous governor for Farah province. For almost three hours that I did not hear from Khan, I called him to find out if everything was okay with him. He was stuck for hours in the crowds in front of the airport's northern gate. Since it was late, and no one could predict the situation I asked him to forget the pistol and children and just make it home. He told me okay, but I saw him with both children and pistol two hours later. Wadan Khan, Shamla, Ghani Khan and the two-year-old Barlas Khan tightened me with their big bear hugs and kept crying like we had not met for decades, my eyes were wet too.

We were supposed to stay another day, but the crying of the women and children opposite our balcony took our attention during breakfast of the next morning. I could not take the risk of standing the balcony to see what happened, so Aunty went out to see what was happening. She came back with bad news. A district attorney had been forcefully taken out of his home by the Taliban. My friend's home was no longer safe for me, most of the citizens living in those four blocks were former governmental staff, so a door-to-door check could be expected at any time. Khan was again there in two hours, and we had to make it home first and then I had to go and spend the night in Pashtana's home on the fifth floor just above our apartment.

Again, we were stuck in the crowd right in front of the Abbey Gate. Everyone was still trying to climb the security wall while the security forces had opened an air shelling on them, and tear-gas-hand-grenades were being thrown continuously, Spogmai and the kids saw such close firings for the first time, they thought we were attacked, and no one would survive. The situation was totally out of control, a young man was shot and was badly bleeding and the women from his family were yelling for help. Shamla, looking at the situation got a sudden shock and started loud nonstop shouts, Spogmai and other kids were badly crying, and I was trying to make Shamla calm, but failed. I kept trying, talking to her, pouring water on her head and even slapping her so I could bring her back from the traumatic shock, but she didn't even recognize me. I started shouting at her and telling her that I was her baba, yet she was not listening and kept screaming with all her inner power. The incessant air shells and massive blasts, the sounds of the tear-gas-grenades made people back up and jump over our car. They broke the windshield and Spogmai and the kids fainted. I asked Khan to keep pushing the gas pedal so we might leave the area since the car horn was not working. He kept moving people with the slow push of the car. Spogmai, Wadan Khan, Ghani Khan and Barlas Khan were faint and sweating, while Shamla kept screaming. I kept Shamla tightly hugged and kept talking to her. Khan did not lose his confidence and had full control over the car and situation, I told him to keep doing his job and I would take care of the family. The smoke and dust had already made their way to our lungs. There was no one to help us but ourselves. Finally, I asked Khan to leave the driving seat for me and get out of the car and try to push people aside from the front, I kept tight hold of Shamla with my left arm and controlled the steering with my right hand. Khan did his job fantastically; it took us about one hour to move around 50 meters. There were thousands of people ahead, but not stuck to each other like they were in front of the gate. Khan was driving now, and the speed meter on Kabul-Jalalabad highway was about 35 mph. The harsh wind had woken up Spogmai and the children while Shamla's lungs had made her tired enough and she had fainted. Now Spogmai had come back round she was extremely concerned about her daughter, Shamla. Khan was also seriously worried. I told him not to worry since she was still breathing. There wasn't any hospital open but thanks God our home had always been full of doctors.

When we got home, the condition of Spogmai and the kids made Moraka and Agha Jan cry. They thought we had been attacked. Of course, the priority was the first aid and emergency treatment, Mallani and Agha Jan could give. The medics started working and Shamla started recognizing everyone, though she was of course still scared. Khan had already brought them some cookies, chocolates and candies from the only open store in the market, which made them feel much better. Moraka had soon served the lunch so I could go upstairs, I took Ghani Khan upstairs with me and asked the rest to confidently tell anyone who should as that I had left the country.

I heard loud talking about 4:00 am the next morning, they weren't familiar voices so I checked the southern balcony attached to the kitchen on the fifth floor to see if I could use it as an emergency exist if needed. I was disappointed since there was no chance of getting out of the balcony. Most of the balconies were made of welded metal, aluminum or PVC cabins, so climbing to the neighbor's balcony had already been blocked. I tried to look downstairs from the little gap between the two purple curtains of the small room. I saw two white Ford Rangers of the border police: there were four gunmen off the trucks and the two drivers were still in their seats. It was not them talking but others right at

Moraka's door on the fourth floor. They started knocking on the door, I then understood that the groom's wedding procession was there to take the groom. I ran into the guestroom to see if Ghani Khan was sleeping, I was scared that if he woke up and found me not next to him, he would cry and that would be a big risk. He was deeply asleep, fortunately. I lit my cigarette and kept my ear on the door, Agha Jan was telling them that I had had some health issues and had already left the country for India two weeks ago.

They told Agha Jan "We can check the houses, but we know he is not here. We are very sure that he is in the city, we are not here to harm him, but we really need to meet him. It will be good for both sides." And then they left.

I was still standing behind the purple curtains, looking downstairs, the three gunmen joined the other four waiting for them downstairs, kept talking for about five minutes and then left, but before they left the area, they stopped at the entrance of the block and talked to Nazar, our watchman from Qala-e-zar Kunduz.

Agha Jan and Moraka thought that I was sleeping, but they did not sleep after that, I could hear them talking, since if you sleep on the floor, you can easily hear through the floor. They were talking about sending me out of Kabul by any possible way within the next twenty-four hours. I don't exactly remember, but I am sure I had smoked about fifteen red cigarettes between 04:00 to 07:00 am. I knew that I didn't have to make it to Moraka's home or mine, just to the opposite door. So I talked to Moraka over WhatsApp and asked them not to come upstairs either. I waited for one more hour and then left. I chose the small back gate of the block, and then left a voice message for Moraka and Spogmai to go and bring Ghani, who was still sleeping, home. I walked through the back street and passed the Markaz Garmi (central heating) office towards Shinozada Hospital. I intentionally went to the only open pharmacy, called Tarakhil medical store, and bought some flu and cough medics. This was the first time that COVID-19 was useful since I had to wear a mask. I booked a yellow taxi being driven by a former army colonel during Dr. Najib's regimes, he was very upset with the changes. He had already lost his two sons; one had been in the police force and the other in the army, and he was very upset about his third son who had been a Captain in Thunder 301 corps Gardez till just few days ago. Macroryan roundabout, now named Abdul Haq, once the busiest roundabout was silently talking of its old days of the 90s once again. The Pul-e-Mahmood (Mahmood Khan's bridge) Road, right behind one of the NDS important directorates including a detention center on the right of the Kabul River, was welcoming every vehicle without the three tight security checkpoints of just few days ago. The beautiful five plant nurseries connecting the road and the river were not only missing the customers' touch and passion but also a caretaker. Pul-e-Mahmood Khan just reminded me of a few days ago, when we were stuck in the huge traffic jams, with crowds and six police, army and NDS checkpoints each at the entrance of Shashdarak and Muradkhani roads, on both sides of the bridge and in front of the Eidgah Mosque when we were trying to attend Shaheed Osman Kakarr's funeral in absentia. Those crowds, traffic and checkpoints had become an island fictional story and the reality on the ground was of the stone age where only few human beings could be seen.

Usman Kakar, who received his degree of Bachelor of Laws from the Law School of Quetta, he had been a human rights activist since he was in high school. Kakar joined the Pashtun Student Organization as unit secretary. Later, he joined the Pashtunkhwa Milli Awami Party (PMAP). Kakar was elected to the Senate of Pakistan as a candidate of PMAP in the 2005 Pakistani Senate election. He ran for the post of the Deputy Chairman of the Senate of Pakistan as a candidate of PMAP in March 2018. Kakar, before joining the Pashtun Tahafuz Movement (PTM) had always been sympathetic, especially the Pashtuns' rights activists and publicly blamed the Pakistani establishment for torturing, kidnaping and killing of tens of thousands of Pashtuns and Balochis. He always raised his voice against the brutality of the Pakistani army in Afghanistan. On June 21, 2021, Kakar died in Karachi from a severe head injury he had sustained at his residence in Quetta. His son and relatives without any fear said that Kakar was assassinated by the Pakistani establishment.

I was dropped right in front of the Eidgah mosque's main gate and started walking towards Kabul football stadium, the place that had always given a message of freedom of speech, equality, peace and democracy during the past two decades. The only positive thing happened that day was the clean air. The sky had spread its pure blue wings over the Maranjan Ghondey (Maranjan Hill), like a mother bird with her chicks under her wings. I was surprised for a while by seeing the area so clean for the first time in twenty years, but soon realized that the Hozori Chaman (Hozori ground) was missing those hundreds of kicks of soccer balls. I also noticed that the muddy cricket pitch was missing those teenage shouts of 'out': yes, there was no dust for the first time in two decades.

I kept walking towards the Kabul cricket stadium where I once witnessed a suicide attack right at the main entrance during the most popular Afghan league called Shpageeza. It was September 13, 2017. The blast left multiple killed and wounded, yet thousands of spectators did not even leave the area, and the international players, commentators and empires kept the matches playing with the highest spirits. While there was no blast or attack today, not only the stadium but also the whole area around was missing the sound of steps of a human being.

I had to book another taxi to Mujeeb Rahman's home in Khushal Khan near the Spin Kalai intersection. We made it via the formerly named Interior Ministry, now Kabul Police Headquarter Road. The road, once restricted, had no barriers now, the police headquarters gate that used to be open 24/7 with vehicles going in and out every five minutes was closed and only two young Taliban were there. Crossing the next roundabout made us witness another scary scene. The Malalai Zezhanton (Malalai Maternity Hospital), once the busiest maternity hospital of the country with roughly one delivery every thirty minutes did not help a young woman. The husband and the mother were slapping their foreheads and chest while loudly crying for the cold body without a soul lying in front of them. The newlywed bride had an ectopic pregnancy and needed an emergency surgery according to a medical doctor living in their neighborhood, while the hospital was still there no more than walls and beds only, the more than 300 staff including gynecologists, surgeons and administration were only on the attendance sheet last time signed three days ago. After hearing the story of the poor husband, I tried to help him with some little cash I had in my pocket, but he refused.

I called Rahman, my old friend from when he was the reporter and stringer for an international media outlet to open the door. He could not sit on the floor mattresses in typical Afghan style since he had two major surgeries in 2019.

Instead, he kept sitting on his double bed and passed me the beautiful fifty-year-old crystal ashtray and said, "you can smoke, don't worry about me, who knows about tomorrow. I have survived from the most dangerous cancer and of course tens of suicide attacks while reporting in Kandahar, but don't know if we live longer after what just happened," and then smiled.

He turned on the 21-inch Samsung TV and asked me to listen to some music on cable and for a while forget about what was happening, he left the room to bring the lunch. As usual, the delicious rice, tasty meatballs and of course my favorite tarwhey, the savory Afghan drink made from a yogurt or buttermilk base with water, were placed in front of us. Rahman had always been a wise man and his sixth sense let him see immediately that I would be facing hard times. I told him that I needed to leave the country in the next ten hours, and he too could accompany me since he also had a COM approval for himself and his old wife. I then called Mobin Ahmadzai who was also an SIV to get ready and wait for my next call that could come at any time. Rahman and Ahmadzai both were worried about the crowds at the airport gate, and of course I was too. We were all SIV and/ or COM approved applicants, but it wasn't helping us with getting into the airport. Rahman told me that since he had two surgeries and was over fifty-five, he would not be able to make it through the thousands of people. I had not told Moraka and Spogmai before, and then called and shocked them with telling them to pack only one small bag with the most important stuff especially some diapers for Barlas Khan and some cookies for the kids. They were not ready at all, but I told them that we had no time to waste, and they needed to wait for my next call. I started thinking about how to get into the airport, since it was totally impossible for people like us to go through the thousands of people who were spending days at the gate and did not care if anyone fired at them.

I called Nasir Khan to see if he could help me with Commander Arsalan, the guy he said was the head of Peace Committee for the Taliban. He had failed to get back to me. Dr. Omid Shah came to my mind then, I knew he had told me just a day before that they would be shifted from Eagle Camp to the airport, I called him and fortunately he was already at the airport. The airport's perimeter was tasked to the National Strike Forces (NSF). I asked him, and he had no choice but to help us getting into the airport. Although he was a surgeon, he promised to wear a uniform and hold a gun at the gate an hour before we were due to leave. I called Naqibullah to be on call so he could drive us down to the airport. Meanwhile, I also called Karimzai, another close friend to see if he wanted to leave because he already had an SIV and worked in high positions. I stayed at Rahman's house for quite a while and called Khan at 9:30 pm to pick me up for home. We reached home at 10:00 pm, everyone was ready but very shocked, of course migration is never easy.

The Journey Of Pain

Since Pashtana, Omid Shah and Hamad Khan were already on the evacuation list and were supposed to leave soon, Jana came from Gardez for the farewell. I didn't know if it was a greeting or a farewell. When we met Jana, she kept crying. Yes, the goodbyes were very hard to exchange. I had already called Mobin and Karimzai to make it to join us at 12:00 am, two hours flew just like two seconds, and the time had come to leave like thieves in the night. Agha Jan, Moraka, Habibullah Khan and Pari had made it to Omid Shah's car driven by Ahmad Shah; and Spogmai, Mallani, Eliana, Faiz Mohammed, the children and I were in my truck, driven by Naqibullah. Although I tried my best to not let them go with us to say goodbye how can one stop his beloved ones from accompanying them at such a time.

I still remember how Jana kept watching us from the fourth floor as we left. None of us had time to pack up or store anything safely. I could not even put my laptop in its bag and put it in a safe place but left it on a sofa in the dining room. About 3000 books that I had brought from India and Dubai were my most expensive and valuable treasure that I left with tears in my eyes. Every book, the chair and sofa that I used to sit on while studying and writing, the study lamp, those Bluetooth loudspeakers in the lights on the ceiling, my jeans, three-piece suits and traditional coats in the caramel color closet were asking me for whom was I leaving them?

Though I had no time, I ran towards my library, the room I used to breathe the most in, I stood at the window and kept

looking at the trees in front of the block that once I used to
water. I lit my Blackstone vanilla cigar and tried to live the
moment, I still wanted to have some more puffs at the window
that I did not know when I would see through again. Naqib
came and said that we were late. I felt my feet were stuck to the
Mazari rug I had bought in Mazar-e-Sharif, I understood that
the rug was not letting me leave it, the relationship between the
two of us had come to an end, as soon I tried to say goodbye
to the window, I hit my pinky finger on the couch that always
hosted me while reading, writing and even watching myself
on TV shows. I forgot the pain but started believing that the
couch, which had been my buddy for ten years did not want
me to leave it.

Jana, her two little daughters and Pashtana with her son,
Hamad Khan were left, since Pashtana was waiting for a call
from Omid Shah before they flew. It was the most difficult
moment leaving the place, which my good and bad memories
were attached to. I felt like a two-day lamb pulled from the
herb, leaving the place that had given me name and fame, that
had given me respect, dignity and popularity not only across the
country but in the region and on international stages. Leaving
Kabul was just like one's beloved is being forcefully taken
from him, he is tightened with the hardest chains, his mouth is
stitched while his eyes and ears are left open so he can see how
brutally his beloved is being taken from him and can hear her
screams and shouts. The moment had totally occupied all my
senses and the midnight was painting the picture of Romeo and
Juliet as they were caught up in between a rock and a hard place.
The delusional love was changing into a reality, my Juliet Kabul
had chosen to go into a dark stone age once again, and I like
wounded frozen eagle could neither land nor fly. Nature had
decided that Juliet had to live with Paris for a while, Layla had

no other option other than going to Ward al-Thaqafi's castle for a period of time.

I turned my eyes to the dark scared, sleeping Kabul, opened the window and watered the soil that is the all-time kohl of my eyes with the drop of tears that had been burning my cheeks for days. For the first time in my life, I felt totally broken, beaten up and a loser; yes, I had lost, I was leaving the city that I never thought of leaving. I had always opportunities to relocate and move to the U.S or Europe but I always preferred living with my Layla, its white snow in January always gave me the message or purity, peace and justice, the freezing cold weather in mid-January making me even stronger. Kabul in snow always looks like a newlywed bride's gown that is inviting her groom to touch, close his eyes and go on an everlasting heavenly journey.

Kabul was not only a place, but also my best friend, a friend with whom I had shared all my good and bad, it was the city I had once told her story to my all-time love and princes Spogmai. Kabul had painted her Mona Lisa on my Spogmai's mind and in heart before she came to Kabul for the first time in 2011. It was the city where for the first time I confidently held Spogmai's hand walked in Babar's Garden and told her of my old days in the garden, it was the city where I experienced my worst financial days after I got married and brought Spogmai to Kabul, yet no poverty could ever upset me since I had both Spogmai and Kabul. It was the city where Wadan Khan, my first and beloved child, grabbed my index finger and started walking. I was remembering the day when on March 26, 2013, the third day of Kabul's spring Spogmai, the one-year-old Wadan Khan, and I went on a long drive to Arghawan, to see the beautiful purple Arghawani flowers. The music of the flowing river and Spogmai's gorgeous green eyes made me write for her:

Be my clothes so I can wear you,
What if you become my skin
And refuse to go out,
Yes, I am not a snake
To shed you off,
But to protect you from
The winter of Kabul
And Summer of Delhi

Kabul was the city where I for the first time gave a revolutionary speech to tens of thousands of people in Huzuri Chaman, it was the city where I started fighting for rights and justice, it was the city that taught me to love, love and only love. But then I remembered Farzan, I started thinking that it was also Kabul that took Farzan and many friends from me.

On January 20, 2018, Farzan for the first time that month woke up as early as 8:00 am, he filled the bath with hot water and lay down for about a half hour. After taking his breakfast he dressed and left for his office, the High Peace Council, and since, his office was close to his home, he walked. On his way, though, everyone passing by looked very comfortable, but he was feeling too cold, he made it to the other side of the road, where the sun was bathing the pathway with warm and shining rays. Meanwhile, he bought some fried peanuts and popcorn from the street food cart to get him some inner heat. He started eating. After his meeting to bring peace and stability to the county he sat at the dining table, and although, he was usually a foodie man, that day he couldn't eat the thin and long white Turkestani rice served in a transparent crystal plate with rolled beefed meatballs. He picked the fat with thinking that life is too short, and he would work out for an extra hour that day.

About 3:30, after he prayed his Asar, he left for home, he again felt too cold and an inner fear, he again made to the other side of the road to get some sun heat. The sun's rays were dying just like the peace process he was struggling for. Farzan picked his phone and called me,

"Hey. What's up?" he asked.

"Nothing much, badly exhausted with translating your article," I said.

"Oh, thank you sir, you have been always so great. Let me pay you back for the article," he laughed. "Poyan, the Afghan Consulate to Pakistan has invited us for a dinner in Continental today, so I believe getting the continental food will pay for what you are doing for me."

"You snake! You are trying to get me healthy with someone else's pocket. Anyways, I am not in the mood to eat outside today, ask Poyan to come to my place, I will get you both a better dinner," I said.

However, since Poyan had already invited other guests as well, his invitation was accepted.

It was about 6:00 pm that massive firings made everyone scream and run to the ground floor. In a scared voice, he called me. I told him to relax and put his phone on silent. I made calls to the Ministers of Interior and Defense, and I asked Farzan and Poyan to lock the room door. They were in the room 402 on the fourth floor, the room's curtains started moving like tornado had taken them, a silence had occupied the surroundings, the only voice that was hitting ears was the fear and terror, the frighten shouts and boots on the ground were the only things broke the silence. All the senses of the people in the room were alert and they felt like they were watching a horror movie on a 3D screen, and every move was making their hair stand up. Suddenly, they were blinded, and their thinking power was paralyzed, but they soon realized that it was the electricity that went off. Farzan and Poyan pushed the bed and the table to the door so the terrorists could not enter the room, but soon, a hole was made by gunfire, and a gassing grenade was thrown in the hole. This not only paralyzed the power of their nerves but also set the entire room on fire, Farzan's and Poyan's bodies were unrecognizable.

Yes, Kabul was the city where death had tried to take me multiple times including the attack on the American University of Afghanistan (AUAF) on August 24, 2016, which I survived, but along with many other innocent souls I lost my dearest friend Prof. Naqib Ahmad Khepalwak.

Yet my soul is so tightly tied to the city, why? I did understand that Kabul was not only a city, it was the spiritual connection we were tied to, it was the hot and cold we were sharing, it wasn't only a geographical place, but part of my life which has provided both laughter and tears. Despite all the bad incidents, Kabul had never let me leave her and kept protecting me under her wings, but this time, her protecting wings held millions of arrows of the monster hunter, she could not protect me anymore, and was asking me to leave with tears, but to come back and make her fly over Himalayas all over again.

Kabul, the city of love, hospitality, diversity of culture and civilization, knowledge, poetry and philosophy – and the intersection of south, central Asia, the Middle East and Europe.

Kabul's beauty and history has been described by many renowned writers and authors including Richard Solomon and Willem Vogelsang.

Kabul owns one of the richest linguistic legacies of pre-Islamic scripts, which existed before being displaced by the Arabic alphabets, after the Islamic conquest of Afghanistan. Sharada, Kharosthi, Greek (for the Bactrian language), and Brahmi are among these scripts.

There is much abundant archeological evidence in the form of coins, manuscripts and inscriptions that has provided traces of the precursors of the contemporary Indo-Aryan languages of Afghanistan such as Dardic languages. Recent archeological evidence shows that Sanskrit in Brahmi script inscriptions was developed in Kabul, and attests to the prevalence of the Sanskrit in Afghanistan.

Sarada texts have been widely found in Afghanistan; one of them was engraved on a marble statue of the Hindu elephant god Ganesh that was found near Gardez Paktia. Another was inscribed on the large Uma Maheshvara from Tepa-e-Skandar (Sikandar Hill), north of Kabul. The Sarada inscriptions all seem to date to the 8th century CE.

Inscriptions and documents in Kharosthi (developed in Gandhara) have been found almost everywhere across Afghanistan. To the far west and northwest, several specimens have been found at sites along the Kabul River as far west as Wardak province, some 20 miles west of Kabul. Recent archaeological excavations have also yielded numerous Kharosthi inscriptions from north of the Hindu Kush, in ancient Bactria, both in sites in northern Afghanistan such as Kunduz.

The first historical account of an oasis around the Kabul River can be found in the 2000 BCE ancient Indian hymn of Rigivida, in which the region was called Kabuha or Kabukha. The ancient city of Vigarute is also said to have been located on the current site of Kabul.

The city of Kabul originated 3500 years ago; Alexander the Great of Macedonian referred to the city in 328 BC and ancient Greek geographer and historian Starbone of the First Century BCE called this city Ortaspana which means " Highland Region". Another ancient Greek geographer, Beltemous, in the Second Century BCE referred to the city as Kaboura and he called its residents Bolitio. According to Gurgasht the city's inhabitants were the Kabolitoi. Some believe that the city has also been called Carura.

The fortress at Kabul is believed to have been constructed at the end of the third century CE. The village of Kabul is thought to have been established during the Koshan dynasty in the Second Century and was located in the Logar Valley within the Chakari region.

During the Second and Fourth Centuries, Kabul relocated a number of times, moving to Shiwaki, Khord-Kabul, and the Takht-e Shah Khanborak valley. The last location of Kabul was the fortress of Bala-Hissar in the summit of Shirdarwaza and Assamahee mountains. Kabul was built northwest of the Bala-Hissar fortress and Kharabad on the left bank of the Kabul River. Kabul became more famous during the time of Arabic Califats (Khalifates) in 645-876 CE.

At the end of the 16th century, Kabul experienced a significant degree of expansion and development when, during the dynasty of Babur Shah, a special initiative was made for the development and beautification of all Afghan cities. Gradually, a number of gardens and parks were created throughout the city. By the end of Seventeenth century, Kabul was a large trade center with a population of 10,000.

In 1773, during the Durrani Dynasty, Kabul became the capital of Afghanistan. During the time of King Timor Shah, the city's experienced additional construction and an expansion. A few large government buildings were constructed around the Bala-Hissar fortress. The construction of housing, mosques, public baths (Hammam), Caravan-Sarai, and new parks took place within the residential area of Gozar. Some new residential areas such as Divanbigi, Sardar Jankhan, Ali Rezakhan, Muradkhani, Ahanghari, Shamrezha, Khakrobah, Sarai Shahzadah Abass, and

Khan Shikh Abdullah were developed within the city's urban boundary.

Kabul becomes a real lover of everyone who spends even a few months there. The beautiful Qargha Lake and the Valley of Paghman gives your lungs the most fresh and cold breezes when the summer is at its peak during August in downtown Kabul. One never needs to have any digestive or appetitive medics if there is access to the water of Chehalsatoon and the historic Dar-ul-Aman. I still remember when, in 2007, with some folks from NATO, I visited a U.S. camp in Tajbeg Palace, they served a well water with the lunch, the water was lab tested and was strongly recommended to drink instead of unhealthy filtered bottled water.

Share-e-Now, the all-time immortal gorgeous area of the capital, where the joys and happiness had always occupied the surroundings even in the very worst days it had been experiencing. The beautiful and big shopping malls, the cafes, the big Afghan, Indian, Arabic, Turkish, Chines and Western food restaurants, the play zones for the children, the lighting and flowery streets for the youths, the teahouses for writers, authors, poets, intellectuals and politicians. Shahr-e-Now was the life living spot for all ages.

The beautiful and landscaped Shamali especially the Gul Ghondi Hill connecting Kabul and Parwan in the north always gives the first news of the spring. Every spring, the cultural dignitaries celebrate with special zeal by writing poems and perform about the ancient festival. Now-roz, celebrated across the country especially in Mazar-e-Sharif, Shuhada-e-Salehin and of course in Arghawani Gul Ghondi, which has its own charm. Beside enjoying the purple Gul Ghondi, tarwhey, the savory Afghan drink made from a yogurt or buttermilk base with water had its own taste.

Yes, leaving Kabul was just like Azarel trying to remove the soul from one's body.

We reached Banaee, where Ahmadzai had to join us, he and his family in two taxis were on the other side of the road arguing with one of the taxi drivers, the taxi driver did not want to go to the airport since he was scared of the Taliban seeing him help people to leave the country. I sent Naqib to talk to the driver and make him drop them at the gate as he had already agreed before picked them up from Ahmad Shah Baba Mena also known as Arzan Qeemat. Naqib convinced the driver by offering him AFN 500 ($6.00). The Abbey Gate was about five kilometers from where Ahmadzai joined us. Ahmad Shah and the two taxis were following us on the Kabul-Jalalabad highway, I noticed that Ahmad Shah's car was missing when we took a U-turn in front of Camp Phoenix, also known OFSOTER Camp.

The global security documents wrote that Camp Phoenix, on the outskirts of Kabul, was home of Combined Joint Task Force Phoenix, which trains the Afghan National Army. Combined Joint Task Force Phoenix was a collection of Army National Guard units that were training the new Afghan National Army.

In early 2003 Camp Phoenix was nothing but a huge junkyard full of scrap metal left from an abandoned tractor trailer park. The OMC [Office of Military Cooperation] needed a large enough area to house up to 800 soldiers and they decided this would be the perfect location, leasing it from an Afghan trucking company for one year.

As soon as the approval was given, the US Army began their work of turning the junkyard into a military training camp. The camp was made up of two force provider kits that come with everything needed to set up operations in a field environment. Normally it took about three to four weeks to have the whole kit set up, but the engineers there set up both kits in about two weeks, which was record time. By 15 May 2003 there was a dining facility, medic tent, showers, latrines and living quarters enough to house over 500 soldiers.

The camp's maximum capacity was quickly filled with more than 300 10th Mountain soldiers residing in the camp preparing to begin their mission. This camp was built to house the soldiers who had to train the ANA. Once the training began, most soldiers remained there but some replaced Special Forces who were embedded with the Afghan trainees.

Members of Coalition Joint Task Force Phoenix began training and mentoring the Afghan National Army in June of 2003. This task force was comprised of National Guard, reserve and active-duty soldiers from seven different countries. By February 2005, Task Force Phoenix had trained and deployed more than 17,000 ANA soldiers at five corps commands located in Kabul, Gardez, Kandahar, Herat and Mazar-e-Sharif, which also have permanent garrisons.

By February 2005 the ANA had over 5,000 soldiers in training. This training was conducted at many sites, including the Kabul Military Training Center, Command and General Staff College, National Military Academy of Afghanistan and the new National Training Center north of Kabul. The ANA themselves were training all the new recruits in the basic training of soldiers, noncommissioned officers and officers at KMTC.

As of October 2008, there had been seven iterations of Task Force Phoenix stationed at Camp Phoenix.

Task Force Phoenix I was launched by the U.S Army's 10th Mountain Division following the collapse of the Taliban regime. Every subsequent rotation had been comprised and lead primarily by Army National Guard commands.

Phoenix II built up the first Afghan Corps in Kabul, Afghanistan. Phoenix III took on the task of splitting that corps into five separate corps and locating them throughout the country at strategic centers. Phoenix IV worked to build those corps to full strength. Phoenix V implemented an aggressive program of dispersing Embedded Training Teams with deployed ANA forces throughout the country.

The mission expanded under Phoenix VI with the added responsibility associated of training and supporting the Afghan National Police, as well as continuing to train and mentor the growing Afghan National Army.

Combined Joint Task Force Phoenix VII was led by the New York National Guard's 27th Brigade Combat Team and was comprised primarily of 1700 National Guard Soldiers from New York and hundreds more from many other states. In addition, there are Active Duty Navy, Air Force and Marine personnel serving along with teams from coalition allies.

But unfortunately, overnight, Camp Phoenix was once again turned into a huge junkyard full of scrap metal. This time it was the US, those who had turned the junkyard into a modern, well equipped and civilized training center, turned it back into a junkyard. Yes, history does repeat itself but mostly in a deteriorating form.

Naqib called Ahmad Shah to find out about their whereabouts, he had taken a U-turn on the Green Village Road before the Kabul Custom office since I had told them that we would go via Camp Sullivan with the gate pass issued by the U.S. Embassy, but after I talked to Omid Shah, we had to make it via Abbey Gate where his teammates were posted for the security, yet I thought Ahmad Shah should have followed us. Some four Taliban gave us a bad look right at the right turn towards BAF and Qasaba Road, they had understood that we were going to the airport since three vehicles with tens of people including women and children would not go elsewhere at 12:30 in this Taliban era. I asked Naqib to drive with limited speed of not more than 20 m/h until Ahmad Shah caught up with us. We kept driving with the exact speed meter for almost fifteen minutes until he found us. As soon we crossed the roundabout that divides the road towards Deh-Sabz and BAF and the airport, we started seeing thousands of people marching towards the airport gates. Omid Shah kept calling me to find out if we were close, it took us thirty more minutes to reach the Camp Sullivan northern gate, since it was about 1:30 in the morning, it felt like we were in the middle of the black sea, and of course my tiredness made me thinking of Sullivan Gate as Abbey Gate, I kept telling him that we were at the gate but he was still giving me different signs, he was looking for us in front of the Shamal Gas station. I then asked Naqib and Faiz Mohammed to walk towards where Omid Shah was waiting for us, they were connected over the phone, I got out the vehicle and lit a cigarette, Ahmadzai had sent the taxis back and I asked him to get his wife and daughters on the truck. Naqib and Faiz Mohammed were back in about one hour and gave me bad news, they said the Abbey Gate was quite some distance away still and the crowds had totally blocked the roads. It would be almost impossible for us to walk with the children and women. I was still figuring out how to make it happen, when suddenly a massive firing began, the firing made people run in different directions, we heard screaming that people had been shot and killed. I asked Agha Jan to get into the car since he was out smoking with me. Everyone was looking at me, waiting for me to make a decision. They were almost disappointed and thinking of going back home. I asked Naqib and Faiz Mohammed to start walking in front of the truck, I would drive, and they would make people give us enough room to get through. Ahmad Shah would follow me. I tried to turn the engine on, but ahh, no more battery since I forgot to turn the engine off after I had opened the window. I had no time to hit my head, cry over our bad luck or create panic. I asked them to find me jump leads and they fortunately found a nice taxi driver who helped us out with the cable, Ahmad Shah had parked his car headlights to headlights and the connection worked. We were just done with starting the engine when Karimzai with his family including his wife, children and parents arrived.

The Deathly Night

Driving through the thousands of people sticking like honeybees, with bullets raining all around, and tear gas grenades made me feel it was a 'do or die' situation. It took us about one and half hours to reach the Shamal gas station through the crowds. Omid Shah had already crossed the road, I saw the gentleman wearing a military uniform with AK47, a night vision and a torch on his helmet for the first time: a surgeon never quits saving lives, if not in the operation theater, then of course in other form. There were dozens of other security officers and soldiers at the gate who were not able to hear each other due the shots being fired and peoples' shouts and screams. I just noticed that he told his team that we were the people he had been waiting for. They already had our COM/SIV approval copies, and they had to count us based on the documents they had in hands. They asked me to verify the family members so they would escort them in lines. As soon the line was made up, people started running and tried to get into our line and pretend to be members of the family, the forces started shouting and beating people with the cables they had in their hands. The line was broken, and I was hit on my neck with a cable, which did not bleed but did hurt. Suddenly they started firing, and some family members including Ahmadzai's family were sprinkled in different directions like drops of heavy rain. The rest of the families had reached the gate, while Spogmai, Shamla, Ghani Khan, Barlas Khan and I were left in the crowd. We had lost Wadan Khan. Spogmai started screaming and crying, I also got upset and loudly calling Wadan

Khan's name among thousands of people, while the forces kept firing at us. I still remember one of the soldiers kept his gun near to Barlas Khan's shoulder as he cuddled Spogmai. The two-year-old Barlas Khan was so badly scared. I was wearing a backpack and holding Shamla's and Ghani's hands trying to hold Spogmai who was struggling because of the gun's barrel right next to Barlas Khan's and her ears while trying to find her missing child. I tried to push the soldier back, but he fired right between my feet. People started screaming that someone standing behind me got shot. I understood that the soldiers were there for the security of the airport and to make the evacuation possible, but I had never seen such violence and wildness from someone calling himself a security officer.

Omid Shah had noticed that we were missing, he and two others of his teammates found us, they kept trying escorting us under the bullets and flood of people towards the gate, the soldiers kept firing but we finally made it to the gate still calling for Wadan Khan. Seeing him being held by Ahmadzai's mother was a second life for Spogmai and me; she hugged him and kept kissing him on his eyes and cheeks. Moraka, Agha Jan and the siblings had successfully escorted us, but unfortunately, I couldn't give my parents and siblings a farewell hug, Moraka could not hug and kiss her Ghani Khan, we were lost on one side of the crowd while they on the other side.

I had thought that the most difficult part of the journey would end there, but it did not. We had to walk for about ten more minutes to the actual gate. This was just the fence before the gate. We were stopped by the Strike Unit 02 from Nangarhar whose security shift had just started. In fact, some of the unit members were accused of accepting bribes and escorting people. This issue was reported by OSF (Orgun Strike Force), so now they were stubborn and tried not to let us in. I tried to talk to their group leader and showed our documents; based on the American government's recent statements and congress approval we were actually the 'right' people to be evacuated even before the overnight change but to a person who had never been to school and was stubborn this made no difference. They started pushing us back, but then the OSF commander arrived and took charge, and we were allowed through. We started following Omid Shah to the gate. By now, the kids and Karimzai's parents were tired of walking. It took us about one and half hours to reach the apartments in which the Strike Force Units members and their family were living. Here, we sat and took rest in the small garden in front of the three-story apartments once used by the ANDSF. At about 6:00 am some SFUs guys got together to receive their coming year's salaries. I also noticed that families with luggage were leaving to a building right opposite to us, I asked Ahmadzai to go and find out what was happening. He came back in ten minutes and told me that the building opposite to us was the hangar being used as a warehouse, and the runway was right behind the building. People were starting to make lines to board the plane. I asked everyone to follow me, we got to the runway in two minutes. There were two lines of people waiting to board the huge grey C-17 on our right. We kept sitting right on the helipad. The plane took off about an hour after everyone in the line had boarded the plane, which then seemed to make it to another runway to pick up other passengers. After about thirty minutes another plane arrived and around 200-250 more people boarded. The planes were not like normal commercial Boeing airbuses with windows boarding at the front: this C-17 opened its whole back. It looked like a shark opening its mouth wide ready to consume everything. Omid Shah had to sign in at work, so he had left us about 6:00 am, and I had no clue of how to make it on plane. Although, there was no boarding or immigration system at the airport and whoever had made it to the airport in the first three and four days had already been evacuated, but now things were more tightly managed. I asked everyone to be ready so we would make it for the coming plane. It was getting hot by 10:00 am, and the asphalt runway and the huge C-17's engine was making it even hotter. The third plane was there about 10:30 am, people who kept coming from the back apartments were making lines, I asked everyone to make it to the line, we started walking when a man came and asked me what Strick Force Unit I belonged to. From his accent he seemed from Momandara district of Nangarhar province, I told them that we belonged to no SFUs but had gotten our own COM approvals. He then told me that the runway was a military runway and only people related to any SFUS, and their families could fly from the runway. And people like us should have made it through Sullivan Gate. I had to face another challenge now, I kept asking them if they could guide me on how to get to Camp Sullivan, but no one was helping.

I lit a cigarette and start thinking of what to do and how to make things happen, meanwhile I had to motivate everyone including Karimzai and Ahmadzai. Later, two Americans wearing red caps, brown waistcoats and blue jeans passed by. I asked them if they could help me with the address; the older one with white beard, gave me a questionable look, and from his body language I understood that they were the intelligence guys, probably CIA, under whom the SFUs were operating. Without giving him a second to ask me a question, I introduced myself, told him the story and showed him the gate pass sent by the embassy that clearly said that I could make through any nearby gate. But unfortunately, their answer was 'no', they did not have a clue how to get to Camp Sullivan, I then called Omid Shah to come and help if his groupmates or anyone in SFUs knew the route to Camp Sullivan, he asked his friends, but no one had any idea how to help us reach to the destination.

I then sent Ahmadzai and Karimzai with their young sons to the eastside of the airport, where we had come from, to find out on how to make it to the desired destination. They returned about forty minutes after feeling hopeless. One of the 02-unit officer who had noticed me came and told me that he had seen me on television, and asked me if he could help me. I thought since the airport's security was under their control and he was driving an American truck, that he could take us to the destination in ten minutes. He apologized; since he was not wearing uniform, he couldn't help. He added that he was tired of always having to wear a uniform for Afghanistan. I said yes, it will take decades for Afghanistan to put on uniforms again, Afghanistan was already ununiformed. At least he tried to explain how to get to the destination. Omid Shah, Ahmadzai, Karimzai and I left according to the map he gave us; we crossed the green container being used as a warehouse, we turned left and walked for about twenty meters to where two security guards and two American soldiers were on duty. Ahead, there were more U.S soldiers on duty at the U.S soldiers' residential building. We kept going towards the southeast wall and finally reached the last corner of the concrete wall of the airport but found no roads that could take us to our destination. We then returned to the roundabout connecting the corner we had crossed earlier; the 0 units residential apartments and a gravel road went north that we did not try yet. I asked if we could succeed, we checked it too, the road went nowhere but to the CIA officials' offices. On our way back to the family, Omid Shah met one of his colleagues on a military bike and asked him if he knew anything about Camp Sullivan, he said his shift was just about to start at that very gate. This was the biggest news for me that day, I asked Ahmadzai and Omid Shah to go with him, note the route and bring back the bike so Karimzai's parents and the children could ride; they were tired enough and had no more energy to walk for hours. They came back in about thirty minutes with badly disappointed faces, the guy had taken them to the same Abbey Gate that we came through the previous night.

Everyone, including myself had accepted that the only way to get to Camp Sullivan was to leave the airport from Abbey Gate, and reenter through the other gate, which felt totally impossible due to crowds outside the airport. We were not the people who could even think of getting through tens of thousands of people at the gate. I took a deep breath and asked Karimzai's parents and the rest of the families to go and sit under the iron roof of the hangar windows, since it was now boiling hot on the runway. They knew that we had lost and would have to leave for the home where we did not know how long I would survive. I was thinking of asking Omid Shah if he could arrange a truck to take us back to the Abbey Gate since the family members were not able to walk anymore. But then I noticed a small building about 250-300 meters to our right. Some thirty people, including women and children and few U.S soldiers with two white 4x4 Ford trucks were there. I asked Omid Shah, Ahmadzai and Karimzai to go and find out who they were and if they were waiting for the flight, since they also looked like civilians. They talked to the U.S soldiers and explained the situation, the soldiers told them that the civilians there were U.S green card holders and they could not help with taking us to Camp Sullivan. I told them let me try, so we all went over. The building had a sign of the Afghanistan military aviation guards, and there was a black 2017 armored Toyota Landcruiser left unlocked. We found tens of badges and national Identity cards and some other documents thrown in front of the entrance to the building. I asked them to sit on the bench in front of the building as I had to wait for the right time to talk to the U.S officers, I noticed that there was a group smoking and drinking energy drinks next to the first truck. I kept watching and waiting for the right time to go and talk to them, a soldier told the captain something and he looked at me, I right away made it towards them before captain could reply to the soldier. I told them the story and requested them to take us to Camp Sullivan. The captain was very nice to me and told me that he needed to talk to his boss over the phone and see if he could help us, but the first sergeant, who seemed to be from Texas from his accent, tried to tell him and me that they would not help us. I left them to pass the request to their boss and went back to my group. About ten minutes later the sergeant came and told me the same story: that those waiting there were green card holders, and they would take them in few minutes but could not help us. I knew that no one of them had even a single document let alone having the green cards because I could easily hear them talking in Dari saying that they were the luckiest people who would soon be Americans while they had worked for neither the U.S nor the Afghan government but had finally cashed the reward of the three nights they had spent behind the gate. Yet, I did not want to argue with the 1st sergeant but thanked him, and he joined his colleagues.

Omid Shah felt bad and apologized that he could not help us. He never needed to be sorry, since he had already done his job and things were not in his control anymore. I told him and the others not to worry, just wait and watch, I knew that those guys would help us. The captain kept looking at me and finally sent those families on the two trucks, but he did not go with them.

He came and told me, "Hey buddy! I would love to help you guys since I believe that you guys are most deserving and right people to be helped out, but I only have two trucks and can't make the third round. You have told me that you are three families of twenty people. I can't take all of you on the two trucks since I am not allowed to take more than five people in the bed of each truck."

I thanked him for the great help and favor he intended to do to me, and then told him that he did not have to worry about the ten more people, I would manage a truck for them, indeed, I was thinking of the little military bike that my friends drove back from Abbey Gate. The deal was made, I sent Karimzai to bring his parents and all the children under five on the bike and ask others to walk as fast as they could, the trucks had arrived. Spogmai, the children and I got on the first truck, Ahmadzai and some of his family members on the second truck and the rest had hardly made it on the bike and hit towards Camp Sullivan on the runway. It took us twenty minutes to reach the camp, but unfortunately, the bike being driven by Karimzai broke down just 100 meters distance from the camp. We passed them and the captain told me to take it easy, they would go back and pick them up. We were dropped fifty meters away from a fenced camp containing approximately one thousand people. The sun was proving its power that day, my face was already burned since I have sensitive skin that burns quickly. Our shoes and pants had changed their colors and were looking like they were made of clay. The children ran towards the water stall the U.S. army had placed, they had tried to find a bottle of water on the runway but had failed.

The Polar Night

As soon we tried walking towards the entrance connecting the trailer offices, the northern gate and the portion of the camp, people started asking us that why we were sent back, they were scared and thought people could be rejected too. I had no clue why they were asking me until I found out that we were coming from the wrong direction. Some U.S. and Canadian soldiers tried to help us and warmly greeted us. I asked Ahmadzai to make it to the gate before me, so I could wait for Karimzai and his family, a 1st sergeant asked Ahmadzai for his documents, he showed him his SIV and gate pass, the officer was surprised and asked me why were we sent back since we had all the legitimate and right documents, I then told him the story that we had not been sent back or rejected, but we made it via wrong gate and we did not know if we had to make it through Camp Sullivan gate specifically. The officer gave us water, verified all the documentation and guided us to the camp and wait for the next destination. As soon as Karimzai and his family arrived we all moved to the other side of the fence. They were very thankful to the U.S. and Canadian soldiers who had helped them making to the gate. For a while, I thought we would be staying there for few minutes, since there was not an inch room to sit, the area was completely covered in trash: there must have been 3000-3500 empty mineral water bottles and about 1000 empty food bags, used napkins, disposable plastic forks, spoons and knives, and pieces of cardboard covered in dust making the place unbearable. The sun was burning and there was no shade, which made the children cry. I was afraid for

Karimzai's parents since they had walked for hours the previous night, did not sleep and eat, and of course had no access to their insulin injection which they needed to take every day. There were only two toilets with three stalls each for men and women separately in a container; the shortage of toilets and their misuse by people who had never used a flush toilet made the entire area smell bad. We tried to avoid using them. We were right behind Camp Sullivan's main gate, and the usual shootings were making our children scared again. There wasn't a tower near us, instead mud had been loaded in an arch shape supporting the RCC wall. Three security points were being controlled by the U.S soldiers in a fifteen-meter distance starting from the north-east making it towards southwest. The soldiers were still and kept their eyes on the binoculars and were ready to shoot if needed. Hundreds of bullets a minute were being fired by Strick Force Units, just fifty meters from us. We saw a woman of about thirty brought inside on a stretcher, the U.S soldiers were running to take her to the hospital. She was still calling for her kids, but the soldiers did not understand her language, they thought that she was cursing them, so I went to tell them that she was asking about her kids. One of the female soldiers said that she would personally go and find her children. The scene had made Spogmai and Karimzai's mother sob. I tried to calm and told them to be strong, things would soon get better. Since it was getting even hotter, Wadan Khan and Barlas Khan got sun stroke. I ran to the toilets and got Spogmai's scarf wet and put it on their heads. We were not getting enough water either, the soldiers kept trying their best to distribute water bottles but the crowd inside the camp kept jumping, hitting each other and some were getting more than they deserved while others remained thirsty. None of our family members had ever practiced the pull and push experience, so we remained thirsty. Standing for almost one and half hours in the boiling heat, everyone except me gave up and had to sit on the trash. My children who I had always protected from even a cold wind had to sleep on the worst trash I had ever seen. A U.S. sergeant bringing in the new evacuees from the verification office had noted us and tried to bring us some water, but as soon he came closer with the bag of water bottles, he was surrounded by the crowd and the bottles were taken from him. He then asked me to follow him to the small warehouse just behind the offices. Although, no one was allowed to cross the fence, he understood that we would remain thirsty if he did not make me follow him. I got enough water for my family, truly saving our lives.

A woman of about forty, wearing three different types of colored shirt asked me for a bottle of water, the request sounded very strange to me, so I asked her what she was doing before. I was shocked by the answer: she was a beggar in Khair Khana and heard of the evacuation, so she headed to the gate. She did not even spend two hours outside, since she knew all the tricks. My follow up question put me in an even deeper thinking that she had shown the verifying office only the copy of her handwritten Tazkera (NIC). Another man, wearing very old clothes and shoes asked me for a cigarette, he told me that he was a cleaner in a restaurant in Kote-Sangi. He had spent one night outside the gate and showed his unpaid electricity bill to the office and was in the camp with us, I asked about ten people, only one of them was a former policeman, the other nine were people had never worked for or with the international forces, organizations or the Afghan government, for a while I thought the U.S was going to evacuate every single Afghan except Taliban members.

We did not even finish drinking the water when a teenager and a young woman were brought in on stretchers; the boy had got shot in his left leg right under his knee, and the woman was shot somewhere in her belly, which meant that they were not only air shelling but ground firing as well. I could not judge if they were right or wrong, because on one hand their security was making the evacuation possible: otherwise, tens of thousands of people would have made it impossible, but people were being wounded and killed. I would honestly say that it was those with no documents or the very low-profile including beggars and shopkeepers who would face no threat at all trying to make the process challenging just to go and live in U.S.

At about 6:00 pm a strong wind made everyone put their heads between the knees and under their arms, I tried to get Ghani Khan's and Barlas Khan's heads inside the shirt I was wearing and closed my eyes, after some fifteen minutes we could not easily recognize each other; look at our tragedy and bad luck, the wind had brought tons of other trash but had not moved any debris from the camp. I wondered about Spogmai; she had always been criticized by me for being extra conscious of hygiene. I looked at her and asked her how she was. I didn't intend to make her emotional but just wanted to make her smile instead of crying over the decades of the misfortune of this nation. People started moving towards the southern gate, where we had to be picked and taken to a biometric center. Karimzai's father asked me to move closer to the gate, so we would not miss any chance, but my sixth sense was telling me that we were going to spend the night there. I told him to wait and watch. It got darker and the lack of lights was making it a polar night. I was badly scared of the next hours, it was getting super cold, and I was worrying about Karimzai's parents and my children. We kept sitting on the trash; Shamla asked for food, although, there were about 1000 empty food bags, we did not see any meals distributed during the day. I thought the bags must have been from previous day and that they had stopped giving out food for some reason. Fortunately, Karimzai's mom and Spogmai still had some cookies in their bags, which had really helped kill the hunger of the children. At about 10:00 pm the U.S. soldiers asked everyone to get ready and make lines. We still kept calm and avoided creating panic unlike the majority. After making the lines and waiting for about one hour, we were told that buses would come the next day and we had to spend the night there. Everyone in the line sat where they were standing. I went to try to find some plastic bags so I could use them as blankets for the old couple and the kids. I saw a few hundred other people had been brought in but kept on waiting on the other side of the trailer-office until we moved and made room for them. I failed to find a single plastic bag or piece of cardboard, but fortunately Spogmai had found two wooden pallets used for the water bottles and had brought them with Zarmina, Karimzai's wife, for the old couple while Karimzai's mom had left hers for the children. After 12:00 am it was freezing cold. The majority of people had come with big luggage and were wearing coats and blankets, but we who could save our lives only, so had nothing to fight with the cold except our strong minds.

Wadan Khan tells me the story of how, that night, I was holding Barlas Khan in my lap and made him sleep, but about thirty minutes later his crying took their attention, he had fallen from my lap while I was sleeping with my head on my knees, Spogmai was shocked because even the sound of a fly or mosquito in the room wakes me up, so how could I fall asleep, then lose control of holding Barlas Khan, and then his cries did not wake me up. They touched me and tried to wake me up, but I fell down and hit my head. They were scared I had died, but Spogmai soon confirmed that I had just fainted. Ahmadzai and Karimzai then put me on the pallet and covered me with Spogmai, Zarmina and Tayaba's scarves. I then asked my back not to spasm today, I had to take care of many lives, and couldn't deal with my back too. I closed my eyes and then with a strong jerk pulled my back from the pallet with all the power my body had. With a loud scream I was able to sit. Karimzai's old mom hugged me and asked if I was in pain.

Her husband said, "he can do it; he is our hero."

The polar night was at its peak, the stars in the sky were witnessing the tragic night waiting to leave on a journey of pains and sorrows.

Suddenly we heard, "get the fuck back, get back, sit down or you will be kicked out and sent back to your fucking homes."

A U.S soldier had been trying to make people sit calmly and wait for the morning, but he gave up. People were still trying to walk towards the next destination, a man with his wife and three kids kept saying that he had worked with USAID in the past and the soldiers had to escort him in.

I asked him to wait, "there is no bus at this time, and everyone needs to wait until the orders come from the next destination, please do not create panic!"

He did not listen and kept on making demands. The U.S. soldiers got angry, but this guy's attitude actually helped me forget about my back. I got angry at him and lost control over my temper; I ran towards him and pushed him, he fell down and I made a fist and asked him if he would shut his mouth or not. Ahmadzai, Karimzai and their sons grabbed me. I told them if he kept creating panic he will be talked to in a different language. He became the ash like a bucket of water is poured on a hearth. The U.S. soldiers and other people then took a sigh of relief.

We were waiting for sunrise to send rays. Finally, a Thai massage of yellow rays of the morning started entering through my skin deep to the bones and muscles, my back muscles started to relax. We washed our faces with the tissue wipes Spogmai had brought for Barlas Khan. The wipes, at the first touch became the chimney soot black. The shooting started all over again right when light of the new morning spread its wings. I noticed the same U.S soldiers at their positions on the wall that I saw the previous night; it wasn't only us who spent the cold and hungry night. I was still thinking about the hard job they were doing that a group of about twenty other soldiers took over, I understood that there was of course a report, and that was not a good news at all, I was not only concerned about us but mostly the tens of thousands of people outside of the gate. I kept my fingers crossed and wished for no more incidents.

A U.S officer with angry eyes said, "I can understand and feel your pains, I do appreciate your patience and I promise, you will have a better life, a life of comfort and success, where no one's husband, son, brother and father will lose his life in a terrorist attack, where no mother will run towards her daughter's school fearing a terrorist attack, I do understand that you spent the worst night of your life last night, but it was all because we do not want you guys to spend an even worse night, we don't have enough resources here, you understand that we just came few days ago to evacuate you guys, to save our Afghan brothers and sisters lives, we did not have enough time to build you guys a better place or a camp, we took our positions right after we got off the plane, we have not slept either. We don't have a proper camp or LSA here since we just came and will stay here until the last flight takes off on August 31st. I request from you much patience and cooperation, so we together can save tens of thousands other lives waiting outside, please wait for a while, no longer than an hour and then make it to the buses as you are requested."

He nicely delivered his motivational speech, but while he did so, three bodies, one dead and two wounded were brought inside. A child of about thirteen years had lost the life he had been fighting for, his long thick black hair did not need a pillow under his head, his white open hand hung down from the stretcher. We could clearly see him saying that he did not have anything or anyone to lose but his life; his torn joggers were telling the story of how close to death they had been before trying to escape it. The soldiers who had thought that they would save his life had turned to stone, they could neither cry nor move. The two other stretchers were carrying a young girl and her father.

The young girl with golden curly hair, and bangles on her wrists, was crying and saying, "Dad! I don't want to go to America, please take me back to home. Where is my mom? I want to go back to home not America."

I kept hugging Shamla since she had already been going through severe trauma for three days, and I didn't want her to see all that scene.

The camp evacuation started about 10:00 am and people as usual started pushing each other, we sat where we had spent the longest and most painful night and kept waiting to be the last ones in the group of about 1000 people. The sun was burning again, yet it was much better than the cold of the previous night. There were two Toyota buses each taking thirty-five people at a time and Hyundai van taking sixteen people. The next camp was about a five-minute drive, but each bus was taking about fifteen minutes to return, so we the last passengers were picked up at about 1:00 pm and dropped in another LSA where there were only four families. The LSA did not have a tent but only one iron sheet-roof car wash. We were told that we would be moved to another place in one to two hours. In order to protect everyone especially the old couple and the children from the burning heat of the sun we moved to the protection of the carwash. The camp was located right behind the main security wall of the airport and from the road on the other side the crowds, especially the single men, were trying to climb the wall but could not escape the U.S forces shouting at them from the towers.

I asked Ahmadzai and Karimzai to see if they could find some cardboard so we could sit on it. They came back with cardboard that they had found at the water stalls behind southern wall of the carwash.

I asked them if I heard what they said correctly, "water stalls?"

Yes, there were hundreds of water cartons. We did not bring any luggage except some cookies for the kids, emergency medics and diapers for Barlas Khan, but I knew that Ahmadzai had brought some luggage including shower kits. Since I now had more dust than hair on my head, the water stall was the greatest news of the day so far, I asked Ahmadzai to pass me his shampoo, and after a good rinse, I felt as if my head was my own again.

It had not been two hours when the camp was unexpectedly filled with 3000 people. All these people were brought from outside of the gate and they did not stay a minute in the camp where we spent over a day. I was still expecting the U.S soldiers who had told me that they would move us to biometrics in two hours. New army tents were installed for the new guests, and our very clean camp changed its look; empty water bottles completely covered the ground. The first tent for about 100 people were installed right at the entrance of the main gate, the second tent was built attached to fence followed by the main gate, nineteen other tents were rapidly built on about one hectare ground. At 6:30 pm the U.S. soldiers brought food for the families, I then understood that we were not going to be moved soon. I needed to smoke and realized that I had run out of cigarettes. I kept trying not to think about them, but my lungs badly wanted one. I then understood that I was a chain smoker. Although there wasn't a single decent thing about the camp, the worst part was the toilets; there were only four mobile toilets, two for men and two for women, for more than 3000 people. While I could clearly see hundreds of brand-new toilets stored outside the fence, I had no clue what they were being kept for, of course not for the Taliban at least. I tried to ask some officers, but they had no answer for me.

It was an area called KIA-North that once held thousands of military and civilian international organizations: most of the NAMSA services to the country were led from this part of the airport, the well-known international construction and logistics companies like Contrack Int'l Inc., Metak and Yuksil had their headquarters in this part of the airport, they were making hundreds of millions USD annually from military and civil services contracts especially in construction. The newest development projects especially the highway roads, urban development, and rural rehabilitation were planned and designed in this part of the airport, which was unbelievably a disaster now. The place where there used to be a trashcan in every twenty meters was covered in trash and debris, the roads and grounds that used to warmly welcome the evening parades of the Afghan and international forces had handed over themselves to scared people wearing torn and dirty clothes, most of whom did not even know why they were there.

The night was much better compared to the previous night since the carwash spot had a roof and three walls, and of course was not very close to the shooting, so the children slept well. The next morning Ghani Khan who had completed his sleeping hours was fresh and started asking me where Burj-e-Khalif was. He thought anyone who goes on plane goes to Dubai, the place he had often watch on most commercials on YouTube, and of course he had seen the photos I had taken last time I visited in January 2021. He then started serious trauma of thinking he was flying to Dubai but finding himself in the trash, I could not help him but telling him to wait until he sees Burj-e-Khalifa, but he kept crying and got homesick. I took him to the clinic opposite to the camp, where he got only few candies.

My condition was getting worse, and I needed to smoke. I started getting emotional about everything. I asked Ahmadzai and Karimzai to go and ask around the camp if they could find me only one cigarette, they returned with bad news: smoking in the camp was banned. I was shocked, since even prisoners are allowed to smoke. At lunch time a female U.S. soldier showed up and asked me to be the tent leader, to help maintain order while they distributed the meal. I was of course not feeling well, and I knew I would not be up for the job, so I introduced Ahmadzai, and he started helping the army distribute the meal and water. Two half liter bottles of water were given per head a day, which made life even tougher. We decided not to eat much because of the lack of toilets: the four toilets were not emptied and cleaned, and they were of course filled within the first hours. Wadan Khan, the poor boy, often gets constipated told me that everything happens for a reason; his problem was helping him now, and he could eat with no tension.

Karimzai's dad who had been walking, sitting under the boiling sun, sleeping on hard wooden pallet in such a cold night, and of course had not been taking his insulin for three days started shivering, and he could no longer stand. Rubina, his youngest daughter started giving him some medicine, but she did not have enough, he needed to be admitted and put on a drip and kept under observation for few hours. He needed to be taken to the clinic and Rubina, as a doctor, accompanied him since only one person was allowed with the patient. He was admitted in the emergency room for six hours. He was given some medicine but unfortunately, they did not have insulin. At about 11:00 pm Rubina called that the security forces at the gate were not allowing them back in, I went to talk to the security forces, but they said they would not let them in, yet he could not explain to me why he was not letting them in. I then asked Rubina from the other side of fence, exactly like a prisoner talks to his visitor for few minutes, to go and talk to the clinic authorities, hoping they might be able to escort them. She did and it worked.

On August 23, 2021, our third day in this camp, I noticed that the majority of the 3000 people were single males between eighteen - forty and at least ninety percent of them had no background of working with any international organization or the Afghan government. They were mostly people who had never been to school either, there were drivers, shopkeepers, restaurant waiters, people who had made to the airport with only their NICs, and some didn't even have them. I met a twenty-seven-year-old young man from Parwan Province with very interesting story: he and his two friends had left home for Iran three days before Kabul collapsed. With the war was at its height and the Taliban having taken over all the business and transit ports of the country including Shirkhan, Islam-qala, Tor Ghondai, Abu Nasar Farahi, Hairatan and Spin Boldak a month before Kabul collapsed, the price of basic goods including fuel, cooking oil, sugar and flour doubled within a week, and the job market collapsed, prompting hundreds of thousands young men to leave the country for Pakistan, Iran and Turkey. Bashir from Parwan had also decided to leave for Iran but he and his two friends did not have enough money to buy visas and air tickets. Iran mostly issued visas for those who were flying by Irani airlines, and of course one had to pay enough money to the broker for the visa itself. So, the three young men decided to go illegally. They had to pay AFN 20,000 ($250.00) to the human trafficker, but they did not have that money either. They asked friends and relatives to lend them the amount and promised they would pay them back soon. They had been living in a local hotel and waiting for the money to receive but Kabul collapsed, and of course after the collapse, people were not even answering their phones. Everyone was trying to stockpile basic goods and couldn't think to lend to anyone else at this point. The three young men were locked down in the hotel since they did not know if it was safe to leave Kabul. So, they stayed in the hotel for four more days and when they heard about the crowds at the airport and the evacuation possibilities, they decided to try their luck for the lands of opportunity. Bashir told me that he loves to sleep. The next morning about 5:00 am his friends tried to wake him so they could make it to the airport, but he kept sleeping and asked them to let him sleep for a while and they would leave shortly. His friends got angry at him and planned to wake him up by telling him that they were leaving without him. Bashir still kept sleeping and an hour later he received their call telling him that they had made it to airport. He, without washing his face or grabbing his bag, got in the taxi and headed to airport. He got lucky and crossed thousands of people and was inside the airport within few hours.

After he had passed the Camp Sullivan gate, he called his two friends to join them, "what? You are at the airport? No way! We were just kidding and trying to wake you up this way, we are still in Company bazaar and were waiting for you."

A young man standing next to us heard Bashir's story.

He interrupted by telling me "You are Mr. Azad, right?"

I looked at him and said yes. He had curly long hair, trimmed mustache and beard and was wearing a grey waistcoat with six pockets on the front and a net at the back. He had a gold chain around the neck and a silver one on his right wrist, three or four rings on his left hand and wearing shoes the way sandals are worn. He seemed to me to be a low-profile gangster. He was very happy seeing me there since he had been watching me on television. I thanked and asked him his name and asked how he made it there. Zaman Khan Hotak was the resident of nearby area called Hotkhil roughly about three kilometers from this part of the airport. He was a professional mugger, and he had gotten caught red handed by local residents of Ahmad Shah Baba Mina and handed him over to the police three months ago. The prosecution in court fought well and the primary court had sent him to jail for twelve months. On the evening of August 15th, the Taliban broke Pul-e-Charkhi the biggest Afghan prison and freed all the prisoners. In fact, the Taliban broke all prisons of the country and freed not only their militants but everyone in the prisons including rapists, murderers, kidnappers, smugglers, robbers, and IS/ISIS. Hotak was freed too, on his first night at home, he heard about the crowds at the airport gates, and this was what people like Hotak were dying for, he joined the crowd the next day and kept doing his job for six days during which time he made tens of thousands of USD in cash and items such as cell phones and jewelry. Of course, people had taken most of their money with them in order to leave the country. On August 21st, he continued doing his job and reached the gate where people were being lined up to be escorted in, suddenly U.S. soldiers called on the people close to get to make a line, Hotak got scared and got himself to the line, which finally brought him to the camp.

The camp evacuation started about 10:00 am. Although the tents close to the gate were people who had come two days after us, but were being evacuated first, the single men were being moved until 9:00 pm. We made up our lines at about 9:30 pm, we had to walk out of the gate for ten minutes where American soldiers and few ununiformed officers were making people wait for the buses. Ahmadzai tried to show his SIV approvals, an American wearing a golf cap asked Ahmadzai to wait on the left side of the road, I, with my family were asked to wait on the opposite side and Karimzai and his family were asked to join Ahmadzai. In general, some people were asked to join one group, and some were asked to join the other without seeing their documents to make sure if one was eligible or not. We were picked up by the van carrying sixteen people at a time, it drove all the way and dopped us about 200 meters from the terminal. We had to walk through broken fence and muddy narrow pathway for about ten minutes, where we had to show our passports, NICs or anything that showed our identity. It was dark so I could not recognize places, but as soon we reached the terminal. It wasn't at all the place I saw in January 2021. The thousands of airport police, intelligence, the aircrews, their offices, the boarding and immigration officers and thousands of passengers at a time had just become a fictional story. The exit at the back reminded me of how frequently I was making calls and shouting at NSC's guys on January 09, 2021, flying to Dubai. Due to fake proof of COVID-19 negative certificates from some Afghan laboratories, Dubai had banned issuing visas those days, but I had arranged it somehow with high profile friends in Dubai. Kabul used to start its day with at least two or three target killings, many of the core committee members of Bawar Movement were assassinated in late December and early January, and I was frequently informed by NDS that I was on the wanted list of the Taliban and should leave Kabul, though I knew majority of the target killings were planned by the circles inside the government. This time I had no choice but to leave Kabul for some weeks. I had received my boarding pass and had made it to the immigration cabins, where the first cabin checks the passports if they are not on the Exit Control List and/or barred to leave the country, a Russian looking Panjsheri officer at the cabin asked for my Tazkera (NIC) after he had checked my passport and told me I was not allowed to leave the country.

It did not surprise me at all, since I knew ARG (the presidential palace) was doing all they could to make issues for me since Bawar Movement was the only opposition that kept criticizing and overseeing everything politically and technically. I tried to talk to the officer, but he was too rude, he seemed that he never had been to school but was brought to the position based on nepotism or favoritism like tens of thousands of others in the past two decades.

I told him, "Listen dude! You know me very well; I will call all the media right now and will tell them that it is you who did not let me get on plane or you need to tell me who asked you to put my name on a no-fly list."

He got scared, he did not know a specific name but said that one of the NSC's deputies (Hamdullah Mohib's deputy) had called the immigration to put my name on ECL, NSC always received the complete list of passengers a day before their flights. I tried to call Mohib, but he did not answer, I then left him a message that this would have a counterattack if I did not make it on the plane right away. Barely five minutes passed when that the same immigration officer apologized and said that he could not go against the orders. However, I was good to go then.

There were no boarding and immigration desks anymore, the windows, chairs, ceilings and information screens on the walls were completely broken. We were asked to head to the right where tens of U.S soldiers were waiting for the next order.

We got in the line on stairs for the next process on the second floor of the terminal. The young soldiers were very cooperative and kept helping everyone with juice, water, formula and diapers. They were even carrying the luggage of those brought many bags. A young lady with blond hair, blue eyes and Afghanistan map on her shoulder greeted us with all high respect, and then gave us all wristbands, we followed her to the next hall where our passports were scanned, and the information was added to the database. We sat in the hall for about fifteen minutes and then we were asked to follow a soldier who escorted us downstairs onto the side of the runway. Since the airport, including the terminal was badly damaged, they did not have a room but had computers and scanners set up here. We got in the line of about 400 people and reached the desks in two hours. Again, it was a freezing cold night, the sleepy children were wearing very thin clothes and I felt very upset thinking about our situation. There were twelve young male and female U.S. soldiers scanning the white wristbands with QR numbers we were given earlier.

We walked with the line and were asked to sit on the right side of the sideroad which was about 100 meters from the scanning desks. I was expecting Ahmadzai and Karimzai and their families since we were together, and they were supposed to come on the next bus. I first called Ahmadzai, and he shocked me with telling me that they were dropped somewhere in the dark and were asked to keep walking straight to reach the terminal, but they found themselves among the crowd outside the Sullivan Gate. I right away called Karimzai, he said they were walking towards the terminal but on a very muddy route fenced by bars, I thanked God and told him yes, they were close to the terminal. They were supposed to show up in five to ten minutes, so after about fifteen minutes, I called him again and could not believe what my ears were hearing; they were told exactly what Ahmadzai was told, and they had joined Ahmadzai outside the gate. The more shocking was when I saw Bashir and Zaman Khan with tens of other single men with no eligible documents and backgrounds, while Ahmadzai and Karimzai had been sent back with their authentic, eligible and SIV verified documents. Spogmai had already understood before I told her, she started crying and told me that we would not leave them, we would not go. I told her that

I needed few minutes to think but she did not listen and went to talk to the U.S soldiers responsible for escorting the evacuees to the plane, they said we could not leave, and they would not send us back, we had to fly on the plane. I tried to calm her down, but I myself got emotional, Karimzai's old parents had spent the three worst days and most importantly they had all the eligible documents that the Department of State had been accepting long before the rapid collapse, indeed the Department of State started the Special Immigration Visa process for eligible Afghans in 2006, so how could the holders of such documents be rejected in the evacuation process where majority of the evacuees were not eligible at all? I felt badly sorry for Ahmadzai as well. He had called his relatives to go and take his furniture and other goods at home and hand the house over to the landlord, and they had done accordingly. It wasn't understandable at all that how could they select people so randomly just like "oh, you go, and you don't go."

The children were shivering because of the cold weather, Spogmai and I were sad and upset, she and Wadan Khan kept crying. Although, we had not brought any luggage since we had to just save our lives, she did have some of her important diaries, jewelries and children's medicines in a bag left with Karimzai's mom. The only thing I was wishing and wanting at that time was cigarette, I was praying to God to make it happen, but of course, I had to go through all trauma, stress and anxiety without the relief of a single cigarette. Kabul is always very hot in August; indeed, the Kabul summer is at its peak from August to mid-September, and of course it was very hot during the day, but those nights kept holding the hands of the collapse like the luck of a prisoner who get free after twenty years of jail but gets hit by a car and dies while crossing the road right after being freed from prison. Suddenly, Ghani Khan's teeth chattering caught my attention, he was freezing cold and shivering. I checked his forehead and chest, and found him boiling hot, he had hyperpyrexia, I kept waking him up and kept talking to him, but he was not able to open his eyes. Spogmai and I forgot the sorrows of the families we had left behind in our fear for Ghani Khan. Spogmai started crying and kept asking me to make it somehow to go back home, our home was very close to the airport and Gul Mama's home was about a ten-minute walk from the terminal, but it did not work. We did not even have an extra shirt for Ghani Khan to wear so I held him inside my shirt to share him my body's heat.

Fight To Breathe

At 4:30 am we were asked to get in the lines and start walking towards the C-17 plane. There were two planes, we had to walk to the second one. Ghani Khan was badly sick, and I also had to take care of Wadan Khan and Shamla, so we as usual, were the last people in the line. It took us about thirty minutes to get on the plane. It was a huge military plane with no windows and seats except some folding seats in an ambulance benching shape attached to the two inner walls of the plane. The plane was completely filled with more than 800 people, there wasn't enough space for us or the fifteen or so more people ahead of us in the line. The soldiers kept asking everyone to move and sit closer, so some room could be made for us. Finally, we were on the plane, hundreds of people were sitting on the plane's floor and their luggage was placed at the back of the plane, where we sat. The plane took another half hour and then took off. The normal temperature of the plane was healing us like a mother's lap and breasts give the comfort and relief to the newly born baby. Being the last people on the plane made us the passenger of business class on one of the most luxury private jet since there were only bags behind us and we could even sit with our legs stretched out, and the children could lie down to sleep. None of us knew where we were being taken to, people sitting close to me were asking me the same question, but since I had heard that most of the evacuation flights had flown to Doha, Qatar, and of course Aimal had also talked to me from Doha, so I told people that it was probably Doha. Others were talking about

Tajikistan as well because according to them a few flights had flown to Tajikistan as well. We flew for about six hours before the captain announced that the plane needed to land and every one had to hold the floor belts tightly. After the plane landed, we were expecting the back door to be opened, we still did not know where we were, but after an hour we were still on the plane. It started getting very hot and fuggy, no one was asking or saying anything about what was going on, so I loudly asked the crew why we were not leaving. The answer was that they were waiting for an order from the control tower. I was scared for Spogmai since she had been an anxiety patient for a year and had always had claustrophobia and nyctophobia, the tight space and closed air used to make her faint. After two hours the doors were still closed, the four central heating/cooling thermostatic pipes of the plane started pumping hot air. The good thing was Spogmai's strong mind and will power, she didn't let her fears take over. Barlas Khan started feeling not well, he was not getting enough oxygen, so Spogmai crossed the people in front of her and took him to one of the airing pipes. Soon, Shamla fainted, I cuddled her and tried to take her to a pipe. An Afghan American sitting on the chair right under the airing pipe would not move to allow me to help my daughter to get some air. I told him that she had fainted, and she needed some oxygen, he said he did not care and pulled out his American passport to show me that he was an American. I knew, from his accent, that he was from Kandahar. There was no one to help, even the people sitting next to him did not say a word except an old couple told me that he was a rude man, and I shouldn't get into arguments with him, but only a father knows a father's feeling when his child in his lap is about to die.

I grabbed the guy's neck and told him, "I don't care who the hell you are, if a single word comes out of your mouth, I will put you right under my feet and I am sure no one will be able save you then."

He was shocked and apologized. I understood that it doesn't matter where one grew up and what passport one holds, some people understand a different language. I am sure any father whose child is about to die in his arms would do the same. I started pouring water on Shamla's head and face and kept her neck up right under the pipe, to revive her.

It was three hours now, people, especially the children and old ones started coughing, yet nobody was doing anything. I then started calling to open the door, the answer on the loudspeakers was to wait, I then walked towards the emergency exits and warned them if they didn't open the gate, I would break the emergency exit with the hammer hanging next to the door. Then they opened the small door at the front right away and started taking people out, but it would of course take another three hours to get more than 800 people off one by one from the small door. People started panicking, everyone was trying to run towards to door which would hurt children and old people, I again shouted at them to open the back gate, or I would break the emergency gate. They understood that I was quite serious, and they opened the back gate then. We got off the plane, it was about 56° Celsius boiling hot, but a lot better than inside the plane where the oxygen saturation was dropping. Strangely, those arrived before and after us told the same story, every plane from Kabul had to be locked for hours after landing.

We waited under shade of the plane's wings for about twenty minutes until the buses arrived. Reading the bus companies names, I understood that we were at the Al-Udeid Airbase, the biggest American military base in the Middle East. The multiple very wide and long runways, the beautiful and big hangers, and the tens of hundreds of Boeing C-17 Globemaster IIIs at every parking lot had created the scene of scientific Hollywood movie. The medium gray C-17 planes parked next to each other were a lot more in number than the yellow-capped rickshaws making the traffic jam in Jalalabad city all the time.

The bus stopped at the nearby parking lot right between three huge white tents installed in a U shape. The security officer on the bus told us that they did not have enough room and more planes were on their way, so we needed to make it to the tent on the left. As soon we entered the tent, we saw it was full with more than 1200 people, I kept looking for a space so we could rest, but it was hard. I noticed about two square meter space near the entrance, and although it wasn't a good place to spend days and nights, we had no other choice. We were still thinking of how to find some mattresses to put on the floor when a short man with beard came and told me that we could not live there, I asked the reason and he told me that everyone in the tent was from Strike Force Unit 02, and they didn't let any outsider live in the tent. He demanded to our cards or said we had to leave.

I told him, "Listen gentleman, the tent is not your property, we all are evacuees here, and we have all been evacuated by the same people, I am not here on my own, but I was asked to be here in the tent by the same people who brought you to the tent. We are tired and exhausted enough, please do not disturbed anymore."

He started calling his other colleagues, about four Pashaees and seven Pashtuns from the eastern region (Nangarhar, Laghman, Kunar and Nooristan) all together came and asked me the same thing. Spogmai had already observed everything. She came to me and asked me that even if they let us live there, we would not. The number of people living there made it hard to breathe. I thanked the men and told them that we would happily leave such a well cleaned tent. We walked out and made it to the second tent in the middle. It wasn't clean enough either, but it was much better than the previous one, but still with more than 1200 people. The only thing we needed now was to sit in front of Air Conditioning for a while since the 56° Celsius boiling heat outside had badly affected all of us. We decided to try the third one and we would stay there no matter how it would be, we could not afford any sun stroke for the kids and of course myself, if I got a sun stroke who would take care of the family then?

Fortunately, we found a decent space in the third tent but on the side where the chillers could not reach because of the cardboard walls made by people for their privacy. A family of eight was leaving for their plane. They had three golden 10cm thick Qatari mattresses. The Kabuli young lady, who was wearing tight jeans and a blouse, tightened her hair and looked at Spogmai and directly asked her if we had just arrived. According to her she was looking for a family like us to leave her well-kept and clean place to. We took the breath of comfort and thanked her. We had sat there for about fifteen minutes when I suddenly felt as if everything around me was killing me. I was feeling that I could not live there any longer, with one thousand people in a tent, with children's noise, and the boiling hot weather. I got breathless and lost all energy in my legs, I was trying to bend them, but they were not responding, I wanted to tear my shirt so I could breathe, I asked Spogmai to take me somehow to the open air, but she knew that I would not be able to stay even one minute under the burning sun since I am a cold weather man and even a minor heatwave had always pushed me to the bed of hospitalization. Spogmai was scared for my situation, but she managed to take care of me and soon my situation began getting better. At the main entrance there was a distribution center not only for our tent but for all the three tents. One of the other reasons that the chillers could not cool the tent during the day was that the large entrance was kept open for the distribution to other tents as well, I told the officer that I wanted to see the commander, they noted my name and asked me to wait. The tall and healthy commander came an hour later to see if he could be of any help, I strongly requested him that since they had the regular flights to Kabul, they had to send us back to Kabul, the answer was of course a big NO. Spogmai then requested him if he could remove the cardboard and trash bag walls that covered the chillers, so everyone could get some cooling, the answer was a no since he believed they were being used to provide privacy. The children got hungry and started asking for food. We had to stand in the line with at least one thousand people at a time to collect our food. It was about 02:00 pm and the sun burning relentlessly. Spogmai who had been ill for the past year was already weak, so I could not take the risk to send her stand in the line for hours. The children started crying from hunger so I had to go and find food for the kids, or they would have got sick. I tried to make Spogmai stay with the kids while I went for food but just then a truck donating food from an Arab Sheikh arrived and parked right at the entrance of our tent and started distributing the food, so none of us had to go and wait in lines outside to get our food.

Although, there were many reasons for my worsening health condition including Ahmadzai's and Karimzai's families being left behind, but the biggest one was the picture I had in mind about the Doha camp according to what Aimal had told me. None of us knew that there would be more than one camp in Al-Udeid Airbase: The camp he was brought to had a big hall, where he got free Wi-Fi, food, hygiene products, all clothing and a help desk processing their documents and getting them on the schedule for their next destination, which was the United States. While, on day two they were moved to a different camp with a separate double bedroom and attached bathroom, with all the required facilities including AC, WIFI, food at door and laundry. But what I saw was totally different, let alone WIFI, there were not even power sockets to charge our phones, the mobile trailer toilets were the place where one would keep vomiting for hours, the showers behind the tent were actually to make you a snake and shed your skin with the boiling hot water. The only thing available all the time was the drinking water stall outside, which was almost boiled by the sun and good for nothing, neither for drinking nor for washing your hands and face, but of course we had to use it at the end of the day for both. Standing under 60° Celsius in lines for hours sounds fictional. The food donated by the Arab sheikhs, restaurant trucks escorted in by luxury cars, was mostly from Indian restaurants and was too spicy for the children to eat. We had the mattresses left by the family before us, but we still needed pillows and thin blankets since the chillers made it cold at night. Unfortunately, there was no management or distribution system, some Qatari Arabs would bring some pillows and blankets and would keep giving to those who were spidermen in taking, one person would take ten and the others would remain with none, there was no mechanism to list and distribute accordingly, so we and people like us, lived all their time with no pillows and blankets.

On our second day, when Wadan Khan had taken a little rest and started asking questions, he asked me if the tents were built right on the beach, I of course asked him why he was thinking that, he said that the fish smell was annoying him. I laughed at what he had thought and told him that we were not living on the beach, it was actually the smell of sweat from more than of one thousand people in the tent.

The arrivals and departures continued 24/7. I was expecting Al-Udeid Airbase to be totally different than HKIA. I thought there would be a system of who and what category of evacuees would be taken first, second and last. There were enough U.S citizens among the evacuees from which only few made it on planes on day two. Many people inside the tent and some from other tents who used to see me out at night would greet me and tell me that they used to watch me on TV all the time. Dr. Hashim Zazai was one of them, he was a tall clean-shaven man. He was with his wife, three sons and two daughters and he kept looking at me from the corner on our left in the tent. The gentleman came and asked if I was Najibullah Azad. He was so happy that finally he found someone who he could talk to. Dr. Zazai had been there only a night while it was our second day in Doha, he was quite confident that he would fly soon since he had COM approval. He was sure some officers would come and call his name and would escort him and his family with all due respect to the plane which would fly them to their luxury furnished house somewhere in the United States. I did not want to disappoint him, but I had no choice and to tell him the reality, which was that the eligibility, documentation, travel documents, deserving people and terms like that had been thrown away with the previous regime. The only categories that mattered now were more to do with access or if the CIA was taking care of your family. They were the people getting into lines for flights.

Dr. Hashim sat on his knees and held his forehead, he was regretting leaving and thinking how they could make it back to Kabul, which I again told him that I had already tried that on day one, it did not work either. He started thinking about his eldest son, the young boy of twenty-one who had thalassemia major, and his condition meant he had to take blood once a week. There was kind a first aid emergency clinic about 200 meters south of the tent. I kept trying to keep his morale high and we went together to talk to the officers at the distribution center at the tent's entrance, but they did not even have a clue of what SIV/

COM was, so they asked us to wait for the commander, who showed up in an hour. I explained Dr. Hashim's son's condition to him, meanwhile asked him on what basis people were being assigned. Was it based on eligibility, first come, first served or any other mechanism? He had no answer except asking us to have patience and that everyone would get to America.

Dr. Hashim and I then visited the E2 tent, half the tent was gone. They were all from SFUs and the rest looking enough educated and well-mannered, mostly SIV/COM applicants. Dr. Hashim shared his concerned with them and asked them if there was a group of those applicants so together, we could talk and make our departure happen. They said that they had already tried but it did not work. A clean-shaven man with dark skin, wearing Afghan dress and a tennis cap, holding a red permanent marker in the right hand met me on our return to the tent, he said he had always been a great fan of mine. Waheedullah Humdard also known as Mike, was from Kunduz and had been a senior terp for SFU 03 Kandahar. Before we continued, I directly asked him if he had some cigarettes. The white Marlboro pack he took out of his pocket was world's biggest gift to me at that very moment. We went outside and I will of course always remember that very first puff of the cigarette after many days. I sat down with the third puff since it had awesomely intoxicated me. Mike was telling me how happy he was after meeting me and offered me his all generosity, he was the smartest terp in the camp I had observed so far. The U.S. officers and their advisors from CIA loved him, they used to meet him frequently so he could push the evacuation process for the SFU members and their families, and they were, of course, listening to him. He for sure knew that only people like him and others I mentioned were able not to stay longer at Al-Udeid, he asked me to be ready 24/7, he could come and send me with his unit at any time. I took and showed him my place of living. It was about 4:00 pm that he came in hurry and asked me to pick up my luggage, he was busy talking to others outside the tent and we walked towards the departure tent per his advice. There were about 250 people in the queue, we stood in the last for almost t two hours, and then a U.S 1st sergeant came and asked everyone to go back to their tents, the flight was canceled. I had already asked the family next to us to look after our place, in case we did not make the flight, otherwise people would occupy it right away. We came back sweating head to toe.

I was mostly thinking about Moraka and Agha Jan, it had been three days that I had not been in contact with them, they did not know that a super power with one of the largest airbases in a secure and developed country could not provide WIFI so people could at least let their beloved ones back at home that they were still alive. Although, I had credited my MTN number for international roaming as Aimal had told me to do, there was no signal for MTN. I met a family comprising an old mother, her sons, who must have been forty and forty-five, a daughter-in-law with three little grandchildren who were all U.S citizens, and the second son's new bride who was flying to the U.S for the first time. The family had come to Kabul two months earlier for the wedding and the woman had already been issued with an American visa, yet they had to stay in the camp and be evacuated with everyone else, since there wasn't an organized mechanism for the eligible and deserving people, so nobody was helping them either. The family had an international roaming U.S. phone number, but the phone's battery had run out of charge, I walked outside to see if I somehow could get their phone charged, I saw a tall U.S officer, Mr. Galley, standing next to his Nissan 4x4 white truck, I asked him if, as a favor, he could please charge my power bank in his truck. Without thinking he put the external battery to charge and asked how many kids I had. He had to visit another camp as well so asked me to see him in two hours.

He showed up with beautiful toys for my kids and the power bank two hours later, the toys made my kids' day, and they forgot all the stress, trauma and homesickness, yes, the only age to live a beautiful life is as a child. I got the neighbor's phone charged and borrowed a hotspot for a while. Moraka, upon hearing my voice started living all over again, she had got severe high diabetic attacks since our departure and she had been crying for Ghani Khan who she had brought up since his birth, she was so attached to him. Talking to Moraka gave me the best relief. Spogmai, the kids and I all felt much better after talking to her.

At about 1:00 pm on August 27, Mike breathlessly came and asked me to pick the luggage which was only one backpack and follow him. Doha in August had always been an oven, but 1:00 pm of 27th August felt like a volcano for us. We did not have proper shoes but were wearing sandals and the sun fried sands were baking our feet. Spogmai was cuddling Barlas Khan, while I was carrying the backpack and had to cuddle Shamla and Ghani as well, since they started crying walking on fire. Wadan Khan, who was also wearing sandals had no option but patience and to keep walking. There were the same 250 people from the SFU 03 in the line, we were last again, but the sun over us and the boiling sands under our feet were making even standing for a second a hell for us, everyone for the flight had to stand in lines for at least one and half or two hours. I am sure they could have erected a shade or tent; it would take not more than an hour and it could have been the easiest job for authorities on Al-Udeid. Spogmai herself could not stand anymore and was about to fall, I asked the guy next to me to give me some water since he and his family had enough bottles, I poured some water on Spogmai and Barlas Khan's heads and then got her scarf wet and put it on their heads, before her condition got worse, our luck came in and a white Toyota truck loading mattresses came and parked it right next to us, I got her and the children to stand in the trucks' shadow. Mike who had noticed us was still busy talking to the U.S. soldiers at the departing tent's entrance, and he finally succeeded, the first family who to make it to the tent was us, it was all because Mike was a fan and did us a great favor! Indeed, he played the role of doctor to my family by getting them on that flight. We waited in the tent for about another hour, but it was cold inside and we were comfortable. The next phase made us forget the previous one. I was expecting a bus to take us to the plane but no, we had to walk, and the burning sands of the narrow-fenced pathway from the tent made our feet numb. I had had plantar fasciitis for almost three months and could barely walk in the mornings. From the day we left home and set off for the airport, the pain in my heel had begun to increase throughout the day, especially walking on hard surfaces like gravel. Now the hot sand and then the walk on the runway made my feet lose feeling, at least I was neither feeling the heat burn nor the heel pain, but I could clearly see that Spogmai's feet had started bleeding. It was the same C-17, the plane had already brought about six hundred evacuees from Kabul and now was taking them to Europe, it landed for about an hour so other 250 evacuees had to be taken, although I was not expecting to make it to the back of the plane since we entered the departing tent before everyone in the line, but there were two planes getting ready to take off. The plane we had to get on was only waiting for fourteen more people and the others walked towards the second plane on our left, so we once again got lucky and wound up at the back of the plane which provided more room to sit. They never told anyone where the plane was flying to, so I asked a soldier that how long would it take us to reach Berlin. He told me that it would take about six hours but that we were going to Ramstein, not Berlin. I told Spogmai that we were flying to Germany since I had read about Ramstein during in 2002 right after the NATO alliance and the U.S. forces invaded Afghanistan.

"The construction of the air base was a project designed and undertaken by the French Army and the U.S. Army Corps of Engineers from 1949 to 1952. It was an example of international collaboration: designed by French engineers, constructed by local businesses and large number of temporary and migrant workers of Italy, Portugal, Spain, Greece, and Turkey and operated by Americans.

During the Cold War, as the wartime cooperation between the U.S. and the Soviet Union ended and tensions between the two countries mounted, the U.S. came to see Soviet expansionism as a threat to its own interests and began shaping a new policy of containment, a policy that crystallized in 1947 when suspected Soviet-backed Communist guerrillas launched a civil war against the Greek government.

Soviet influence in Greece threatened U.S. interests in the eastern Mediterranean and the Middle East, especially Turkey and Iran.

American reactions resulted in the Truman Doctrine, which called for large-scale military and economic assistance in order to prevent communism from taking hold in Greece and Turkey and thereby lessen the threat to the entire Middle East.

The congressional appropriation, which followed, reversed the postwar trend toward sharp cuts in foreign spending and marked a new level of commitment to the Cold War.

The result was NSC-68, a report that recommended an increase in U.S. conventional forces. In the ensuing buildup of forces, the number of U.S. Air Force combat wings increased from 48 in 1950 to 95 by June 1952.

The increase in air assets and personnel required additional facilities to house them. More importantly, planners began to reassess how best to deploy their aircraft and associated facilities. That rethinking led to the decision to build six new bases in Rheinland-Pfalz, which at the time had two existing military airstrips, one at Pferdsfeld and the other at Baumholder.

Pferdsfeld had been built by the German Luftwaffe in 1938. In the 1950s, it was periodically used by the U.S. Air Force to conduct exercises.

From 1961 until 1997 it served as a German Luftwaffe base once again. The airfield at Baumholder, built in the early 1940s, came under U.S. Army control in 1951 and was used exclusively by U.S. Army air assets.

There was also an auxiliary Luftwaffe landing strip on a portion of the old autobahn between Landstuhl and Ramstein. It was here that two adjoining bases, Landstuhl Air Base and Ramstein Air Base, were to be located.

From a strategic perspective, the decision to construct six bases on the west side of the Rhine made sense because it placed them behind a natural barrier, and in the majority of cases, surrounded by protective topography. It also placed them in a straight-line approach to the Fulda Gap, from where the Soviet attack on the bases in the Rhein-Main area was expected to begin.

The tactical air assets based at these six bases could be used in an offensive or defensive capacity to counter the Soviet advance or they could be employed to provide close air support for army infantry units meeting the Soviet advance head on. Evidence of planning for the latter contingency was seen on Feb. 11, 1952, when the 86th Fighter-Bomber Wing, based at Neubiberg, furnished four F-84-E Thunder jets for a combined infantry-artillery training exercise with the 2nd Armored Division at Baumholder.

The bottom line for military planners was that these bases would be better protected and in closer proximity to the forward edge of the battle area and easier to integrate into joint operations. At the time, these bases were situated in an area of stability near an area of potential instability." (Wueschner, 2012)

The inside of the plane started getting cold after two hours, it wasn't like normal commercial Boeing planes that keep a level temperature all the time. The captain announced about six hours later that we had arrived at the Ramstein airbase, but the plane could not land due to the bad weather. The plane started getting colder and landed at 2:00 am after flying over Europe for four hours. We still had to wait for one more hour until the control tower authorities allowed us to get on the buses that were waiting for us. Life had been playing a hide and seek game with us, once we fought for the oxygen saturation while locked on the plane arrived in Al-Udeid, and now fighting with the stinging coldness locked on the plane in Ramstein.

Aug. 16, 2021, mobs in 1 mile from HKIA

Aug. 22, Camp Sullivan, Kabul

The USAF plane coming from Qatter, landing at KLIA

Aug. 23, Inside the USAF C-17

Aug. 24, Al-Udied Airbase camp, Qattar

Aug. 25, thousands of people getting food

Aug. 27, inside C-17 towards Germany

3:00 am, Aug. 30, children sleeping in Ramstien Biometric office

Aug. 31, Barlas Khan, I and Shamla, Ramstein, Germany

Sept. 7, Shamla and Ghani Khan playing soccer

Sept. 8, Wadan Khan & Ghani Khan, line for food

Packing and cleaning the hanger before leaving for flight, which was canceled.

Aug. 10, Ghani Khan trying to escape the camp

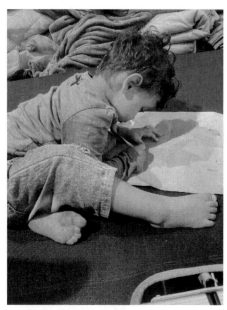

Barlas Khan finally got some Crayons

Sept. 10, enjoying the Ramstien rain

Sept. 11, Ramstien sunset & Refugee tents

Sept. 12, Shamla and Wadan K enjoying the rain

Left to right, Barlas Khan and Ghani Khan build a house

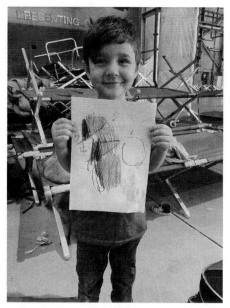

Ghani Khan tried to draw his national flag

Attan in Ramstien, Emma and I were enjoying it

The old plane in Ramsiten Airbase

Ghani Khan drew spiderman on a food box in LSA5

Barlas Khan playing with the Shamla's only doll

I got Ghani Khan the hair cut after 3 months

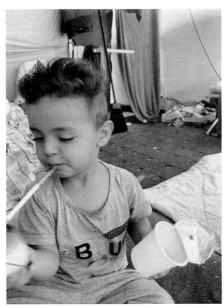

I got Barlas Khan a hair cut after 3 months

Oct. 13, cleaning the tent in LSA5 before departing

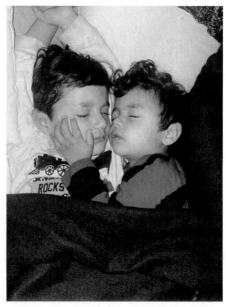

Ghani Khan & Barlas Khan sleeping in white tent

Barlas Khan used the paint brought by Shakir

Wadan Khan & Shamla had fun with musicians in LSA5

Shmla and Ghani Khan had fun with their dearest uncle, Shakir Azizi

Oct. 16, Fort Pickett, South Virginia

Dec. 5, Fort Pickett, South Virginia

Dec. 5, Barlas Khan, Fort Picket, South VA

Dec. 6, leaving Pickett village for Buidlings 2000

Jan. 3, Barlas Khan enjoying the 1ˢᵗ snow in VA

Ghani Khan & Barlas Khan swinging in trailer

Pickett Village mobile sleeping trailers

Wadan Khan, Shamla and Ghani Khan loved the French Fries for the 1ˢᵗ time after 4 months.

USAF plane, and Ramstien sky during sunset

Left to Right, Spogmai, Shamla, Wadan Khan, Barlas Khan and Ghani Khan, LSA5 ROB

Jan 3, 2022, in memory of Kabul snow.

Under The Rainy Sky

The buses drove us all the way to similar white tents, where again about eight hundred people had to live. We were given one black sleeping bag per head, and since we were exhausted, I fell asleep right away, but soon someone shouting kicked my legs and asked me to get out of the tent. The former SFU 01 Panjesheri soldier and with his three other colleagues including two translators who spoke very bad English had decided that all the men needed to sleep outside. I asked them who were they to take that decision? They only had the right to decide about their own families not others, but unfortunately all other men kept quiet although they did not want to leave their families alone inside, since families like mine needed their heads of the families to take care of them. Spogmai could not manage all the four kids, but who cared, the rude guys who did not even know how to talk were not listening and I did not want to get into a fight with them. They still believed that it was Afghanistan, and they had their weapons, they kept saying "we are from unit 01, and we have decided that all men will sleep outside."

I took my sleeping bag and tried to find a place outside, the 50x25 meter tent was fenced in an area of approximately 60x30 square meters, so there was only ten meters of space at the front and on the right side of the tent, which was already filled by six mobile toilets and hundreds of people on the left. I did not find a place to lay down in my sleeping bag but wore it and kept sitting on the northeast corner of the fence and then heavy raining started. People sleeping outside were cursing those five gangster type uncivilized guys. The rain stopped at about 10:00 am and the Army brought ready meals for breakfast and some warm jackets. The same two translators grabbed all the jackets and distributed them to their friends and families, the army again like in Doha were simply throwing the jackets so some even got two while others like me kept just watching the scene and getting nothing. I was still thinking of what would happen next when a tall man wearing the U.S army uniform with a colonel rank on his chest accompanied by female and male sergeants from the other side of the fence passed the morning greetings and asked me if he can be of any help.

I asked the Colonel to move us from the tent, "there are many things to ask for" I laughed, "but the only thing I believe being a Colonel you could do is relocate us." I told him the story and asked him to help, "I want to be relocated to a tent where I can live with my family, I have kids under ten and they are all locked down inside and I am not even allowed to find out if they are good, if they need anything."

The Colonel asked for an hour to find us enough room in another tent where I could live with the family, and he also said that he would investigate the issue those guys had created. He came back in about ninety minutes and asked me to collect our luggage, at this point some others also noted that we were being moved and asked me if I can also move them to the new tent where they could live with their families. I asked the Colonel and he accepted. I went and brought Spogmai and the kids outside the tent, and those guys who had been practicing ruling over the tent were shocked and thought that we were being taken to the plane. I did not have any luggage but had the sleeping bags this time, of course, I was unable to carry all six and take care of the kids at the same time. The Colonel, the most senior officer in the camp, carried four sleeping bags, despite my telling him that I would come back a second time, but he did not accept, he was not only very nice but also a real army man. Indeed, most of the American soldiers and officers, from Kabul to Germany, I had seen were very nice and cooperative, but unfortunately there had always been the issue of management and evacuation mechanisms, which I believe were in the control of others rather than those who were deployed to help us with meals and accommodation. Unfortunately, August 28 was the Colonel's last day on that camp, and he had to hand over the command and leave, otherwise he would have come back and see if he could provide more help.

It was a big tent and there were approximately 200 families with about 1500 people in the tent. The tent floor had just been installed the day before and the tent itself was only installed that morning, so the wooden floor had been soaked by the previous night's rain. The rest of the people already in tent had been moved from an open hanger just few hours before we made it. There were four other white tents about the same size all in a row. The tent had hardly 10x10 meters space at the front, of which 5x5 meter were occupied by eight mobile toilets. The soldiers had provided a small distribution center with two small tables for diapers and hygiene behind the fence. About thirty minutes later a group of soldiers led by a female captain brought warm clothes for the children, they again started distributing as usual, and my kids being the children of a spiritless father in such cases, remained in their only one pair green sleeveless summer shirts. The other four tents were also fenced at the front and residents of those tents were looking, waving and talking to their friends in other tent exactly the way prisoners of one barrack talk to the prisoners of another barrack.

Although we could not sleep because the floor was wet and the place where we were living was near the main entrance, so everyone was walking in and out and the kids were running on the wooden floor, yet it was much better than the previous tent where it was nice and warm inside with the central heating system, because at least here we were all together.

The next morning at about 9:00 am, buses started taking people from tent A to the next destination where their biometrics and scans were being taken. Everyone thought that this meant we would be flying to the U.S in about a day or two and that this was farewell to hard times. A major who had just replaced the Colonel came to our tent to see if everything was fine. I explained to him that since the tent had been built just a day before, the floor was wet and there was not heating facility and no electricity, and the kids, women and old people were struggling in the tent, so if he could help by sending them before the other three remaining tents which had all the amenities. The Major, being a good listener observed the tent condition and made a call to his boss right away, he explained the situation and got permission to send our tent before the other three.

As soon we made the announcement in the tent and asked people to get ready for the buses in the next hour, everyone grabbed their luggage and ran towards the exit. The first thing I ran to do was to save my children from this stampede of horses just freed from a stable. The Major got angry and stopped evacuating the tent, a German Afghan translator from Hazarajat who was a very nice and decent man tried to explain that everyone would go, but not this way. He, along with the U.S soldiers then started evacuating the tent by columns. The bus drove for about fifteen minutes inside the Ramstein airbase and dropped us in a parking lot where thousands of bags were waiting for their owners; they had already asked us to take our sleeping bags with us so we could use them in the next destination. Before we got off the bus, those who had bags had to collect them. Everyone was angry at seeing their bags left out in the rain. Indeed, no luggage was given while leaving the planes from Doha but had been brought here. We were lucky, neither we had luggage, nor we were weeping over the conditions of the bags.

There were eight khaki tents, four on each side of a fenced area. We were asked to go into the second tent on the left marked with a D. Everyone, including myself, was surprisingly happy to see the power sockets in the tent. We were told that we would not stay there long but every bag was opened and the only words to be heard were "which bag did we put the phone charger in?" Most were quickly disappointed to see that their Asian adapters did not fit the U.S. sockets. I spread out two sleeping bags so Spogmai and the children could sit. There were twelve benches beautifully placed under the iron sheet roofs right in front the entrance of the tents. For the first time, I enjoyed the rain in Germany; the rain on the iron sheet roof relaxed my mind and the water flowing from the grey edges of the roof all the way down to the ground made me think of how we had been flown with the flow of time so far. Of course, something that you have always loved heals your pain, now, the journey of pain that was taking us to an unknown tomorrow was a little healed by those drops of rain. I did not know if it was the support of the column of the roof I was standing with or the column was holding me, but I had totally forgotten my heel pain for the first time. I was looking at the hundreds of evacuees holding the hands of their innocent children, carrying and pulling bags, yet the rainwater was not able to wash out thousands of questions the lines on their foreheads were asking. Suddenly the long shawl stuck in the gate's fence caught my attention, the innocent shivering hands were trying to get the shawl freed from the naughty and shameless gate, she was busy trying to fight with her thick wet black hair that kept bothering the blue eyes like bees with their feet stuck in their own honey. With one hand, she was trying to get the honey freed from the bees while tightly holding her white shawl with red roses print so the moonlighted face would be hidden from the evil eyes, but she failed. The crowd from the next bus caught her eyes, she accepted her defeat and pulled shawl with all her power she had in the two snowy white hands, the thick black long hair all the way on her back and the two blue eyes, and pomegranate shivering lips on the moon alike face were portraying the human Orion's belt which was lightning the space we were living in at that very moment, the black terrace got even more confident and beside the blue vintner eyes, it started owning the red shivering lips, when she inevitably tried to free the blue oceanic eyes from the usurpation of snake-like hair, the shivering wet lips yelled to be rescued.

Suddenly, I saw a woman by the gate in the rain. The brazen German rain had completely taken her in its arms, and a part of her chadar was stuck in the gate. She bent down to rescue it, and her eyes incidentally caught mine. She looked at me with so many questions in her eyes: Where I am, and where I am going to? I have not even smelled fragrance of fresh flowers of my village fields, the wedding henna had not left its color on my hands yet, that the whole village turned red with the blood of my handsome beloved. Who I am and where I am going? I could see all her questions: Why did I fight with the fence for my chadar, which is not more than a shroud now. Do you know where a living corpse is taken to? Oh, I think to America.

She was the fiancée of a commando officer who had just lost his life a month ago, and his family including his parents, sisters, brothers and she were evacuated with us. Maybe she will marry her martyred fiancé's brother. Bismillah Khan a former KPF commander from Khost told me her story.

People in tent A and then B were being taken to the eighth tent, where they had to leave their luggage, go and wait in the second portion of the camp, so the security would physically check the bags. It was the first time that people's luggage was checked. They did not check the bags while entering HKIA, then getting on the plane, Doha or even flying to Germany. It of course surprised me and left me scared from Kabul to Ramstein.

We left our bags in tent H for the checks and waited for about thirty minutes in the third tent of the back portion of the camp. Then we collected our luggage and started following two soldiers, it was a narrow pathway where only one person at a time could walk. We were taken to a very clean and well decorated small meeting hall, where there were twelve rows of cinema seats, each with thirty seats. The thing that made Wadan Khan and Shamla happy was the clean and modern toilets. There walls were adorned with Team Ramstein "welcome back home" slogans and photos. Three officers started guiding the 'audience' on how to fill the forms and the next steps of the process. They asked if anyone spoke English so they could help them translating their speech and also guide others on how to fill the forms. About fifteen people including two ladies ran to the desk and started taking the class, which lasted for about fifteen minutes. I kept waiting and watching until I got six Locator and Processing Card forms for the family. Only one U.S officer stayed at the desk while the rest left, and by now most of the people who were supposed to help others filling their forms were seeking my help with filling in their forms. The process took about four hours, and all three halls had to leave for the biometric date processing at once. The three-meter-wide corridor was divided by the safety tap into two parts, we had to make a U-turn all the way to the right from the beginning of the corridor. We finally made it to the biometric room after about an hour waiting in the line. There were fourteen desks with two operators each in the room. We made it to a desk, and became the first family done in five minutes, although the process was a lengthy including the rolling finger biometrics, scanning and providing height and weight details too, but since all of us speak English, our process was completed before everyone else. We had to submit the forms we had filled in the hall and received receipts in return, it was about 2:00 am and the kids were exhausted, so they kept sleeping on the floor and I had to pull them around in their sleeping bags. We walked to the second room where we gave the slips and got a printed paper for each of us. The paper had our photos, a title with Locator ID per family and personal coding number, which wristbands were given at the next door accordingly. The paper also had the bed-down assignment marked with P2, most of the people thought they were put for the P2 (priority2) visas but actually there were seven refugee camps called P1, P2, BLDG-2231, ROB, 51A 51B. P1 and P2 stood for POD1 and POD2.

From the beginning to the end of our process in the biometric office everyone kept wishing us safe travels so I thought we would stay there maximum a day or two. After the blue wristbands were issued to us, we were escorted to a khaki tent where about fifteen people were waiting in the first two rows close to the narrow door. There was a female soldier keeping the door closed and waiting for the call from the next bus. More people started coming to the tent, the buses arrived about one hour later, and more than 300 people in the tent ran towards the tiny door. I kept watching out for my sleeping kids so they would not get hurt by the crowd. We again became the last people and made it on the last bus at 4:30 am. Of course, we did not know any places, but everything was looking awesome, the road and vehicle lights reflecting in the rain looked like stars twinkling to the kids. The sidewalk of the wide military runway finished at a stop where six women welcomed us with hygiene kits, blankets, cookies, juices and cakes at the entrance gate. I was still praying for a separate room in a building, where we should have electricity, internet and a clean toilet above all. We kept following two soldiers in the rainy dark early morning all the way across a big hangar to tent B19. There were thirty-six army cots with lemon colored sleeping bags in the khaki tent. I was disappointed that we did not even have electricity in the tent, let alone a clean toilet and WIFI.

A thin short man was busy trying to place seven cots the way he and his family would feel comfortable with his mobile torch. I noticed another man speaking Turkmani/Turkish with his wife, the couple was trying to decide whether to keep their five cots in the middle of the left side or move them down to the right. Since there were already other tentmates, I claimed the first six cots from the door on the right side, the remaining eight were taken by another family. We were not done yet, that a soldier entered with another family of five and asked Sharifullah, the Turkman to make room. They tried telling the soldiers that the tent did not have enough room, so if they could move them to another tent, it would be better, but the soldiers had decided to bed them down in the same tent.

Since we all were very tired, we went to bed at about 5:30 am and woke up at about 10:00 am. I greeted other three families who we were meeting for the first time, there we found a small and beautiful Afghanistan in the tiny tent. We were five families from the five different parts of the country namely: Paktia, Helmand, Wardak, Juzjan, and Khost.

The 30th August was a beautiful rainy day. After breakfast of cake and juice, Wadan Khan and I walked out to see the camp, there were 117 tents in nine columns with approximately 3500-4000 people just in POD2. But the worst part was again the toilets, there were about 40 toilets for thousands of people. I was eagerly looking for a shower since I had not had a shower for almost two weeks, there were two trailer showers each for men and women, but unfortunately the pipe was broken, so I had to wait for another day. Since I had also not trimmed my beard for two weeks and had not gotten a haircut for almost a month, I began to look somehow a Taliban. I was expecting either a barber or a trimmer, razor or scissors, but these were only not available but also banned. No one had an idea of why the trimmers were taken from their luggage by the security.

POD2 had become a small Afghanistan, the first four rows of A tents had people from around fifteen provinces of northern Afghanistan including Pashtun, Uzbek, Turkmen, Kerghiz, Turktabar, Hazaras and Tajiks. The B and C sections had people from the west, southeast and southwest; and the D section had mostly people from Khust who were all the KPF (Khust Protective Force of Strike Force Units), and some from other provinces as well.

The beautiful Ramstein evenings were healing everyone's pain thanks to gorgeous sunsets over the green mountains that faced the military runway. The broken old plane would catch my eye from this side of fence every time I walked by. It took me back to the old British tanks, cannons and mortars caught by the Afghan warriors in Anglo war in Spin Boldak district of Kandahar, that had been kept as the victory symbols of unarmed Afghan warriors over the British, the most powerful, and the only superpower at that time. But after the collapse of the Taliban regime and involvement of the international community in 2002 in Afghanistan, those tanks, cannons and mortars were taken out of Afghanistan, yet the history could not be removed by removing symbols of victory. The huge and strong aircraft was also telling the story of one's victory and the other's defeat. There was no mark on the plane to tell me if it was an American or a German plane, but the way it was kept told a story of being the prisoner in an American airfield. I always wished that I could cross the fence for once and sit next to the plane who had just wanted to tell its untold story for decades.

POD2 was quite a tiny place, approximately 20 hectares for more than 3500 people, yet its evenings especially the rainy ones always felt romantic.

I was again standing and thinking about the plane during a rainy sunset when a voice said, "the history of tens of thousands of massacres. Hi, my name is Emma, I'm a Captain in the German Army." (name changed to protect that captain's identity)

The beautiful tall young German captain joined me watching the place during that rainy sunset. She had been noticing me coming and looking at the plane frequently. I had started an emotional relationship with the hushed plane that was witnessing the days I had been going through. Emma's father was the only child of his family who survived during the WWII, her grandparents and all their children except Emma's father were killed in an airstrike. Her father grew up in three different families. She cried while telling me her story, and was surprised that her story had not made me emotional.

"I know what you are thinking Emma, I am sorry to hear what happened to your grandparents, see you only heard the story from your father who was of course told the story by the families that brought him up. I can understand how cruel the time was to your father's family, but see, I am myself a story. My dad did not tell me any story, but I have seen what he and I have been going through, and I don't have to tell my son the story either, since he also suffers with me on the pendulum of the polar night that has been over my country and countrymen for decades. Oh, by the way my name is Azad which means freedom, the freedom that we have been looking for, for decades." I smiled.

"Wow, I love your name, you must be still thinking of giving your name to your country. I am sure this will happen one day."

Emma started joining me in the rain and sunset frequently. One can't trust in Ramstein's sky, it rains a lot, which of course I loved the most about Ramstein. Emma, wearing red tracksuit tightened her beautiful silky blond ponytail and held out her hand for a handshake. I, for the first time, couldn't take my eyes off her and her wonderfully blue eyes. She began to blush, her hand was as soft as the newborn baby's cheeks, I could even see the red marks my fingers had left on the back of her hand.

"You look a fairytale, Emma. I would have marked your forehead with ash to protect you from the evil eye, ah, but you guys don't even allow us cigarettes. See! I can't protect you from the evil's eyes now," I smiled again. "How did you make Cinderella ununiformed today?"

She kept her face up to the sky, closed the deep ocean eyes against the rain, opened her arms and gave herself a rope to swing just like a stunned lover moves on her beloved's drumbeat, and then breathlessly asked, "guess, Azad!"

"It's red, while it's neither a skirt nor a gown but a tracksuit, so you are not the birthday girl either...hmmm, let me think, okay, I quit."

"It's Sunday, the weekend Azad."

"Ah, my mistake, honestly speaking, I only remember August 15 and then 20, I didn't know what day or date was today, my apologies to the gorgeous Cinderella." I passed her an innocent look.

"I am not Cinderella," she said with an angry tone.

And then she held the fence and kept looking at the green mountains miles behind the plane that had introduced us, took a deep breath and began telling me how her heart was broken, he cheated on her, while she did not only give him her heart but also her house, car and bank balance as well.

I started thinking that there can't be anyone without pain on the earth; some like me who have left his soil, parents, siblings, friends and left for an unknown journey, while others, educated and beautiful souls like Emma who creates beautiful yet fragile lives that can crumble within seconds.

Emma wanted me to seek asylum in Germany, she tried to explain how Germany would be the best place for me to stay. I knew that Germany, as a European country and of course the heart of Europe would offer me more benefits, but I did not leave my country for benefits. She kept convincing me and of course offered all her help and support including her three-bedroom house and enough cash. But an inner voice of my own kept telling me that there are some undone tasks that I have to do, I didn't know what tasks, but I knew my journey did not end in Germany, I had to keep traveling. I couldn't thank Emma enough for her generosity and love she had for me, but my journey did not end there.

We started losing weight and getting sick in few days, Wadan Khan had abdominal pain, so I took him to the clinic at the POD2 gate. The first tent from the left was the pharmacy and medical staff room, there were five other tents for men and women separately. People who had to seek medical services had to stand in lines on one side of the fence, talk to the translators to be called for a checkup if needed, otherwise everyone was given pre-packaged pills. Many people used to get the same medicines for different health issues. The translators mostly those brought from the U.S did not know enough English, Pashtu or Dari. They reminded me of most of those Afghan translators working with the international forces in Afghanistan, who were one of the reasons for the chaos created between the Afghan nation and international forces. Many operations failed, went wrong or had innocent people targeted just because of poor translations.

An Afghan terp, Waheed, now in India told me the story of a night operation conducted by the U.S. forces in 2009 in Arghandab district of Kandahar province. The special forces, in three groups, were searching nine neighboring houses in a village, all the three groups included female soldiers. Group A took more than an hour searching the first house, then they called Waheed who was with the B group to help them with translation. In fact, the group A's Dari speaking translator had kept asking the men and women to go to separate toilets, the head of the family, a 60 plus man, kept telling that they only had one toilet in the house which did not have the capacity of two people to stay at one time, and why would they go to the toilet? Indeed, the officers asked the men to go into one room and the women to another, the translator kept asking them the same but used the word "Makan" which is Dari word for the room, but the same word "Makan" in Kandahar Pashtu is used for toilet.

I saw the same condition in POD2 medical clinic. Really, it seemed like most of the medical teams were just brought on contracts from their homes, the majority were either nurses or paramedics with no experience. Wadan Khan was feeling an abdominal pain on his left side, it wasn't the kidney since he had no pain at the back. It was probably constipation, while three doctors had kept seeing him for an hour and were thinking it could be appendicitis. I then told them that he had pain on the left side, while he could easily bend his legs even with a jerk, so it could not be appendicitis. They still could not figure out, finally I requested them to just give him painkillers, antibiotics and some laxatives.

The nurse gave a strange look to his long nails while checking his pulse and oxygen saturation.

"We neither have nail clippers nor scissors to clip his nails," I told her.

Unfortunately, no cigarettes, no trimmers, no disposable shaving razors, and no nail clippers were allowed on the camp. I even talked to the POD2's colonel that to ask the contractor opening a PX shop, so people could at least buy cigarettes since smoking is even allowed in the prisons, and thousands of chain smokers were going through a serous anxiety and trauma. In addition to that, nail clippers really are of the most hygienic importance, we had not clipped our nails for almost three weeks; children were scratching other kids and their own skin. I even requested to keep some nail clippers at the clinic so people could clip their nails at the clinic, but the answer was always the same "we cannot do this."

The food was not only bad but also too little as well. we were given two meals a day: 25g toast, with 25g jam and 10g butter per head for breakfast; and the same size of toast with about 75-100g boiled rice or beans were provided for dinner.

When we came back from the clinic, we found Ghani Khan in the corner of the tent, crying, I hugged him and told him that I had taken Wadan Khan to see the doctor. We would go for a walk together. I thought he was angry with me that I had left him but took Wadan Khan.

"Baba! We were rich in Kabul, we always had something to eat at home, at least potato chips, yogurt or just bread, but we have become very poor here, I don't want to be poor, I have abdominal pain, please get me something to eat," my four-year-old Ghani Khan kept asking me to get him something to eat.

I pulled him to my chest and cuddled him tightly, while my eyes dropped tears on his face.

He looked at me and told me "Baba! Please don't cry, I am not hungry anymore, I won't ask for anything again, but you promise that you won't cry again," he with his innocent babbling accent said, and then tried to wipe my tears with his small and soft palms.

I still tried to talk to the administration tent to either increase the meal or get some cookies, biscuits or just simple bread for the kids only. We adults can understand and be patient, but the kids can't. Unfortunately, the answer was a simple NO. it wasn't only the food, but also the formula and diapers issue for the babies: every baby got only two diapers and 250ml formula feed a day.

Every tent was given a meal card with the numbers of people in the tent; there were thirty-one people in our tent. The lines for the meal started from the main gate all down to the women's mosque close to our tent. Hekmatullah Khusti never showed up at meal pickup time so Zabiullah Wardak, another tentmate requested me to pick up the meal for his family. Most evacuees had some kind of trauma but for Hikmat it was different. He, as a soldier felt that 'as you make your bed you must lie on it.' He had been evacuated like all the other thousands of SFU members. He had been married for six months only and had brought his old parents and younger brother of fourteen but had left his newlywed wife behind. I was shocked. How could a man leave his newlywed wife while bringing his old parents?

"Of course, you had to take care of your parents and I appreciate that you brought them with you, but what made you leave your wife? Do you know that it might take you years to apply for the family reunion and bring your wife to the U.S.?" I asked.

"Well, you know our culture, you don't have the power over your personal life in a joint family, it's for your parents to decide what and when to do things. My parents told me that west is not a good place for young women, the culture is totally different and very democratic, I had to leave my wife and will keep going to Afghanistan whenever I can," he said.

Looking at other families especially the couples from his own province made him super depressed, he would leave the tent early in the morning and make it to the D section where he had friends from his village, spend half day with them and half walking and weeping all alone on POD2 roads. I started counselling him, telling him what is done, is done," but sit back and make sure to put things in their right place the next time. There were many others especially from Khust province who had not brought their wives with them but cousins and uncles.

It had been a week in POD2 Ramstein that we neither had an internet nor electricity in our tent. I kept requesting the administration to install electricity in the tent, since after 6:00 pm, we could not even see each other, let alone see our meal and eat it, but they did not help. The next day Zabiullah found out that people from Tent C27 had been moved to the hangar, where they would stay for a day or two and then from there would leave for America. We asked Maj. Nomack, a gentleman officer, to get us that tent's cables since we already had circle D Junction box in front of the tent but needed connection to the inside. He could not help but asked us if we could do it our own. Zabih and I went to the tent and tried to uninstall the wiring, which was quite a tough job. The ceiling of the tent was about four meters high and there was no ladder or table to stand on. I asked Zabih to hold his hands so I could climb his shoulders to remove the cables. It took us about thirty minutes to do the job, but before I removed the last tightened socket, he lost control and I fell down. For a while I felt that I had broken my left knee or leg. It wasn't a fracture, but I had badly hurt my knee and could hardly walk to the tent. I had already had plantar fasciitis that sometimes made me unable to walk in the morning, and this knee injury made my days even worse, but we had our dinner in under the light at least.

Two days after the injury I started a limp walking again, that beautiful sunny Ramstein day became my day when I saw Emma waiting for me at our spot with a pack of red Marlboro.

"Where have you been, Azad? I tried to ask the administration about your tent number then I thought that it would give a bad impression, so I just kept walking by and thanks God my eyes are seeing you again," she passed me the cigarettes.

I without waiting for a second asked her if she had forgotten a lighter with the cigarette, she gave me one.

"What a world! I am giving you something that I never liked since it killed my dad, I had never thought that I would have cigarettes in my hands, and today I am motivating you to smoke by providing you with tobacco."

"Ah, Emma!" I called her name with an intoxicated tune after the first puff of the cigarette, "you are awesome, sometimes even a single cigarette means a world to a smoker," and then I told her the story of how I had hurt my knee and was absent for two days. She kept sadly looking at me, her blue eyes were trying to ask and tell many things.

"Hey, you want to tell me something, right?"

"I ah, um, no, I just want to see you smoking, you look good while smoking, ahh. No, you don't look good," she said.

"Ok, lets walk down the road," I stubbed out my cigarette.

"Aren't you tired of walking for thousands of miles?"

"Well, I have not walked yet, I have been just chasing the life, which has become the marathon track and I am the hunted deer. Life is a battle, not a feast, I just want to take a break from this race so I can live the moment by walking with you today," I said.

This time I was seeing the sunset in her eyes only, the brave and proud captain I had seen the first day had become an innocent sparrow, I could easily hear her heartbeat. We started walking down the road towards the sun hiding his face behind the poetic green mountains like a warm lap of mother trying to persuade her baby to nap.

Although there were tens of people including the U.S soldiers leaving their boot prints on the road but we without noticing anyone had reached to the fence that divided POD2 and POD3. It wasn't raining that evening, but a strange silent had incubated its wings like a broody dove on her warm eggs to give life to heartbeats with her waves.

"Can you see those big iron birds?" She broke the silence by pointing to the big U.S air force and Omni Boeing planes parked south-north down on the Ramstein runway. "One of them will soon take you away."

I then understood that she had feelings for me, I was running out of words to make the fairytale calm, while I hated to give her the lecture of how cruel the nature is sometimes. I unexpectedly pulled out the packet of cigarette and lit a cigarette. She gave me a look with thousands of questions but asked none, she again gave me a deep look.

"You are wearing the same dress that you wore the first time we met, I have just noticed, but I like the dress." I then realized that I hadn't changed my own clothes since leaving my office before heading to HKIA.

Before I could say any more, she said, "you have never told me about yourself just your name."

"Well, you know my name, right?" We both laughed.

"I was only ten when Dr. Najib's regime collapsed, and we left for Pakistan. We were taken to Haripur a district of NWFP now KPK, where we had to live with my uncle and his family. Since we had lived all our life in Kabul that had harsh winters, it was hard for us to live in Haripur which hits 45° Celsius in the summer, so we moved to Abbottabad, another district about

45km from Haripur. Some call it Osamaabad now," I smiled, "since Osama Bin Laden was killed by the U.S special forces in 2012.

"None of us knew the local language, yet my siblings and I were admitted to Pakistani private school, because there were no Afghan schools since Abbottabad did not have an Afghan refugee camp. I still remember that we had a tea kettle but did not have tea and sugar. We were living in a one-bedroom house. The first few weeks were the hardest time we spent there, but in the summer, life began to change.

"Abbottabad was a cold, rainy and green city, so rich Afghans living in Peshawar and other hot parts used to come and live for four or five months in Abbottabad. My mother was the only Afghan gynecologist and of course my dad was the only Afghan pediatrician, so all the Afghans used to see them for medical services. I also started with a small shop after school time, where I used to sell Afghan dry fruit brought from Peshawar. I later moved to Peshawar for high school, and then got my BBA, MBA and MA-English. I taught English language since high school, and later started teaching in Alkhair university.

"After the collapse of the Taliban regime in 2001, I returned to Kabul in 2005 and started working with an American construction company called Contrack Int'l Inc. Later I joined NAMSA/NATO as senior political and cultural advisor in 2009. Being a political and cultural advisor, I had to meet the Afghan politicians and analysts from time to time, and gradually I began to get involved in politics. Being heard and making a difference; those were the reasons I had wanted to get into politics since I was a teenager in college. My passion for social justice, making a tangible difference in the community and resolving people's problems made me earn another degree, in law, from the American University of Afghanistan.

"In 2015, I established a watchdog organization and kept investigating the corruption in the Afghan government. In 2017 Mohammed Ashraf Ghani, the Ex-President, offered me the position of the state and national spokesman. I kept working as the national spokesman for about a year and had no choice but to resign because the circle around Ghani. I ran for the Lowerhouse in 2018 but did not make it to the house because I did not have money to pay. Later that year, the Ex-President called and asked me to run his campaign for the 2019 presidential elections. I took the position of Secretary General, basically CEO of his campaign team for a year. Our roads were diverted once again before he started his second term, and I then founded an intellectual political opposition for almost one and half year till the regime was collapsed. And also, I have been a columnist, writer, critic and an analyst for eight years. And now, I am standing with a moon under the stars." I looked at Emma.

"I wish I could give you hug," she said.

The night had spread its darkness all over the Ramstein, and the boots of hundreds of people making a parade were now taking the breath of comfort in their owners' tents, so we could hear each other's breath.

"Although, I want to stop the time here, but I think it doesn't end here, I can't keep your family waiting for you any longer, we have to walk back, and shall continue from here," she pointed to my dress and we laughed loudly.

I activated a AWCC sim card, while the other Afghan networks I have been using did not provide international roaming, I needed to talk to Moraka, it had been a long time, and I knew she had been thinking of me. I had to credit it with AFN 2000 ($25), and I also knew Naqibullah back in Kabul did not have enough money to load the credit. Then Dr. Mujeeb all-time great friend and Bawar

Movement's core committee member came to my mind, but I had to text him and that needed internet, so I borrowed a hotspot from a neighbor who was also using AWCC and sent a message to Dr. Mujeeb. He had already helped me with my office rent and vehicle fuel and other things a few months ago. Dr. Mujeeb was on his way from Khust to Kabul and loaded the credit some three hours later. Interestingly, I had been meeting Emma but it never came to my mind to ask her for a hotspot so I could talk to Moraka, Agha Jan and my siblings.

Ramstein had begun welcoming the cold breezes of beautiful autumn, my all-time favorite season, the colorful leaves give me the philosophy that every start has an end, and every end has a beginning. Indeed, autumn is naturally the time of departure, every living thing is a nomad in some way; humans have developed their lifestyle by inventions, while naturally all the birds leave their homes and the murmuration flies towards a warmer place with a hope of returning in the next year.

The Attan

The Ramstein sunrise recalled my last mornings of Kabul in my office, where after taking a shower, a light breakfast and a cup of coffee, I used to sit and take the therapy of the beautiful sunrays of Kabul. In Ramstein, I would sit on the blue cot in front of the tent, getting the Ramstein's morning sun therapy and taking green tea made by Zabih in the electrical tea kettle, while trying to read the thousands of messages I received on WhatsApp. Two gentlemen of about thirty passed their greetings.

"You are Mr. Azad, right?"

"Right."

"We have been seeing you for a few days and have been hoping to meet you," they said.

"Pleasure is all mine."

"How did you get the internet?" They asked.

"Do you want to talk to your families? You can only send them either text or a voice message since the data I have got doesn't support any calls."

Amanullah, a thin man with curly hair and a wondering eye, sent a voice message to his family in his native Uzbeki language. His friend, Khanzeb, sent few voice messages to his family and friends. He kept telling everyone that they did not have to worry about him, he was alive, and all was good in Germany. He also asked them to send a reply to the same number and let him know if they knew anything about Gulzeb his older brother, and then cried, thinking of Gulzeb.

"Is everything alright?" I asked him.

"I am from Momandara district of Nangarhar province. My older brother Gulzeb and I drove taxis from Kabul to Torkham for fifteen years. When the Taliban took over Kabul, we could not make it to home for the first three days, due to the flood of people leaving Kabul for Pakistan; we were making good money. On day five, Gulzeb had brought passengers from Nangarhar to HKIA, since everyone had known about the evacuation by then, the five passengers from Nangarhar had a money exchange business in Jalalabad city. Gulzeb also thought of going to America after dropping his passengers near the HKIA gate, he parked his taxi on the roadside and joined the crowd and got to the airport after about three hours.

"Gulzeb called me to find out about my whereabouts, I had got my passengers seated and was just about to leave for Torkham. I apologized to my passengers and requested them to get out after Gulzeb asked me to go and get his taxi. I parked my own taxi at the station and left for HKIA, I got there at about 4:00 pm and finally found the taxi, which was locked, but I had the copy of the keys. We always had copy keys for our two taxis in case of emergency like that one. Looking at children, young and aged men and women, everyone including shopkeepers, porters I asked myself, 'what I have made in this country so far?' I have been a taxi driver for fifteen years, but my one taxi has not brought the second one, I don't have to lose this opportunity, I too have to go to America where I will be able to make good money and my children will have a better life than me. So, I also started pushing those before me and being pushed by others behind me, and we made it to airport in about five hours. I tried to call Gulzeb and saw that I had dozens of missed calls from Gulzeb. I then opened his voice message that he had left for me from the plane before the flight. I tried to call him but did not reach him. I spent the night at HKIA and then nine days in Qatar and have not seen or heard anything from Gulzeb yet. I don't know if he contacted our family or not because I had no resources to contact anyone, my wife, children and parents must have been badly worried about us, since none of us had told them about going to America. At the airport I called my cousin who also had a taxi to come and take Gulzeb's taxi, but before I flew to Qatar, he called and told me that he did not find the taxi, I am sure he did find it, but since he knew that we both brothers had left for America he stole our taxi, and I am sure he has not told our families that we left for America," Khanzeb slapped his forehead with a long sigh.

Mohammedullah from Kunduz province had his own story.

"I had been a cook in a local construction equipment rental company for seven years, my family was living in Imam Sahib district of Kunduz province, but when the fight between the Afghan forces and Taliban reached at its height, I moved my family to Kabul before the Taliban took over the province. Most of the excavators, graders, loaders, forklift and crane operators from different provinces were living in the office. Many of their friends, operators in other companies kept joining the crowds and most of them had made it to be evacuated. Operators in our office also started joining, some had spent a day while others two to three days to make it to the airport. It had been five days since the evacuation started and Ahmadgul, the only remaining operator asked that we too had to try our luck. I was in two minds as to whether I should accept the idea or not, and then I told him that I would take my family with me as well. The next morning before the sunrise I brought my wife and five children to the gate. Ahmadgul kept telling me not to bring my family, but I had no one in Kabul to look after them. We spent the whole next day in front of the gate, my children kept crying due to the shooting from the control towers and at the gate. My arms and legs stopped working when I saw Ahmadgul had got a bullet in his neck, I started yelling for help. Some Americans along with the Afghan forces reached out to us but it was too late, Ahmadgul had taken his dream of living in America to his grave, yet the soldiers took the soulless body inside. My wife kept crying and asking me to go back, she emphasized that there was no threat for people like us, why we would put our lives on risk and flee. She was right, but I told her that the majority around us were also people like us, most of them were facing no threat or risk, but since we had already spent a day and lost a close friend we should not give up. Some thirty minutes later, the American and Afghan soldiers came and asked me for Ahmadgul's family's contacts, all I had was our office's address on Kabul-Jalalabad Road. They said that they would send Ahmadgul's body to his family.

"I don't exactly remember but we made it to the airport sometime around midnight, we spent another day without eating anything at the airport and then made it to Qatar. I was very happy when I saw Khanzeb here the other day; he used to take and bring our company's machine's spare parts to Torkham time to time, so I have known him from the past," And then he hugged Khanzeb.

The two gentlemen who were accommodated in section C of POD2 were happy when they got replies from their families.

"By the way, where did you get your beard shaved?" I asked Mohammedullah.

"Mr. Azad! I am a cook; I know how to get the salt out of the food. To be honest with you, I did not know that they even take trimmers, I had simply rolled my trimmer in my clothes and put it in the bag just to make sure it didn't break, and they did not find it while checking my bag."

"Let's make a deal, I will get you the internet whenever you need it, but you have to lend me your trimmer at least once a week. I really hope we don't stay here for another week." I winked at him, "Just kidding, you can use the internet as long I am here, but I seriously need your trimmer right now."

The nice Uzbek man left and brought the trimmer, an old Panasonic that he had bought in Bush bazaar.

The two Bush bazaars in Qwa-e-Markaz and Pul-e-Kheshtee were the Free American Market and Black Friday markets of Kabul. The markets were named after the former U.S President George W Bush, since all American products including electronics, energy drinks and protein powder, clothes, bags, dried fruits, boots, toys, simply almost everything was available at very reasonable prices. The products were actually brought from U.S. airbases. It was almost impossible to find a parking next to the bazaar in Qwa-e-markaz, where the front shops mostly sold blankets, pillows and mattresses. The first two middle streets contained shops for school bags and luggage, while the following three streets sold army uniforms. The left corner from the east had mostly electronics including running machines, kitchen appliances and televisions, while the last portion of the bazaar had furniture and mechanical tools, all American products. I heard that Taliban have named the Bazaar after Mullah Omar now.

The trimmer made my kids happier than me; they wanted their dad to look the way he used to.

I always used to go to bed after 12:00 am, but since there was no activity at the camp, I started sleeping at 10:00 pm. I had just fallen asleep when the beautiful beat of an Attan woke me. I was half asleep and kind of intoxicated, and thought I was dreaming of some beautiful event, but the drumbeat woke me up. There's a proverb in Pashtu "'the drumbeats coming from far away always sounds beautiful.' I opened my eyes and found myself in Krubera cave. I slowly freed myself from the prison of my sleeping bag and got my shoes out from under my head where they were being used as my pillow. We were sleeping on the floor as the cots we were given were really good for nothing but acting as walls. Sleeping on them was so painful that we preferred to sleep on the wet floor.

Because of my plantar fasciitis, especially right after getting up, I walk with a limp. Now, like a thief in the night, I went out the tent and followed the drumbeats. As I was getting closer, the drum was leaving its echoes all around Ramstein, there were tens of tall, young Khusti men with long hair, walking in time, clapping. What well-organized and powerful steps were moving the Ramstein soil under these angry feet. A man with long hair and a moustache was hitting the steel trashcan with his large hands in front of the hangar. There were hundreds of people, including U.S. and German soldiers surrounding them. I could not move my eyes from the boots on the ground, I kept cursing the plantar fasciitis. I made it to the women's park fence at the right corner of the hangar and lit a cigarette. I was still enjoying the drumming when a sweet voice in my ears diverted my attention "Azad also likes the music, I love it."

"Hey-Emma, how beautiful to see you here."

"I just thought that I might see you here, so I made it.," she said.

"How sweet."

"Is it kind a local dance? I can see they follow every single move all together, its beautiful, I love ballet because it is well organized and everyone follow the exact steps, but I have never seen a dance like this before, it's so energetic," Emma said.

"Attan is actually an Afghan traditional and national dance, the origin of which lies in all Pashtun tribes' pagan past. It usually involved men performing a ritual dance. Later, the dance was modified and practiced as religious and patriotic dance, performed to get closer to God and also to attack the enemies, and at the end to celebrate the victory.

"Generally, now, Attan is performed at events especially weddings, national days and other private celebrations. Often, you'll see different instruments such as barrel drums, flute, rubab being used but it should be performed with a Dhol, which is a double-headed barrel drum that has deep and low resonant sound. The technique behind different Pashtun tribes' Attan differs.

"Attan ranges from two to hundreds people, and the performers need to follow each other going round and round in circle led by the first dancer who does not only lead other dancers but also plays the Dhol. It starts from a slow beat and goes from faster to the fastest."

"Can I tell you something? If you don't mind," Emma asked.

"Do you think I would mind?"

"No, I just asked to be polite," she grinned, "Some of those Afghan translators and evacuees standing next to the American soldiers were cursing the dancers, they were telling the Americans that the dancers were shaming them, they have lost the entire country, everything was gone, that these former security and defense soldiers, instead of crying and grieving were partying and rejoicing that their country was lost. Don't you think they are right?"

"Do you agree that music belongs to emotion, and it has a direct connection with our feelings?" I asked Emma.

"Yes, of course.

"Excellent, so you would also believe that emotions and feelings are not only about happiness, I mean, you don't only laugh but cry too, right?" I asked.

"One hundred percent."

"So, music has both laughter and tears. You might have also seen when a soldier loses their life, especially in battle, the coffin is carried by uniformed soldiers with a guard of honor, the firing of volley shots as salute and drumming?" I asked her.

"Absolutely right."

"I don't know if you have heard about Hazrat Hussien, the grandson of Prophet Mohammed PBU, who was brutally assassinated in Karbala, his date of assassination ashura is also made with singing Marsiya and Soz Khwan, two songs of lament from the battle of Karbala, and there are many other examples where music is also used for mourning. And I am sure some music in your daily life might still make you sad or even cry," I said, "I can clearly see the same mourning and anger in tonight's Attan, this is the only way they can express their frustration. You can't see any happiness or joy on any of these dancers faces, see how grim they are. Some have kept their eyes closed, while others are making their moves with a red fire in their eyes. So, they are dancing for their country not celebrating its loss. Also, you must know that this Attan has a strong message that where there is a will there is a way. We will come back with more energy, because chaos always gives birth to opportunities,"

"Wow, just wow Azad. Will you please teach me Attan?"

"Only if you can cure my damn plantar fasciitis."

"Azad! Please seek an asylum in Germany, please do accept it, Germany is a beautiful country, and also very close to Afghanistan, while America is too far. You will have a lot of opportunities here." Emma said.

As usual I did not have enough words to convince her as to why I wouldn't be able to stay in Germany, so I asked her to take another walk all the way to the end of the POD2.

We left the drumming and the loud steps of Attan and were by the C section when she broke the silence by saying "you did not answer."

I held her hand for the first time, she began to tremble; I could feel the fast blood circulation in her veins. She did not say a word but kept holding my hands with her eyes closed.

"Emma. You are not only the prettiest woman I have ever met but also the most beautiful soul, our world is really too small, it brought me to this prison, yes, a prison, where I am locked in by the steel fence, but here I met you. Any man with half a brain would beg to hold your hand. But we are the passengers of two different boats, you already know that I am married with four beautiful kids, and my wife is not only my first and last love but also the most beautiful mother in the world. Moreover, I am not the right person for you, I have burdens of liabilities on my shoulders, I believe God has protected me for something big that I still don't know. I have left a war-torn country behind; it will take me very long to get back to my personal life. We will always be best friends. But I believe that you deserve someone much better than me, someone with no burdens on his shoulders, only you to care for. Let's be the best and proud friends, I shall expect you to receive me at Hamburg airport next year, and you will show me the beauty of Germany, I want to explore it one day with my best friend. I am sure you won't reject the offer."

She did not respond, I looked her and found that she had her eyes closed tightly holding my hand. I then called her name a bit louder.

"Oh, Azad, you did not answer."

"So, you didn't hear anything. It's late now and I think we need to go back, please don't forget to bring my cigarettes tomorrow."

She said yes by blinking her beautiful but sad eyes.

The maximum days people had stayed before us on Ramstein were ten. About half of both A and B sections were taken to the hangar, which had the capacity for about 1,000 people at a time. On September 04 at about 08:00 am, as usual I was getting the beautiful warm sunbath when six American soldiers led by two military police officers, Maj. Lynn and Capt. Cunningham were doing their routine patrol, stopped by my cot. After the morning greetings we started friendly chitchat and during the conversation they came to know about my background. Although, the hangar was already filled with those waiting to fly to the U.S., a wait of up to three to four days, these two gentlemen talked to each other and told me that they would come back in about an hour. I thought they would have something about more security control since there had been some arguments and disputes between Sharifullah and another man from C section the previous night.

Maj. Lynn showed up one hour later and offered me to move to the hangar so I would be able to catch the next flight. I requested them to take the other three families with me too, if possible. We went to see if there was enough room for the four families in the hangar, and fortunately we got the best space there. There were about 200-250 families in the hangar, and every family had built walls with their cots for their privacy and used the floor for sitting and sleeping. It was a huge hangar with thick and strong steel chain lifters hanging on the ceiling. We built our forts at the right end below an iron sheet flax board with the USAF logos, aircraft photos and a slogan "PROUDLY REPRESENTING OUR TEAM" next to a two-story blue trailer control room. My children loved to see the photos of planes on the board. The worst thing about the hangar was that there were no power sockets so we couldn't charge our phone batteries. The big spotlights hanging over our heads 24/7 were very annoying and caused migraines. Moreover, 500 children in one place meant nonstop noise. Adults often had their hands on their ears. Additionally, the twelve big powerful air conditioners over our heads were set on an automatic cooling from 4:00 am to 10:00 am used to make the hangar freezing cold. I personally requested the administration multiple times to get them turned off, but they had to wait for the contractors to come and they never did. We had thought that we would stay there for one or two days, but who knew that we would spend weeks in such condition.

The next morning, I was grabbed by some ten ISAF radio reporters and started chatting in front of the hangar. Capt. Cunningham showed up and requested if I could help the main administration with high level translation for all Ramstein, I of course accepted the request.

The afternoon Ramstein sky once again wore a cloudy black and grey shawl. Looking at the sudden clouds I believed that at least there was someone who often cries with me. Yes, nature feels everything and the Ramstein sky was always very generous. It wasn't like autumn's leaves that were scared of falling down from the branches but had always kept weeping for our fate. I kept standing outside the hangar, the strong wind from the north made the tents shake, everyone including the MPs took shelters inside. I still wanted to be completely taken by the clouds and the cold winds. I was thinking that the clouds would soon migrate because they are also refugees and then they began dropping tears. I opened my arms, held up my face towards the covered sky and closed my eyes to feel the fragrance of the wet soil which took me to the muddy and broken streets of Kabul, where once my beloved had walked. I was still walking on the streets of Kabul when a massive blast opened my eyes. I thought my Kabul was hit once again but it was the thunder from the Ramstein clouds. I am sure my heart had asked the sky to send me an angel, as soon I opened my eyes, I found the angle right in front of me.

"Azzaaaddd!"

"Shakirrrr!"

I gave a big bear hug to my childhood best friend, Shakir Ahmad Azizi, I could not believe my eyes, I again hugged him to make sure that I wasn't dreaming, yes it was him, my buddy.

"Ohh, my God, how did you make it Azad? I kept calling you to find out about your whereabout and of course I was scared something bad would happen to you, since I knew they would not let you go. Oh, my goodness, how sweet it feels seeing you're here, where are the children? Did you bring them with you? I want to see them, please!"

"Shakir, my brother, they are all here and they are all good, it's a long story, can't answer all of your questions right away, let's go inside and see the kids."

He cried at seeing my children and how they were dressed.

"I have something to do. I'll be right back," Shakir gave the children a hug and left.

He showed up about three hours later with three bags. He had brought everything he thought we needed, and of course we needed everything since we had nothing except the clothes and shoes we were wearing. I sometimes wondered how others had managed to go with full bags, then I had to answer myself that they did not leave in the face of threats as we had. If we would have planned to leave Kabul for the U.S, Spogmai, the kids and I would have had shoes, clothes, socks, towels and even toys. Shakir had driven to a market outside the airfield and bought all that stuff for us.

Ghani Khan wearing the new pants and T-shirt said "Baba! We are not refugees anymore." He thought those with only one outfit for three weeks are called refugees.

Seeing Shakir in those days reminded me of the proverb Moraka often used to say, 'patience is bitter, but its fruit is sweet.'

Shakir Ahmad Azizi was one of the bravest and best reporters until 2014 when he left to pursue higher education in Germany. He was busy with his master's in mass communication, and also worked as a senior linguist at Ramstein since he speaks Pashtu, Dari, Turkish, German and English fluently.

During helping with translation, I noticed that the majority of Afghan refugees needed legal, cultural and social awareness rather than just with translation. I talked to Capt. Cunningham, he loved the idea and shared it with his boss Col. Everett. Col. Everett called Spogmai and me for a meeting right away, he did not only love the idea but promised to provide all the required materials and facilities. Spogmai and I drafted a detailed curriculum for both men and women, which contained the basic federal and state laws and regulations, culture, norms and ethics, English language, hygiene awareness, cultural diversity, advocacy and more, and handed it over to Colonel the same evening.

The Measles

Usually, people in the hangar did not have to stay more than three days. On September 08, at about 11:00 am they started moving the first two rows from the right side to a white tent. Every family including us was asked to pick up their luggage and to be on call for the flights. There were six rows on the right side where we were in the third one. At about 11:00 pm the USAF and the German forces came and started moving the third row, they were getting everyone to wear the white wristbands with special QR codes, the wristbands were given out by the only Afghan-German female soldier, she was speaking fluent Dari. The Afghan-German soldier kept providing wristbands and sending people to the white tent. About 300 people for the next flight were taken till 04:00 am, and then she made the announcement that the next movement would be started at 09:00 am, but no one showed up until Capt. Nowack and Maj. Steller came at 04:00 pm, they told us to keep our luggage packed and we all would fly before 11:00 pm.

We started rebuilding our tiny houses at about 02:00 am the next morning since nobody showed up to take us to the white tent, we did not hear anything the next morning either. At about 11:00 am, Shakir came with three more bags containing more clothes, shoes, toys and cookies bought off the camp. The kids started waiting for their Shakir uncle all the time and he would bring many things for them every day without fail. Shakir told me that because a lady gave birth on the last plane, it returned to Ramstein, and the people were taken to another camp. He also said that two measles cases were found in one of the camps in the U.S., so all flights were cancelled for an unspecified period. I understood that the last flight wasn't called backed because the woman had given birth on plane since those Boeing planes have enough facilities. Secondly, she had already given birth, the baby and the mother both were all well, so it did not make any sense to turn the plane back to Ramstein instead heading to the U.S. It was of course the measles issue, because of the time difference between Germany and the U.S., Ramstein received Pennsylvania's message late and the plane had already traveled for about two hours, but it had to turn back at the control tower's call. The plane returned and the passengers were relocated to different camps rather than the hangar, the Afghan-German soldier had indeed done good to us by not letting us on the plane or we would have spent the long night in the white tent, waiting for hours and would have brought back at the end of the day. The news of postponing the flights for unknown period had made everyone sad.

Furthermore, there were reports that no measles cases were found in either camps Ramstein or ROB in Germany, there were also some assumptions that the huge and sudden evacuation had overwhelmed the U.S. military camps and the resettlement agencies were having a hard time finding houses for the refugees. Thus, the measles excuse was used to slow the movement of evacuees from the Middle East, Central Asia and Europe until those already in the U.S. were processed.

I kept helping with translation and waiting for the Administration to facilitate the required classes we had decided to start. How the world outside those fences looked like, I did not know but of course kept thinking of the Kaiserslautern and that it must be very beautiful, the people of the most romantic clouds and mountains would be taking comfortable sleep in their houses, while the nights in POD2 waited for their lives to restart.

Eating twice a day was not enough and the same food every day was making everyone sick. The noises and big spotlights in the hangar were torturing Ghani Khan like the hot rays of the sun tortured the innocent Prophet Yousuf's (Joseph) eyes when taken out of the well. Yes, my handsome and innocent Joseph (Ghani Khan) did not know that where those ironic Egyptian camels were taking him. He started crying for his Moraka, his home, his toys and his school, he even started getting angry at Khalil Kaka (our driver in Kabul) for not coming to pick us up. The POD2 fences started to feel like the plastic handcuffs that get tighter as you try to move your wrists. The only good things about Ramstein were Shakir and Emma, the two had become the only flowers in the desert, while my surroundings were fragmenting. The beautiful and honest smile on Shakir's face entering the hangar became like an oxygen cylinder to a COVID-19 patient, I never showed him the volcano of stress boiling inside me, but it always fell dormant at seeing him.

On September 13, when Wadan Khan and I went to bring our lunch, a beautiful green eyed and blond hair teenager girl of about sixteen and her handsome younger brother were in line to get their food. There were only two people on the meal card, I asked them if they were the only people in the family.

A flow of tears from the little Hamasa's eye made its way on her red cheeks, the cute Abdullah held her hand and asked her not to cry or he would cry too. I hugged Abdullah and asked others to let them go ahead so they would get their food without standing in line for another thirty minutes. The two little souls did not let me sleep the whole night, I wanted to go and see them in their tent, but it was midnight. I could not wait for the morning, but I had to. I kept walking before the hanger where the lines were made up to get the breakfast, and finally they showed up.

"Good morning gorgeous babies! I hope you had a great night."

"Good morning, we had a good night, thank you."

"Hamasa! Would you mind if I ask where your parents are, I may be of some help," I asked her.

"No, you can't help. We were living a happy life in Ishkashim Badakhshan, my dad was a high school teacher at the district school, I went to class ten and Abdullah to eight. Dad used to teach at his private tuition center after school and would return home after sunset.

"I can never forget that Thursday, Abdullah and I were done with our tuition classes at 5:00 pm, and asked dad to go home with us, my heart had strange feelings, I could not explain but I told dad that I wanted him to go with us. Dad gave me a warm hug and a kissed on my head, 'my hero daughter, you must be feeling low, I am sure you did not have a good lunch, please go and ask mom to get you something to eat right away, I will also bring your favorite sweet tonight.' I again asked Abdullah to force dad to go with us since Abdullah was very dear to dad, he had never refused his requests, but that day for the first-time dad did not listen to Abdullah either. We left for home, and I kept looking behind, I just couldn't relax. I made ablutions and prayed maghrib, yet the strange things kept coming to my mind. I went to spend time with mom in the kitchen, 'what happened Hamasa? You don't look okay today.' She told me she was making my favorite spaghetti and told me to go watch tv. I explained my situation to mom, I could see some fear in her eyes too, but she tried to make me feel better.

"Although, the tik-tik sound of the wall clock was annoying, it felt as if the clock hands weren't moving, as if everything had stopped. That stillness was actually the message of the storm that none of us were aware of. I couldn't move my eyes and ears from the main gate, the eventually I grabbed the cellphone and dialed Dad's number, it did not ring, I felt my heart in feet, my hands and legs started getting cold, I called mom and told her that I knew that something bad would happen, dad's phone was not ringing, we need to go and find out what happened.

"Mom made it to my paternal uncle's home next door, I could not wait and watch at home so I left with my uncle, we walked for about ten minutes and saw a crowd on the main road, my uncle said to avoid it and that we should keep going to dad's tuition center, which was about to ten minutes more walk, but without answering to him I made it to the crowd. I saw a stream of blood under my feet, which scared me. I had never seen that much blood before, I was about to leave the area but the unique fragrance of the perfume my dad always wore pulled me back, I called uncle's name and jumped into the crowd, I saw my dad's white shirt had changed its color to red, the pages of his notebook were being moved by the wind. I wanted to scream and cry loudly, but my tongue and eyes were paralyzed, I could not speak. The ambulance carried two bodies, one with, but the other without a soul. We have never come to know who and why killed the only teacher of the village; I am sure those who believes in offing the light of education killed my angel dad.

"It had only been two months; our tears were not dried yet that the Taliban took over Badakhshan province. I was one of those girls in my district who could not even think of living under the Taliban but hearing about their taking over the province I was neither shocked nor sad, I did not have any space in my heart or my mind for more laments. Grief for my dad had completely broken me head to toe. I had forgotten the day and night, cold and hot differences, I left remembering time, date, day and month, but some moments in my life could never be forgotten. It had been only a few days of the Taliban being in power that one day our Mullah told my uncle after the maghrib prayers in the mosque that some people would come to our house later that night, so he had to be ready, my uncle did not know who were coming. We were just about to have dinner when four people were brought by my uncle to our guestroom. Dad had built a bigger house than my uncle, so even neighbors used to bring their guests to our guestroom.

"It did not take half hour that we heard uncle begging them, we were so scared, we were thinking to send Abdullah to the guestroom to find out what was happening when the four gunmen dragged my uncle into the room. They were accompanied by the old man who had been our mosque's Maulawi forever. Dad used to take extra care of the Maulawi all time, they did not even care that there were women inside the building or that they needed to knock before entering the family part of the house. Maulawi knew every man and woman by name in our small community of about fifty families, he called my mom by her name:

"Zarmina, I have brought you good news, the bad days are gone, you will begin a new and happy life once again, very few women in the world get this chance, you must be very dear to God that he has showered his special blessings on you. You are as lucky as those respected ladies during the prophet's time whose husbands had been killed in the battlefield and they were married to As'hab right after the victories of Muslims over infidels. The Islamic Emarat's mujahedeen are here to marry you to one of their bravest Mujahid friends. We have already talked to your brother-in-law, he will take care of your children just like his own children, if he fails to do, the Islamic Emarat will prosecute him.

"Mom started shouting at him. 'Maulawi, I have always respected you like a father, I didn't know you are a broker, you call yourself a mullah? Don't you know that I have been a widow only for two months, and I have not even completed my Iddat (period of waiting, a woman must observe after the death of her husband or after a divorce), did you forget all the favors my husband did for you? How could you even think that I would remarry? Please get out of my house right now!'

"Then one of the Hazara-looking-Taliban said something in Uzbeki to his friends and then told Maulawi that they couldn't waste time, they had to take my mother forcefully and would do her Nekah at their place, since they believed that mom would not accept the Nekah at any cost. The man then grabbed mom's hand and tried to pull her. Abdullah, my little brother, sister and I kept pulling mom and screaming loudly. I kept begging those gunmen not to do that to us, he kicked me and told my uncle that their Ameer had ordered that all young widows and unmarried girls between fourteen and thirty should be married to Mujahedeen, 'we will kill all your children if you keep resisting,' he warned my mom. We kept begging and crying but they pulled our mother, she was not even wearing her scarf and shoes but was pulled like a sacrificial sheep. I tried to run after them, but my legs wouldn't move, I was paralyzed. Abdullah kept crying and hugging me, my uncle who could do nothing against the guns were also crying like a child and hugging my younger siblings.

"The next day, uncle asked his wife to pack luggage for Abdullah and me, he had to take us to Kabul. I didn't want to leave my younger siblings, I cried to uncle not to separate us from our littles ones. He cried and tried to make me understand, he was scared that the Taliban would take me too, they had clearly said that they would take all single girls between fourteen and thirty and marry them to their people. Uncle was also afraid if they would take Abdullah to fight for them. We left later that day and spent the night in one of our relative's home in Faizabad and left for Kabul the next morning. I did not know where we were going since we did not have any close ties in Kabul, but uncle knew many people from Badakhshan living in Kabul. On the way to Kabul, I realized that nothing is beautiful or ugly but your own mind and eyes. Once the most beautiful, mountains, river and greenery all the way from Faizabad to Kabul looked ugly now. I remembered the trip to Kabul with my dad just five months ago when he had to get his new position approved by the Ministry of Education. Dad explained the specification of every mountain and river on our way, it was the same bus but a different world, a world where everyone looked alien to me, the world was full of sorrows, sadness and tears, the world that was created for tyrannies and oppressions only, the world with a sun and a moon, indeed the world without a God.

"I noticed thousands of people camped next to the main highway at the entrance to Kabul. Uncle told me that they were all refugees from the northern provinces including Badakhshan due to a massive ongoing war in their provinces. We took a taxi to Reeshkhur where hundreds of Badakhshi families were living, Nazari uncle and his family cried with us the whole night after uncle told them our story. Abdullah got insomnia, he could only sleep for an hour or two in 24 hours and would scream in that short sleep. The sword of death was always hanging over our heads, we began to believe that death was the only comfort. Abdullah kept telling me that dad had started calling him, Nazari uncle took us to a doctor one day who prescribed us some tablets that helped us with sleeping.

"I don't remember how many days we spent at uncle Nazari's home, but it wasn't much time before the Taliban took over Kabul. Uncle Nazari heard of the evacuation and told my uncle that he had planned to leave the country. He asked my uncle if he could take us with them. We finally came to the airport gate where we spent two days, it was midnight when people in groups were allowed to enter to the airport. We got separated from Nazari uncle's family in the crowd of thousands of people. Abdullah and I were taken to the airplane after spending long hours at the airport gate, we neither have a mobile phone nor anyone's contact number. We then spent two weeks in Qatar and then were brought to Germany. I still don't know if Nazari uncle and his family left Afghanistan or not, we don't know anything about our uncle and our two little siblings and they don't know about us, I don't know if we will ever be able to contact them," Hamasa tried to wipe her big tears.

Hamasa and Abdullah went to their tent but had left their tears with me. I couldn't stop weeping for them. I couldn't sleep at all the next night, so I went and sat on the same cot in front of the hangar which had cruelly absorbed the tears she had poured on the cot. At about 5:00 am, Capt. Cunningham came and asked me to grab our luggage including the sleeping bags within thirty minutes, as they had to move us to another camp. He then made the announcement to everyone in the hangar. It was very hard to do all the packing at such short notice and then clean up the entire hangar including folding about 800 cots and putting them in the left corner of the hangar, we were all done by 5:30 and started making lines to leave POD2.

I just thought of Emma and how I had promised her the previous day that I would start teaching her some Pashtu. I tried to press her name on the WhatsApp screen, then I thought it was too early in the morning for her, meanwhile, I did not want to give her the news of our leaving. One thing that kept sticking in my heart like a needle that she asked for a selfie, but I told her that we would take one the next day. I felt a strange worry in her voice that evening, I thought she was tired or missing her friends back home, but I realized too late that she was scared of the next day.

She had been telling me she had weird feelings, almost as if she was waiting for an exam at school.

"I think you have been too busy without taking a break throughout the week, I guess you need more sleep, that's it," I said.

"I don't know, but I had the same feeling when I was only thirteen and my parents were separating in court the next day, I kept knocking their doors the whole night. I entered each room tens of times and kept begging and crying to them not to do this to me, I still remember how hard I cried before my mom not to leave me and my dad. I asked dad to compromise, but all my tears and sobs died in the court the next day. I don't remember that I have ever cried after that, I believe my eyes dried up that morning. I grew up in the same city, but I never went by that court again, indeed I always try not to go close by any court. I have the same feeling Azad, trust me I have the same scary feelings tonight,"

I was very sure that it was simply stress from work. I did not want to end it this way, but I had no control on time, I then made my mind and convinced my conscious that ROB was only about 12-15 miles from Ramstein, I would send her the location and she would make it there.

The Flooding House

The U.S. army escorted us outside the POD2 behind the clinic in two hours where our meal cards were scanned and reprocessed, three buses had to leave at a time escorted by MP vehicles, the entire process of the three buses took about four hours.

The smooth Ramstein runway road soon ended into a posh area of Weilerbach where we saw Mitchel Avenue, the Skytrain lane with beautiful double, triple and four-story luxury buildings. The four-story building looked like it would be either a beautiful and calm library or an art museum, but to the left of the entrance was a sign with 'Elevator, Flight Medicine, Med. Special Operation and Mental health' telling us that it was a hospital. It was totally different to any hospital in my country where one would always see tens of people bleeding and crying outside.

The Weilerbach lane took us all through a beautiful and thick forest. The lush green trees on both sides of the road shaded the asphalt road like a tall Kochi Pashtun lady's eyelashes cover her eyes. I closed my eyes and took a deep breath; I was thinking that how lucky Germany is that it doesn't have a country to its south that wants to cut its beautiful trees.

About fifteen minutes later the buses crossed the highway tunnel, and we for the first time saw the outside world since leaving Kabul city. The vehicles on the beautiful wide highway surrounded by tall and green trees made this the land of beauty for living. Looking at the outside world from inside the buses reminded me of the Afghan prisoners when they used to be escorted by the Afghan security forces to court and back to the prison, they had to look at the outside world the same way we were doing.

The sunny sky of the Ramstein Neaubau High School Road forced me to ponder whether earth has four different skies or if it was divided into four, the one we had lived under was the resident for Azrael, while the other three were for Gabriel, Michael and Israfil.

The buses stopped by a gray ironed sheeted hangar, we took our luggage and entered a partitioned area of the hangar where we went to do the exact scanning process that we had done few hours ago at Ramstein. Since we had left early in the morning so the kids neither had breakfast nor lunch, they started getting hangry. The scanning process took about two hours, and the buses took us to our final destination, ROB.

ROB looked like a very important military base for NATO. The Rhine Ordnance Barracks (ROB) is across Kaiserstrasse from Vogelweh and houses the 29th Support Group, TSC's forward-deployed contingency logistical command.

The shuttle bus kept stopping almost in front of every fenced camp to find out if there was enough room for us. Shamla kept her fingers crossed for a private room with an attached bathroom for us not those tents she had suffered at Ramstein, but she wasn't lucky. The bus finally stopped by a fenced gate where two U.S soldiers and one 1st Sergeant welcomed us. Everyone except Zabih's family and mine had taken their luggage to a big white tent just by the gate, we were asked to wait. About thirty minutes later, we took our luggage to the same tent where Curry a U.S officer registered us, we were taken to the last tent, tent four. The first tent was an administration tent, which was used for food distribution, Friday praying and events, while tents two and three were almost full with people who came from Doha a month ago.

All the other families in our bus were placed in tents two and three. Tent four was emptied a day before we arrived, there were about 300 single men in the tent who had been relocated to another LSA, so this, LSA5, was made only for families.

The tent had about 200 cots in five rows, mine was the first family making it to the tent, about thirty minutes later more families from the Ramstein hangar arrived. We started making the same refugee castles with the cots, since we knew that we would not leave in a day or two, and every family was comfortable with their privacy. We were just done with covering our areas when Curry and two other soldiers came to the tent and asked everyone to take the walls down and use the cots the way they were placed. I tried to make her understand that nothing should have bothered them as long as the families are comfortable and happy and making no disturbance for the administration. She then called her boss the 1st Sargent Mr. William. William was a gentleman who was a great listener, I told him that every person deserved one cot, a family of six deserves six cots and they should have the right to use cots for either covering their areas and use the floor as their beds or simply use them as beds, he loved the idea, and thirty-three colorful forts some square, while others in triangle and round shapes were built. Tent four became a beautiful community where people from almost every part of Afghanistan started living. Since there were not enough cots to provide for every family's privacy, we used blankets and sheets tightened to the cots placed on each corner of the area.

LSA5 was built on approximately one and half hectare area with four tents and about 600 people. There wasn't any difference in the rules and regulation between Ramstein and LSA5, we were not allowed to have nail clippers, disposable razors, trimmers or cigarettes. The food was much worse than in Ramstein. We were given the same exact food for one month: boiled white rice for breakfast, the same ready meal for lunch and the same chicken piece and boiled rice for dinner. There was no place for a morning or an evening walk, there was hardly any space at all. The kids managed to play soccer and some adults played volleyball, and we were expecting WIFI so people could contact their families back at home because everyone did not have AWCC international roaming, which was quite expensive, one had to pay $25 for only 1GB weekly data bundle, which lasted only a day or two.

The good thing about LSA5 was we could at least touch the green leaves of the trees on the other side of the fence, the mobile toilets were cleaned three times a day and there were nice and warm showers right behind the tent.

At about 5:00 pm, a 1st Sargent came and told me that the camp commander wanted to meet me later that evening. Captain Adam Wiener, the commander, was a quiet gentleman, yet I found him a brilliant manager and friendly person.

We introduced ourselves to each other. He already knew that I had helped the Ramstein administration with translation for 34,000 people, and he requested me to help his team as well. I recommended he make some smart people as tent leaders who would share people's needs, and suggestions and pass his messages to them. We called two people from every tent and the tent leaders were given blue belts. They represented both parties, the U.S. army and the Afghan evacuees. We set up another meeting the next day after dinner, in which I had to provide them with a detailed plan, needs and management mechanism.

When I left the tent, it started raining, which reminded me of Emma. It had been two days since I had moved from POD2, but I had not heard anything from her because I had no more internet, and I was very sure that she had sent me a message and had kept calling me but could not reach me. I was then expecting that she would find my location and would come.

At about 2:00 am, I was woken up by water while I was sleeping in. The moment I checked, I thought a heavy flood had come, almost everything in the room had got wet, the mattresses the children were sleeping on were totally wet, and the sky was still showering, the next family to us were in the same situation, we tried to take the water out with our hands, but it was impossible, I went outside to find something that could stop water flowing to the tent but nothing worked and I got soaked in my thin sleeveless T-shirt. I even asked the security guard to find me a shovel so we could use the mud next to the central heating machine to stop the water, but there was no shovel in the camp, all the mattresses were completely wet, I took the cots down right away and got the kids to sleep on the cots. There was no tool to stop or bail the water out, so Spogmai and I kept trying out with our hands. The sky had a hole and was unable to stop the shower. The floor was built with rough cement chips with a space in the bricks so water would be absorbed but the fertile soil became helpless to absorb the heavy rain. I had already got soaked trying to find something to stop the water from outside. Since Kaiserslautern is often rainy, one would see greenery even in the concrete and asphalt cracks, the little left space in the floor bricks had rough gross and roots which had badly wounded Spogmai's hand, but she still kept protecting her home from the water. I cried looking at her hand bleeding, the woman who once used to take extra care of her beautiful soft hands did not care now if they were injured. Almost every kid in the tent was crying, our small village was flooded and the recently made small homes were taken down, some were busy getting their kids in bed, some their old parents and pregnant women, while others were trying to protect their luggage from water.

I looked at Spogmai and told her with a smile "see, you always wanted to see Europe, you are in the heart of Europe, honey."

"If there is anything more painful than dying gasps, it's of course migration," she replied.

Despite the children crying and the noises of moving the cots, the sound of deep sobs grabbed my attention. I walked down to the other end of the tent where a woman was badly grieving, cursing her luck and the German sky at same time.

"I hope everything is okay, may I help you?" I asked.

She kept crying, I understood that there was something not okay with her and I had to help her.

"My dear sister! You know every one of us here has their own story of pain and nuisance, there is no medicine for these annoyances but only sharing can heal. You can share your infuriation, maybe I can help." I said.

"I wish this rain could wash out the fate lines of my hand or maybe I should cut them out. I wish God had heart while writing our destinies, why the nature does not get tired of playing with our souls? I have no money, I don't have enough clothes, I don't even have enough medicine, yet I didn't complain to God. All I had was my mobile phone, but this barbarous rain has taken it from me, I don't remember my sons' contact numbers. I had my WhatsApp and other applications on my mobile phone, how will my lost two sons find me now? Ya, Allah, why did you do this to me?" She started screaming all over again.

"Your two lost sons?" I asked.

"Yes, the apples of my eyes, the only hope I have been living for, my fourteen- and sixteen-year-old sons. I have been dying for their voices for two months, I have been knocking the American's doors from Doha to this camp but no luck."

She started cursing her heart for not failing. I tried to convince her that I would get her phone fixed, which she brought to me the next day.

Zahira and her husband were ANDSF officers, her husband, Sarwari, lost his life defending Helmand two months before the fall of Kabul. The Herati officer kept working for her soil and moved to Kabul with her two sons after Herat was taken over by Taliban.

I had noticed her just the previous day, she looked different than most of the women I had seen so far, she used to sit on the wooden bench next to the small soccer field behind our tent all alone. I didn't see anyone sitting and walking with her. I saw her, bringing only one meal the previous night. I had understood that she was traveling all alone, I then asked Spogmai and Wadan Khan to see if she needed help.

Zahira, after the Kabul fall ran towards HKIA with her two teenage boys, she spent two nights outside the airport gate, where she had witnessed many casualties.

"The wound of losing my Sarwari had not been healed, yet that the flag Sarwari was rolled in was taken, the anthem he lost his life for stopped singing. You have worked in high positions, you have been involved in politics, I am sure your heart burns as well, but being a soldier and a woman, I can't forget the dark night of August 15th. Kabul was wearing the black shroud, I started thinking that where did we start at and where it just ended, I have been to many countries including the U.S and some European countries for training and workshops, I could have claimed asylum long ago, but I just wanted to work for my soil. I was only fourteen when a group of Mujahedeen, commander Ismail Khan's people, gang raped and killed my elder sister who was only sixteen. A year later the Taliban came to power, and we took a breath of comfort, we thought they were angels sent by God to throw the devils out of our wounded soil. It wasn't long after that the Taliban brutally killed my dad for being a former officer in Dr. Najib's regime. My mother, two younger sisters, a brother and I migrated to Iran then. We were not even allowed to study in Iranian schools, we were not even treated in Iranian hospitals except some basic and emergency medical services.

"My mother brought us up struggling day and night. She worked in a tailoring factory fourteen hours a day just to make sure that we had shelter, food and enough clothes. I then married my cousin Sarwari, and life took a happier turn for me. Sarwari was working as a skilled labor in a brick factory where he had to bake the bricks all night, sometime his hands got so stiff and burned that I had to massage them with salty water and oil all day, yet we were living a happy life. He was a real man, one who always loves and protects his wife, that is how my Sarwari was. We returned to Herat right after the dark regime of Taliban ended. Sarwari told me that it was the right time to take our revenge from all oppressors and that we had to join the Afghan Defense and Security forces to defend our motherland and people. I enrolled in the National Police Academy while Sarwari enrolled in the National Military Academy. We started living a happy and proud life and after two years of training we planned our first baby. I sent Waheed and Hameed to the Turkish school, the best high school in Afghanistan just because I wanted my sons to show Iranians that if one door is closed tens of others are open, I wanted to show to people like Isamil Khan and the Taliban that a man is man with a pen in hand and mind in his head.

"Sarwari and I kept working shoulder by shoulder for the soil and the family, his big dream was to see his sons graduating from the high school. Yet I did not quit even after we lost the sun to our small world, I kept working as a police officer just because I had made the commitment to myself and Sarwari, but August 15th abolished all the commitments millions of people had made. What a woman, especially an Afghan woman, needs most is a shelter and a protector, but I lost both. Sarwari my protector and Afghanistan my shelter, I accepted my defeat, the lines on my hand had won once again over my hands. It left me nothing to stay in Afghanistan for, not even Sarwari's grave. I didn't even receive his dead body, but only a letter from the Ministry of Defense confirming his martyrdom in Helmand province.

"We spent two hungry and cold nights at the HKIA gate and then made it to the airport on August 17th, the last time I saw my sons was in the crowd inside the HKIA gate. I kept calling their names and screaming, the U.S and Afghan forces kept taking everyone on the plane, there was not a one percent chance to talk to them about my sons or to go back. I kept dialing their numbers, and fortunately Waheed's mobile worked, and he picked the phone, he could only tell me that he had been taken on the plane, but he did not know about Hameed. Then his phone went off, I have not heard from either of them since then. This is the story of three generations; my dad, me and my sons, and this is not the story of mine only, but of all Afghans, every Afghan in the last four decades has lived a similar life, did God really create us with the same fate lines that other nations have?

"Oh God, why don't you stop my heart beating, please do so, please do so, I am neither alive nor dead, oh, God you can't do this to me."

She continued crying, there was so much pain in her voice, Spogmai kept hugging her and tried to heal the pain, but even a stone would melt with those tears.

I looked at her smart phone, the rain had stopped but had done its job to the phone, it wasn't fixable, yet I kept it and told her that I would send it outside to get it fixed. She was right, it wasn't only her story but that of most Afghans. The evacuation had become the Berlin Wall for many Afghan evacuees who left and lost their loved ones and had no idea when they would be able to see them again.

The meeting with camp commander Capt. Adam Wiener took place about 7:00 pm, he was accompanied by a female officer. I thought she might not like her job but later found out that she was workaholic, Lieutenant Girlado was the first American who could pronounce my name the way Afghans do. Although Girlado did not talk to everyone, but I got lucky, she started being very friendly to me.

ROB was not different than Ramstein in terms of regulations, and we faced the same issues. I provided a brief of community needs and the resolutions, that razors should be provided by the U.S soldiers at the entrance of the shower trailer, they could be put in the trash upon leaving the shower. One trimmer should be provided to each tent. The distribution of clothes and hygiene had to be done by list, every tent leader needed to list the families with their details and distribute the required stuff based on the listed needs. A separate meal card had to be issued with the unique number for each family so one person could get the family meal according to the number of family members on the card. There had always been complaints about the single food menu, so I suggested they should sign a contract with an Afghan restaurant, hire an Afghan cook, we had few in the camp, or provide Afghan ingredients to the contractor. Most of the proposed suggestions were implemented except a change in the food.

I also told Capt. Wiener that we had been in the row for the next flight at Ramstein, so would we still be the on first list when the flights restarts? The answer was that there were about 6500-7000 people in ROB, and he had no control on the flights, only USAF knew about the flights, so all from the Ramstein hangar had to start all over again.

The food distribution did change and become based on meal cards as I had proposed. As tent leader, I oversaw the food distribution. A woman and her young son was finding it hard to wait in line for her meals. She had been a university lecturer at the Kabul university, living in a beautifully apartment in Kart-e-Char the most desirable residential area of the capital. Neelum, as well as being a literature lecturer at Kabul university was running one of the largest kitchen businesses. She used to provide high quality food to weddings, parties and events. After finishing the food distribution, I left the tent to go and sit on the bench next to the soccer field where I was still thinking about how this woman who was once made food for thousands of people was now standing in the line for hours to get the boiled chicken leg for her son and herself when a hand on my shoulder brought me back to LSA5.

"You were thinking of this, weren't you?"

"Oh, I wish I had asked something else from God! How did you know that they moved me to LSA5?" I asked Shakir, taking the cigarettes from him.

"I might be a little dude for you, but I am a big man for others, I can do anything," Shakir hugged me, "But I have brought you much better gifts. You will love me for this for the rest of your life." He smiled and then gave me a German sim card with 90GB internet.

Truly, all one wants in such condition. The next surprise changed the prison into a heaven for me, a brand-new laptop, that became my psychiatrist, relieving all my stress and anxiety with the sound of its keyboard. He also bought every one of us branded clothes and shoes as well. Shakir had to leave after a short chat and promised to see me the next day. I had just begun to enjoy my first smoke in three days, when loud shouts and screams made me run to the tent. A family of twenty-one including two old men were beating up a young couple from Khost who didn't even speak their language. The two families lived next to each other. I tried to get the poor couple away from the punches and kicks, but I failed. I asked others to help but everyone was scared of that family especially their women who were using the most vulgar and most abusive language that I had ever heard from someone a woman. I then called the U.S. MPs, who helped and took Hazrat Gull and Shabeer and Ali Taimuri to tent 1 where Capt. Wiener, I, some other officers and a guy from CIA who had been KPF advisor where Hazrat Gul had worked in the past tried to find out the reason of the attack and abuse and to mediate between the two. Shabeer and Ali Taimuri from the family of twenty-one were found guilty of beating up the couple without any reason, all they were blaming was that Hazrat Gull stared at them while entering to his cabin, which was also found to a false statement. However, the family was given an oral warning not to repeat the inaction.

Since I started enjoying the fastest European internet using the sim-card Shakir had brought, I received hundreds of messages as soon as my WhatsApp got connected. The breezy wind, the cigarette and that wooden bench: it all felt like old college days. I was scrolling down the messages without reading any when I saw tens of missed calls and a text message from Emma saying, "It must not have ended this way Azad!"

I tried to call her but could not reach her, I thought she had got angry at me and blocked my number for what I did not do, yet I was feeling guilty and kept smoking outside. I had to check my email inbox as well, the most recent among hundreds of emails was Jan's email that made my mood.

Jan Karl Staab had always been the man of words, Jan and I started working together to provide construction, reconstruction, rehabilitation and health services for Afghanistan in 2006. Our professional relation soon changed into personal, I became the little and Jan the big brother. I can never forget how hard he used to work for Afghanistan and then at the end of the day, instead of making money for himself, he used to donate most of his salary by buying food, blankets, clothes, shoes and medications for the poor Afghan families. Jan was extremely valuable, and his actions were in keeping with the highest traditions of working in accordance with the Afghan traditions. Specifically, Jan made himself singlehandedly responsible for helping and providing personal donation to needy families. He never came up with something like 'it's too late at night, I am tired, etc.,' but he always smiled and said, 'don't worry Azad, I am here to bring smiles to faces.' We used to go down to Chicken Street on Holy days, buying antiquities, silk carpets, and just being out with people. Jan was not only worried about me but had already arranged a beautiful house for us, he even tried to buy us plane tickets and to allow us to independently depart the military camp in Germany, but it was not possible. I couldn't wait, responding to his email with my German phone number. He called me right away and started crying with relief that I was alive. His moral support had always changed the journey of pain into the journey of hopes.

When I got back to the tent, I saw Wadan Khan crying with severe abdominal pain. I took him to the clinic, which was set up in kind a garage place with two chairs and a table in the reception and a single bed in the checkup room behind. I tried to explain Wadan Khan's condition to the two gentlemen sitting in the reception, but they were not doctors, they did not have a clue about any types of abdominal pain. They gave Wadan Khan some juice and asked us to see the doctor during the day.

The White Tent

The morning of September 17th brought good news for everyone: about 600 people in LSA5 were getting MMR (measles, mumps-rubella) and Varicella vaccinations. The vaccination started from Tent 2, they had to get into lines to get vaccinated but some people from Tent 2 fought over their turn, they thought whoever gets the vaccination first will fly to the U.S. first. The vaccination was then delayed for three hours, which meant Tents 3 and 4 had to wait a day for their vaccines.

On September 18 I started getting everyone vaccinated first and got my family done last so I would not be accused of misusing the position of tent leader. Two men wearing sports caps and pretending to be members of the medical team were taking photos of adults for their medical records. Their black glasses and James Bond stance made it obvious they weren't medical staff, they were for sure intelligence guys most probably CIA, and were taking the photos of individuals for background checks.

After the vaccination I met a twenty-two-year-old-boy from Tent 3 who I had noticed before playing loud music on the speakers connected with his mobile. He disturbed a lot of people. It was him, his mother, an older brother, a younger sister and the older sister with her husband and a son who were evacuated. I tried to talk to him nicely to make him understand that he could enjoy his music without disturbing others. He listened but kept doing the same thing. I then talked to his brother-in-law and told him that people were complaining about him. The poor brother-in-law had no control over the family. No one, including his own wife was listening to him. Their story made me think that the collapse of the Afghan regime had been something of a lucky break for some; people like this family who believed that if the Taliban had not taken over, they would have never been able to make it a country like America.

"Their father died just a day before the fall of Kabul. We buried him the same day and planned the Fatiha and Qur'an Khwani event for the next three days. When the news of the crowds at HKIA's gate reached my in-laws, they left everything including the funeral and ran to the airport, I tried to tell them that they should have stayed for a day or two at least, but they did not listen. They were not among those who were at risk or being threatened, they were not even eligible to be evacuated but got the golden chance like other tens of thousands, and I also had to leave everything and go with them since my wife went with them. Now I regret it. I left my old parents who badly needed me to be with them," his brother-in-law said, weeping.

On September 23, 2021, the issuance of new white wristbands, known as flight tickets, began. In Ramstein, those wristbands were given right before the flight, so people were happy, thinking that they would fly in a few hours. There was no biometric screening this time but instead passport and NIC scanning. The thing that made some worried was taking their social media in particular WhatsApp and Facebook IDs and previous telephone numbers.

Since no flights started even after issuing the new wristbands, things started getting worse; we were hundreds of people fenced in with the same food every day. It became stressful and people started to get depressed, especially after they came to know that everyone had to stay for four more weeks from the day of vaccination. The early excitement died away as people understood that the vaccines were not an immediate ticket to the U.S.

I was enjoying smoking near the small volleyball port where middle-aged men were trying to take their stress out, when loud shouts from the small soccer field next to our tent caught everyone's attention. A young man had beaten up a young boy of about eight. The young man and his friends had borrowed the young boy's soccer ball and had been playing with it for an hour, the young boy who had been asking them to return his ball finally grabbed it and tried to run but they had caught him and started beating him up badly. The MPs took them to the TOC for investigation.

The young man, his older and younger brothers, two sisters and parents did not care if they were in the heart of Europe where beating a child is a serious crime. The two brothers and his father had a street shop of Chinese and Pakistani sandals in Cinema-e-Pamir. On August 16th their mother went to see their relatives in Qasaba where she saw the crowds surrounded the airport. She did not even go back to home but called her husband who with the rest of the family came and joined her. They also called their other relatives living in Kotel Shamali to leave for America, but because they had not been in contact with anyone since they left Kabul, they did not know if their relatives had made it or not.

October 01 started with getting COVID-19 vaccinations, it started from tent 4. Everyone had to make it to Tent 1 in lines, I was making sure that everyone was either getting the shots or they already had got complete doses with the proof. Spogmai and I already had two shots in Kabul, yet we had to get the new U.S. cards, so we were still in Tent 1 when our neighbor came and gave me the news that the rainwater once again was washing everything inside our living area. We were already done with the cards, and I asked Lieutenant Girlado to take care of my tent's people as I had to take care of home. Fortunately, we had been using cots since the first flood, yet all our bags of clothes were swimming in the water, which reminded me of the popular Pashtu tapa/folkloric poem, 'migration is not easy, you'll be shivering in the rain, yet you won't be sheltered by anyone.' Since I had already made a request to the camp commander for sandbags, I knocked on his door and asked him to get me the bags right away. He had already brought some but forgot to give them to me. Some soldiers and I tried to stop the water with those sandbags, but they did not work. I then emptied the bags and used the mud to fill all the gaps, which did work. I was still busy with this when poor Wadan Khan made my day even worse: he slipped in the water and broke his already wobbly tooth. He was all bleeding, so I left the water to take refuge in a refugee's home and took Wadan Khan to the clinic. There were no specialists there, let along an ENT doctor, but the remaining tooth needed to be taken out. The clinic staff did their best but failed to help, so they called a doctor from ROB Military hospital. He was not an ENT doctor but at least he was a doctor. Together we took out Wadan Khan's tooth with floss and a simple Kelly forceps he had. The poor boy got only one teaspoon of painkiller syrup, and after he could not eat anything for two days, since there was no food for him except the usual chicken legs which he could not eat, He needed some softer food, but not even toast was available. Shamla, looking at her brother began to curse her teacher and schoolbooks that often talked about the beauty and facilities Europe and America have. She now believed that the books and the teacher had lied to her, here in Germany we had neither had a dentist with medication nor simple toast or any other meal except the chicken legs. The poor daddy's girl did not know that her books and teacher told her about Germany not a refugee camp in Germany.

The only good thing we had in the camp was that we all were alive, it was only us who could change negatives into positives, the big tea machine in the middle of the tent became the TV round table hard talk show every evening, the water pipe outside the women's shower trailer being used as a laundry became the newsroom. The children and women had attached to each other like they had been neighbors for decades, the empty spot at the western end of the tent became the story telling, cards and chess playing spot for the men until midnight. The tiny colorful blue, green, red, yellow, brown, purple and white protective walls made of curtains and blankets in the tent made the community a Basant event, which always reminded me of Sardar Harjeet Singh.

Sardar Ji was over sixty, six feet tall with a long, pure white beard and moustache. He wore a white Shalwar Kameez with a black waistcoat and a red turban and had a clothes store in the beautiful and crowded Kabul Mandi behind the jewelry bazaar and historic Pul-e-Khishtee mosque. Sardar Ji was the clothes seller with the fairest prices and all types of materials including the original Banarasi. Spogmai and Khan used to buy most of the raw material for their business from Sardar Ji. One day Sardar Ji wanted to see their factory where, by chance, we met. He had seen me on television multiple times, he then invited me to his big store, which was of course very well decorated with Allah's name right above the entrance door and a Guru Nanak photo next to Allah's name. I asked him if he did that for his business, so he would attract more customers.

"We live on the same planet created by the great God who is known by different names and worshiped differently, which shall totally be related to one's personal appearance and way of calling his God, just like a man has many children one calls him baba, while others father, dad, ata, plar or peta. Similarly, his children never look exactly the same, one is short, while the other is tall, one has beautiful thin nose while the other has an ugly fat one like mine, and of course their fingerprints and eyes scans are totally different, it's just like that, my appearance is different than yours and yours is different than others," Sardar Ji filled my cup with green tea and passed me the sweets, "Yet, the area police commander often makes trouble for me just to fill his mouth with money every day because according to him I am an infidel and he is protecting me from the ISIS and Taliban," he added.

"What if the Taliban comes again, will you justify keeping Guru Nanak's photo with Allah's name the same way you did to me? I asked.

"Can one explain or justify things to God? Taliban are Gods themselves." We laughed so loudly.

Sardar Ji had been a great and professional family businessman; his grandfather was one of the richest Afghans during the reign of King Zahir Shah. He used to gift expensive carpets to the King and to the Indian President, Zakir Hussain. He was basically from Paktia province but had six bungalows and villas in Kart-e-Parwan, which were forcefully taken by Fahim Qasim and his people. Faim Qasim was a Jamiat Islami commander and Ex-President Hamid Karzai's first vice president. Half of Sardar Ji's family migrated to Canada in those days, and the rest to India during the Taliban regime, but he did not leave his country even in the worst conditions for people like him.

The colorful clothing-made protective walls inside the tent were just like Sardar Ji's clothing shop where every shelf was portraying the colors of life. But the colorful shelves of our tent were made black and white by the family of twenty-one and another family of five sisters, who just like the area police commander used to uncolor the colorful shelves of Sardar Ji's shop. Shabeer's family, especially the women used to fight with anyone in the tent or outside, and if they found no one outside with whom to fight then they would fight with their family inside the tent. They used the worst language that made every man and woman cover their ears and seek protection from their evil. They again fought with a decent man from tent 2 claiming that he was staring at them, after they were done with the poor man, they started fighting among themselves over a blanket.

The five women who pretended to be sisters were traveling without a single man. Once a UNISEF team came and confirmed that the babies and children traveling with them were actually not theirs, so they said they were their other sisters' children who did not come with them. These sisters were all-time troublemakers for everyone, they kept fighting over meals, donations even over disposable teacups, which were given in dozens. I never heard a single decent word from them, they even used the worst vulgar language among themselves as well. Baseerat was about thirty-five. She was dark and thin. She was also the oldest and rudest one. The five sisters and fourteen children in the family often disturbed people with their constant screaming and shouting. Later, it was found that the two families were also among the ineligible people who just made it to HKIA by passing the wastewater stream by the HKIA northern security wall. The families in the tent submitted a written complaint to the commander who relocated the family of twenty-one but did not find another spot for the five sisters. Professor Hatim, a man of about seventy from Kunduz was with his well-educated and decent family. He would often look at these two families and cry that destiny brought a person like him who educated and trained tens of thousands of people over forty-five years and those two families on the same page. They were sometimes treated even better because of their selfishness and shamelessness.

Finally, October 11 brought good news for the LSA5; it was the day to be tested for COVID-19 and get vaccinated for Influenza. Those with no COVID-19 would fly by October 13, which started with a smile and tears. It's true that no condition makes a man happy, on one hand we were happy that a part of our painful journey was ending, while on the other hand, we were used to this place, and did not know what plane would take who to which camp in the U.S., would we meet up again or not? Taking down the beautiful and colorful protective walls felt like we were destroying our childhood houses. The once the beautiful village started to be demolished at 10:00 am, and the tent became an autumn field in five hours after all the cots were folded and taken to the warehouse. Everyone made it to Tent 1 and left ROB for Ramstein. We were wished a safe journey by Girlado at 5:00 pm, and the three shuttle buses escorted by two MPs vehicles each drove for about thirty minutes via same beautiful route and dropped us in front of the famous white tent that everyone had heard of. There were six tables where the officers were checking every family's documents. After checking the documents, they gave the sealed medical records containing all the vaccination and medical records for the stay in Germany. It didn't take more than five minutes, but unfortunately, the developed technology and updated database had made a big error: my family number on the record with the officer showed twelve people in the family while we were only six. After checking the documents of another family who also lived with us in LSA5 they saw that we had the same family code. It took them about one hour to issue us only separate sheets, but they were not able to change the family codes since the database was controlled by the State Department in Washington DC and military wing in Pennsylvania.

We were escorted to the next tent where hundreds of people with their luggage were in lines. We had been waiting in lines since afternoon, so the children were hungry and tired. Spogmai had to take care of them, and I had to carry our four bags, which were full of clothes mostly sent by Wajihullah, Spogmai's brother from Italy to Shakir who brought them to us with other stuff he kept buying for us. There were again two gentlemen wearing sports caps taking every adult's photo with their cell phones and stopping some individuals for hours until they received their clearance.

It took about three hours for all the luggage to be physically checked and for us all to be given new yellow wristbands. The sealed medical records were taken by a woman who escorted us to the third tent, which was being used as the departure terminal. My friends, Said Ahmad Safi, Sayed Ali, Khan Agha and Obidullah Bowra were waiting impatiently for me in the second hall, they thought I might have been stopped by the cap wearing guys for some reason. The hall was very cold since it was 2° Celsius and we had no blankets. Shakir had told me to take blankets and leave them in the hall, but the two hands could only pull the bags. Shakir as usual was our angel and just showed up in front of me. The first thing he noticed was that the children were shivering, so he left and returned with two blankets within ten minutes. It was about 1:00 am and Shakir had to leave, our goodbye with him was truly difficult which made us cry. Since the children had blankets, they fell asleep right after Shakir left but Safi and Khan Agha and I kept fighting with the freezing cold until an announcement was made to get on the shuttle buses at 3:00 am. The shuttle buses dropped us at the airstairs of a beautiful and huge Omni Boeing aircraft that Emma and I used to look at. Once onboard and in our comfortable seats feeling warm, Spogmai and the children fell asleep right away.

Across Seven Oceans

After a seven hour journey the captain made the announcement that the plane would be landing in about thirty minutes. Looking out the window, Shamla was surprised by the twinkling stars on the earth. She happily asked me to look too, and we saw New York, the city that does not sleep. New York was welcoming us to the land of opportunity. I began to think how lucky and happy the people were living with these lights far away from bomb blasts, suicide attacks, poverty, drought, desolation and the smell of human blood.

The plane landed on the wide and smooth runway of Philadelphia airport, and we were escorted to the immigration desks. Here they checked our biometric data, our passports and NICs and we were issued with two-year parole visas. I had no idea how those with no documents would be processed. Two of our tentmates' passports were passed to other colleagues by the immigration officers, saying 'they are red'. We were then taken downstairs for further processing, which included giving us our sealed medical records and family code documents from Germany, and an A12 Samsung mobile phone with two months' worth of internet data and national calls, and new green wristbands.

We waited for about thirty minutes at the departure hall of Terminal A and then got on the city bus next to the beautiful metro track which looked very similar to Delhi metro. The beautiful ports where tens of huge red and white ships and hundreds of containers made me believe that I had come seven oceans far from my homeland. We reached Fort DX in about thirty minutes where we waited on the bus for about one hour and then after receiving our luggage we walked into the big hall where we were again processed for biometric and screening and issued new orange wristbands. I did not gift this many bracelets to Spogmai in our ten years of married life as she got during those three months. We spent about two hours there, where they also gave us a buzzer and walked us to the next huge hall where we had delicious food for the first time in three months. The hall was divided into two parts with about 500 cots in each. We thought we would stay there for a day or two but some three hours later the buzzer started vibrating which meant to get in the lines to leave for the next destination. We stood in line for nearly two hours and were screened once again, finally the city buses left for Fort Pickett at 6:30 pm.

The children and I wanted to explore the places from New Jersey to Blackstone South Virginia, but we were traveling at night so did not see anything but just had to get to the destination where we could finally take a nap after traveling and standing in lines for forty hours. The buses finally stopped in front of a one-story building with a wooden board announcing Pickett Theater above the entrance. We were taken to the cinema hall and had seated in the rows. Three hardboard cabins were built where three medical staff in each were checking families for skin disease and headlice. The next stop was in front of a white tent at the Pickett village at about 2:00 am, where Maj. Michael Kuiper welcomed us. Maj. Kuiper was a marine commander and Pickett village mayor and had been in Helmand, Afghanistan. Before we were given blankets, bedsheet and pillows, getting registration and meal cards at the mayor's cell took another three hours. We started following the marine soldiers who were carrying our luggage to the white trailers. We and another family were accommodated in one section with fifteen triple beds in B55B, but Maj. Michael moved the other family to another trailer the next day.

The white lodging mobile sleepers, made to be used in emergencies and natural disasters, were here being used for refugees for the first time. The triple beds were about 50 cm high and did not even allow the five-year-old Ghani to sit, only to lie down. There wasn't enough space for the luggage either, but we got lucky that the other family was moved the next day, while families were living together in other sections. The trailer was divided into three sections A, B and C with twelve-fifteen-twelve beds, and only family members with exact bed numbers were lucky to live as a single family, otherwise two-four families were made to live in 2x6sqm filled with prison type triple bunkbeds.

Our section was the middle one with three beds right opposite to the entrance door and six on each side. The next day after some three hours rest, I wanted to see if we were locked behind a fence like in Germany or if we had the opportunity to walk around. The tall pine trees forest on the left of Pickett village was telling me that sky is the limit, the thick forest on the right of the huge soccer field right behind our trailers gave me a fresh and energetic breath. There were 216 trailers with approximately 6500 people, some living in double bed while most were in triple bed trailers.

The Commonwealth's Guardian writes that Fort Pickett was originally named Camp Pickett. The name was chosen to honor Richmond, Virginia native Major General George E. Pickett, whose ill-fated charge at the Battle of Gettysburg in Pennsylvania during the US Civil War holds a unique place in the history of warfare. Situated just east of the town of Blackstone, Virginia, the location of Camp Pickett was chosen for its central location and access to natural resources. Approximately 46,000 acres were acquired and cleared, and construction began in January 1942. The camp was formally dedicated in ceremonies at 3 p.m. on

July 3, 1942, exactly seventy-nine years to the day and hour of Pickett's Charge in Gettysburg.

Development at the base continued at a rapid pace after the United States' entry into World War II, and by the end of 1942 approximately 1,000 barracks for enlisted soldiers, seventy officers' quarters, and another 400 buildings were completed and in use. These other buildings included twelve chapels, a post hospital, six fire houses, warehouses, and headquarters and administrative facilities.

For recreation, there were four movie theaters, a gym, several enlisted clubs, and a main post exchange, as well as several satellite PXs. Transportation infrastructure was critical and involved both an army airfield and railways being constructed to facilitate moving troops on and off base. Blackstone Army Airfield consisted of multiple runways, an air-control tower, and the post's only hanger. Two rail spurs to the camp were connected to the nation's existing rail infrastructure.

The army also built and maintained its own water and sewage plants to assure adequate sanitation and potable water for the post. In the 1980s, these facilities were transferred to the control of the town of Blackstone. Two prisoner-of-war camps, and nine smaller satellite camps in nearby counties, housed approximately 6,000 German POWs. Many of these POWs were brought to the United States to perform farm work and other non-war-related jobs as allowed by the Geneva Convention.

According to taskforce commander General Richard, the Pickett village was built in nine days by the rental trailers for bed downs and showers. The only way we really knew we had left Afghanistan was the lack of blasts, suicide attacks, torture and corruption. Otherwise, we may as well still have been there. We did not see the outside world at all except on short bus journeys. We saw US forces with us in HKIA, then Doha, Ramstein,

ROB, New Jersey and then Fort Pickett. Every trailer and street was populated with people from different parts of Afghanistan. I would see people speaking Uzbeki on one street, while the next streets would give me the colorful norms of Pashtu, Dari, Hazaragi, Peshaee and Turkmeni. Fort Pickett had become a small Afghanistan where Pashtu speaking people from Kandahar had hard time understanding the Pashtu speaking from Khost. Children who had never spoken Dari started speaking Dari like a nightingale. One thing I noted was that Pashtu speaking children who had never been to school were very good at learning another language; they started speaking Dari and English just in few weeks.

Since the mobile sleepers were built for sleeping only, the soccer field became the picnic spot, everyone would bring their meals to the field and have them there. Every family had to take a blanket or a bedsheet early in the morning to occupy a spot for their family. Some would also keep walking all day since there was no space to sit in the trailer, and there were other families living in the same section, so the men used to go to their trailers only at bedtime. The first days gave everyone bumps on their heads, as we got used to the tight bunkbeds.

Fort Pickett was warmer than Ramstein yet the trees, like those in ROB kept holding my hands, they too started shedding their skin and left for a journey of immigration. The golden leaves of fall covered the ugliness of dust and cracks. The first thing Spogmai and the children asked for was a long walk, we were not prisoners anymore, the huge Fort Pickett was all open for us, but we still did not know if there were restricted areas, so we walked around the Pickett village only which took about half an hour.

After taking rest for a day, our names came in the list on notice board for IRC biographic forms. After scanning our passports, we were asked in which stated we desired to be resettled. What surprised me was that they asked for any U.S. ties. Those who with any links to specific states had to provide IRC with contact information so that a resettlement agency could try and find them a house nearby. Those who did not have any ties in the U.S. would be sent anywhere decided by the IRC. Before taking us to IRC office in building 2406, we were briefed in the Pickett Theater that we were not allowed to choose resettlement in some states especially Virginia and California since many had already chosen those places. I thought the IRC would have some preference or priority based on an evacuee's skills and educational background and would suggest states around their jobs and skills, but unfortunately it wasn't the case. Most of unskilled labor and totally uneducated people were sent to metropolitan places in particular areas close to Washington DC, which I was sure would mean that they would not be able to afford to live there once they had to start living on their own. Since I had worked for some American media outlets, organizations and had political connections, I wanted to select a resettlement place close to DC, but they had already closed the Virginian door on me, despite many contacts and friends confirming the availability of reasonable housing in North Virginia. I chose Maryland which was neither on the No list nor far from DC. Maj. Michael had already become my U.S. tie and had provided all his contact details. He and his wife, Sherry Kuiper, were helping me look for securing housing for us. Maj. Michael transferred to another camp in Maryland two days after we arrived at Fort Pickett, yet, he had been doing all he could to help.

On October 19, we were called for biometrics. There were about 150 people, but the process was taking quite a long time, so we had to wait outside for our turn. The bad thing about Pickett village was that the AT&T mobile phones given to us did not have internet coverage in the village, but was fast enough around the biometric office, so I thought to use the opportunity and made video calls to Moraka. During my conversation with Moraka, a man asked me, "Mr. Azad, please ask her to pray for me too, a mother's prayers are heard."

The tall man with green eyes, blond trimmed beard came and asked me if I had asked Moraka to pray for him?

"Yes, she did."

"Thank you very much Mr. Azad, may your mother live long. Amen," he prayed, "By the way, my name is Ayoubi, I have been watching you on television since you were President Ghani's spokesman and then his critic. I tried multiple times to meet you, but unfortunately destiny had decided that we would meet like two tired and breathless horses who after losing the race look and ask each other that who they ran for? They then realized that they didn't only run for the bet they had no idea of but had run too fast and gone far away from their home ground."

There was a deep pain in his eyes and words, I understood it wasn't the pain only for the soil but also accompanied by another grief.

"Do you smoke?" I offered him a cigarette and we both started polluting the beautiful climate of green Fort Pickett, "Are you on your own or with family?" I asked.

He tried to hide the tears, but they started burning his cheeks.

"I am sorry, I didn't mean to upset you," I said.

"Ah, you don't need to be sorry Mr. Azad, I am glad that I have finally met someone whom I can cry in front of and lighten the burden on my heart. I am all alone, I don't have a family anymore."

I asked him to walk towards the beautiful trees on the other side of the road with me, I didn't want people staring at him, so he would hesitate to let out this grief that had built up in his heart.

"I worked as translator for the coalition forces from 2004 to 2012, and then enrolled in a medical university. I graduated with an MD in 2017 and started doing my specialization in cardiology. Life was at its peak, my parents and younger sister wanted me to get married, they had already chosen a girl for me, but I was in love with the girl from my first year of MD, and we had decided to get married once we both are done with our specializations. I told Tahmina about what my parents wanted, so we married before the completion of our specialization in 2018.

"Although, I received my COM and KBR approval in 2019 I wanted to heal my people's hearts, I preferred staying and working for my country and countrymen. I was already a doctor yet people in my village still called me Tarjuman Sahib (Mr. Translator) because I had worked as a translator for eight years, and I was the only translator with the coalition forces from my district Imam Sahib of Kunduz province. Everyone including the Taliban from my district knew me. Tahmina was on a maternity leave at home, and I was in Kabul continuing my specialization when on August 08 the Taliban took over Kunduz. The first thing they did in Imam Sahib district was they went to my home asked for me, when they did not find me, they brutally killed my old parents, the nine-month pregnant Tahmina with the baby boy who had not even seen this cruel world yet, and Farkhunda my younger sister who was a law student.

"Fawad, my cousin called me at 1:00 am and gave me the news that took the earth away under my feet, my legs became paralyzed, I was not able to figure out what to do what not to, my wardmate at the hospital took care of me somehow and tried to get me out of my shock. I tried to leave for Kunduz about half hour before sunrise, but neither my wardmate nor Fawad, my cousin, let me attend my world's funerals. Fawad told me that they actually came to kill me so I couldn't even see my family's dead bodies. So, all I could do was see the photos of four innocent faces asking thousands of questions."

Ayoubi started sobbing. I had seen many, including myself cry, but I had never seen a young man with such painful crying like Ayoubi that day. His sobs broke me. His pain took over my nerves and for a while I thought that my spasm had dominated my movement. I slowly laid my legs out on the dried autumn leaves and leaned against a thick pine tree. I didn't even realize that there were dried leaves and branches in the tiny forest. I lit the cigarette, and a sudden wind moved the dead leaves and broke the killing silence that had made both of us statues. I passed Ayoubi a tissue to wipe his tears.

"It had been almost a week of grieving when the news of the fall of Kabul fragmented everything. Our staff at the hospitals, like everyone else, left everything and went hiding. Those were the days when I started smoking, my wardmates kept coming to my place and we kept our eyes and ears on the television and radio to know what was going on. Every second news after the collapse was the crowds at HKIA and the evacuations. My two wardmates decided we should try our luck. I told them that I am just like a broken boat whose helmsman has drowned and the boat is moved by the waves, so you guys are the waves, you can take me wherever you want. My two colleagues Dr. Safiullah and Dr. Maiwand, their families and I made it to the Camp Sullivan gate at about 4:00 am on August 25, where it seemed like the whole nation was leaving, men, women, old, young and children were trying to cross the barbed wire like the birds of a burning jungle are trying to flee. We were badly affected by the continuous shootings, we were exhausted, but Maiwand said, 'we can't quit, we do have to make it, otherwise we will all be killed just like your family, we need to save our lives so we will be able to save the country and countrymen then.'

"Maiwand was still motivating me when a huge red fire flash took my vision, and the massive blast made my ears ring for a while. I tried to bring all my senses under my command, I saw the dirty blackwater stream had changed to red, human bodies had covered the road and the stream, hundreds of old, young and little bodies were covering the water in the stream, the shootings and people's screams made the area the second Babara massacre[2]. I could not smell the explosive and dust anymore but just human blood. I touched my head and face, which were badly covered by the dust, flesh and ashes of clothes. I thought I was injured but the pieces of flesh on my face were not mine, I then remembered that a man who showed some documents to the American soldiers had crossed the stream and passed his bag to the soldiers by the control tower. The soldiers then pulled the man to help him enter HKIA, and then the huge blast took hundreds of lives including those American soldiers trying to save that man's life. He had been a suicide attacker.

"I started looking for Maiwand and his family who had been to my left but did not find them, I kept calling his name, and then started looking at the nearby bodies. My phone had run out of battery hours ago, at this moment, the American and Afghan forces arrived and took control, they did not let anyone move from their spot. They asked everyone to sit down and not move. As I sat, I saw Maiwand, his baby and his wife drowning in their own blood. I tried to run to them, but the soldiers shouted at me of course for everyone's security. I started crying and told them that they were my family. They were busy getting the bodies

---

[2] The Babrra Massacre was a mass shooting on August 12, 1948 by the Pakistani military commanded by Punjab in the Mardan city of Khybar Pakhtunkhwa. Hundreds of innocent protestors including women, children and old people were brutally killed.

from the stream and road, it took hours. Some bodies were taken inside the airport and the rest were taken by ambulances escorted by the Taliban. Maiwand and his family's bodies were taken too. My mind had stopped working, I had lost decision making powers. The soldiers were taking some people to HKIA, I was among them, I just started walking with them without thinking if I should go or leave. Some others and I were taken to the clinic inside, I believe they gave me some anti-depression pills, which I took right away. There were thousands of people inside the airport, I spent another day at the airport where Dr. Safiullah and his family came to my mind. I had only seen Maiwand and his family before and after the blast but had no idea about Safiullah. I tried to make a call and thought that I would borrow someone's power bank to get my phone's battery charged I then realized that I had lost my phone, and I did not know his number.

The plane took us to Doha the next day, where they kept us locked inside the plane for about four hours. The boiling heat and lack of oxygen made many faint. The shuttle buses took us to the big white tents. I did not even have a wallet, all I had were the clothes and shoes I was wearing. I did not care going to the tent first but asked for a shower. Although, I had been working in operation theaters for five years and was used to the smell of blood now it was burning my nostrils. I had been feeling vomiting since then, I wanted to tear my clothes and shed my skin, I made it to the shower, and I did not take my clothes off but stood under the shower for almost an hour, I didn't even feel the water that was boiled by the Doha sun. I could still feel the innocent souls hanging with my clothes. I got out of the shower and knocked the next cubicle door to borrow some shampoo or soap, I emptied the whole bottle on my head and clothes and then started feeling better. I stayed in Doha for four days and then were taken to Spain where we stayed for about one and half months. We just arrived at Fort Pickett last week," Ayoubi ended his story with a deep breath.

Every next story was marking the cruelty of the skies, the painful stories had started tenting on the desert of my heart but totally different than the tents that had been built for us because we were leaving every tent in a few weeks, while the tents on the desert of my heart will last as long as my heart and mind keep working. Ayoubi had taken the fire out that had been burning him inside for three months. The tall Chinar and Pine trees on both side of the E Parade Road had started wearing the grey scarf with the orange shades of the sunset through the tree branches. We left for the biometric office where we still had to wait for fifteen more minutes for our turn to come. An American gentleman came downstairs and escorted us to the first floor where two women welcomed us and offered crayons and painting notebooks to the children. Although, the screening and photos took few minutes but the rolling biometric for our work authorization and social security cards took quite a long time.

The Flowery Soul

The beautiful sunny morning of October 20 made me leave for a walk early in the morning, the E 24th and E 23rd streets of the E Parade Road made my day; I was still leaving my footprints on the road when a young man, wearing a mask came from the opposite side, gave me a smile and a wave to talk to him.

"Salamona Azad Sahib! I am very happy to see you here, my name is Atal, I met you twice in your office, but of course with a group of hundreds of people, you would not remember me because you were meeting hundreds of people a day. It's really an honor seeing you here. Actually, I saw you last night in the Dining Facilities Administration Center (DFAC) and wanted to talk to you, but you were surrounded by bunch of people."

"It's very kind of you Atal, I am also very happy to meet a young gentleman like yourself," I gave him a hug.

"I need your help, indeed your favor," Atal said.

Atal was a young captain in SFU01. He had successfully raided seventy-two operations against the Taliban and ISIS in the last four months in which he had shot and captured 283 militants. Atal was from Paktia where people normally have arranged marriages, the parents choose the girl and the sons accept the choice, the couple normally meet on the third night of their weddings. The girl is married either in Badal/Exchange (the groom's sister shall marry the bride's brother) or against Walwar (cash between USD$6,000-USD$10,000), which the father of the bride takes and spends on buying gold, furniture and kitchen appliances for his daughter. Some fathers also keep most of the money for themself and spends a little for the daughter. This can be called a dowry but it's different from an Indian dowry because in India the groom's family asks from the bride's family, while in Afghan culture its vice versa. The bride is also given Mehar (cash, gold and/or property) by the groom. Mehar is agreed at the time of Nikah (tying the knot), but it is generally only on paper or a verbal promise. The bride never actually receives it because divorce in most parts of Afghanistan, in particular in Paktia, is unheard of and unfortunately, in her married life she doesn't ask for Mehar and the groom normally doesn't give it to her. The fiancé is not allowed to be seen around his in-laws' house until after he gets married, so normally the lucky couples are those who somehow see each other's photos, or they are cousins or close relatives who have seen each other before.

Atal got engaged six months before the fall of Kabul, he did not even see his fiancée's photo. Atal was one of the last men who was evacuated on the last plane on August 31st, he had been one of the officers who was deployed for the HKIA security since the August 20th. Atal, like all other SFU officers and staff, had to leave for America or he would most likely be killed. He had not seen his family for three months and had no chance to see them before his departure. Although, Atal's parents, especially his mother like my Moraka, did not want him to leave them and the country, but they wanted him to survive. They barely convinced Atal's in-laws to let their daughter go with him because nobody knew how long it would take for him to come back to his motherland. Gul Bashra was brought to the Abbey Gate by her and Atal's parents and siblings in the evening of August 30th, and the couple, without any ceremony or wedding, were waved off with tears. Atal did not even have enough time to hug everyone, then the couple walked under the lightning bullets instead of Qur'an which is normally done in Muslim communities. The groom and bride who are considered to belong to each other were not each other's so far. The girl without a bridal dress was carrying only a small bag of two dresses. She kept following this man without even knowing what name she had to call him. Newlywed brides normally don't call their husbands by name, because it is considered disrespectful. They are told by the in-laws by what nickname she has to call her husband.

Atal, like all other SFU's officers was allotted a room in the buildings on the north side of the military runway. He took Gul Bashra to his room, brought her food and water but spent all night in the garden in front of the building, he did not even have the confidence to sleep in the same room as her.

The next evening, after handing over all the gates and the airport he, along with his other colleagues and the U.S forces, left Afghanistan for Doha where they spent one day and then flew to Germany where after the biometric process, they were taken to LSA2 in ROB, which became a Guantanamo Bay for the innocent girl who had never been outside her home and family. In the LSA2 families were divided, males above ten were separated from their families, while all females were accommodated in a separate tent, about 500 people were in each tent, the men and women could only meet for ten - fifteen minutes behind the fence during the day. Atal and Gul Bashra had not started talking yet, but Atal realized that his fiancée had become badly homesick. she was not telling him anything but kept weeping behind the fence, he did his best to motivate her, but she kept crying and begging to him to send her back to her village, otherwise she would die. Indeed, she had been going through severe anxiety and stress, and many people especially the kids who were attached to their fathers got sick, and they lived that way for almost fifty days. The same thing happened in the Indiana camp where my sister, Pashtana and her two-year-old son, Hamad Khan, had to live separately from Omid Shah. Hamad Khan was very attached to his father and got sick and would cry all night without him. In addition to that, hundreds of families in 1600 buildings on Fort Pickett were also living separately, they could only see each other outside their blocks during the day.

"Now, we have been in Fort Pickett for one week, Atal said, "I already told my baba last night that you are also here. He always watched you on television so the first thing he asked me was to pass his greeting and respect to you and then request you to do our official Nikah (marry us). Baba wanted someone like you to do this, and I saw your son with you last night in the DFAC, which means your family is here too. How beautiful it would be if your wife could be the maid of honor and make Gul Bashra up. I will be grateful to you for the rest of my life, please Azad Sahib," he added.

"Oh, wow man, indeed I am not going to do any favor, but you are doing me the big favor, you are giving me a reason to smile and feel good for the first time in the last few months. Thank you very much for choosing me for this great and sacred responsibility. Oh Atal, you made my day, let me give the good news to Spogmai so she can meet Gul Bashra and arrange their part of the job, and you let me do mine, you don't have to do anything but relax and let your elder brother and sister do everything."

After the walk I took shower and gave the good news to Spogmai, I was sure that the news would make her so happy since she had not smiled for almost two months, and she had always been first to volunteer to help others. I went to see Atal in his trailer where he was living with another family of nine. I asked him to bring Gul Bashra to the soccer field where we all would have lunch and plan the event together. The innocent Gul Bashra was meeting Spogmai for the first time, but she kept weeping and hugging her so tight just like she was meeting her own sister after decades. I felt so sorry for her because the only happiness for people, in particular the women, over the last five decades in our war-torn country had always been their weddings. They have so many wishes for their weddings, the friends, especially cousins often start coming to the bride's home a week before the wedding, they plan her dress, make up and tease her about her future husband's name. There is a famous Pashtu proverb, 'she only pretends to be sad leaving her parents' home, but she is celebrating it in her heart.' Culturally, since the bride is leaving her parents, siblings, friends and the home she grew up in, she cries on her wedding day, while naturally she also celebrates the happiness in her heart and may secretly shares her joy with the close friends because getting married is considered one of the sacred and most beautiful chapters of one's life. In Gul Bashra's case it was different, she was not pretending but truly sad, there was no family, no cousins, no friends, no music, no celebration but only her and the man she was marrying. This typical arranged marriage sounded like a deep love marriage for which two lovers leave their homes, families and even country in order to become each other's forever. The twenty-year-old Gul Bashra was just like her name which means 'the flowery soul', her never tweezed thick black eyebrows were making her big hazel eyes looked like the frigate birds' murmuration flying over the Atlantic Ocean.

I asked Atal to pick up his lunchbox, he and I would take our lunch behind the volleyball net so Spogmai could counsel and motivate the innocent scared girl. After their two-hour chat, Gul Bashra looked better. We planed the Nikah for Friday for two reasons. First, Friday is considered a sacred and religious day. Secondly, Spogmai and I needed a day so she could arrange the basic things needed for the bride. On the day of our interview with IRC, Spogmai and I saw a PX store and some shops outside the PX store. Spogmai was worried that we did not even have a penny, and culturally we could not ask Atal for any money. I told Spogmai not to worry, where there is a will, there is a way. I asked Sayed Ahmad Safi to lend me a sum of $400, he had always been buying me cigarettes and medicines from the PX because he knew that I had no money, he loaned me the requested money right away.

Spogmai, the children and I got on the shuttle bus on E Parade Road. It took about ten minutes to reach the PX store called Exchange, on Southeast side of the Pickett village. There were about twenty people waiting in a line to enter to the store for shopping. Only three people were permitted to enter at a time, while the soldiers were exempt from standing in the line. The beautiful iron sheets with white paint were installed on the wooden wall like most American houses, made the building resemble a Hollywood tuck shop. The store did not have enough stuff but did have a lot of soft drinks, some alcohol, chips, chocolates, military boots, gloves and caps, cigarettes, trimmers, hair dye, a small makeup selection, some medicines and a few T-shirts and trousers, but the prices were talking to the sky. We had no other option but to buy chocolate cakes, cookies, makeup, and some chips for the children. There were four female cashiers who seemed to be somehow rude with the refugees especially with the ones who did not speak English, for a while it sounded like they thought that the refugees were excluded from human rights. We also checked with the outside cabin run by a Pakistani Punjabi American old couple with very low-quality stuff but with world class brands prices. For instance, a one-liter low quality Chinese electric kettle was $75.00. In Kabul it was $5-7 and later I found out it was about $20 in Walmart. Spogmai bought some henna, bangles, an Indian suit and some creams and bleaches for the bride. We had done enough shopping and because of Gul Bashra, the children also got the opportunity to grab some chips and chocolate for the first time in few months. We decided to walk instead of going by the bus, the graveled pathway right in the middle of the thick forest between the PX and the clinic made Spogmai and me look younger than we were. The children were enjoying running and playing hide and seek behind the pine trees, and I, after years held Spogmai's hand walking through the small but very romantic forest.

Based on the Islamic law, there shall be at least two adult men witnesses for the Nikah. Atal did not want many people to attend the ceremony, so I only invited the old professor Hatim who had lived with me in the same tent in Germany. We planned to marry the couple at 02:00 pm after the Jumma/Friday prayer. The Jumma prayer used to be prayed in the tent mosque opposite to the mayor's cell. Gul Bashra was already in our trailer for her makeup. Atal wanted his and Gul Bashra's parents also to attend the event online, but there was no internet signal in the village, so we decided to walk down to the green ground on the Southwest side on the road opposite the medical clinic, where no people walk by.

We took the white blankets given by the American Red Cross to be used as rugs, some juice, the cake, Qur'an Karim and some sweets to the green ground under the trees who had been the witness of many military trainings for decades but that day they were witnessing the Afghan Romeo and Juliet exchange of souls.

The skype video call was made, the two hearts were beating fast, the blushes and confusion on their faces were making them the pupils of grade one on their first day at school. A strange and beautiful fragrance was scattered the air which was sending its blessing by dropping the golden, and purple leaves on the couple.

"Mr. Atal Khan son of Mr. Alam Khan, do you accept Ms. Gul Bashra, daughter of Mr. Zabit Gul, who does not have another daughter with this name, as your wife against the raej-ul-waqt Mehar/currently accepted Mehar?"

"Yes, I, Atal Khan, son of Alam Khan do accept Ms. Gul Bashra, daughter of Mr. Zabit Gul who does not have another daughter with this name against the raej-ul-waqt Mehar/currently accepted Mehar."

"Mr. Atal Khan son of Mr. Alam Khan, do you accept Ms. Gul Bashra, daughter of Mr. Zabit Gul, who does not have another daughter with this name as your wife against the raej-ul-waqt Mehar/currently accepted Mehar?"

"Yes, I, Atal Khan, son of Alam Khan do accept Ms. Gul Bashra, daughter of Mr. Zabit Gul who does not have another daughter with this name against the raej-ul-waqt Mehar/currently accepted Mehar."

"Mr. Atal Khan son of Mr. Alam Khan, do you accept Ms. Gul Bashra, daughter of Mr. Zabit Gul, who does not have another daughter with this name as your wife against the raej-ul-waqt Mehar/currently accepted Mehar?"

"Yes, I, Atal Khan, son of Alam Khan do accept Ms. Gul Bashra, daughter of Mr. Zabit Gul who does not have another daughter with this name against the raej-ul-waqt Mehar/currently accepted Mehar."

"Ms. Gul Bashra, daughter of Mr. Zabit Gul, do you accept Mr. Atal Khan, son of Mr. Alam Khan, who does not have another son with this name as your husband?"

"Yes, I, Gul Bashra, daughter of Zabit Gul do accept Mr. Atal Khan, son of Alam Khan who does not have another son with this name as my husband."

Ms. Gul Bashra, daughter of Mr. Zabit Gul, do you accept Mr. Atal Khan, son of Mr. Alam Khan, who does not have another son with this name as your husband?"

Yes, I, Gul Bashra, daughter of Zabit Gul do accept Mr. Atal Khan, son of Alam Khan who does not have another son with this name as my husband."

Ms. Gul Bashra, daughter of Mr. Zabit Gul, do you accept Mr. Atal Khan, son of Mr. Alam Khan, who does not have another son with this name as your husband?"

"Yes, I, Gul Bashra, daughter of Zabit Gul do accept Mr. Atal Khan, son of Alam Khan who does not have another son with this name as my husband."

The beautiful couple was married, the couple and the parents on the Skype video call were weeping, which made us cry too.

"From now onwards, you call Atal, Jan Agha," Spogmai told Gul Bashra.

"I will do my best to give you the most love, care and respect, Jan Agha," Gul Bashra said.

I understood that the sentence was taught to her by Spogmai.

The beautiful sunny morning of October 21 led us to one of the most important parts of our process: the medical. The buses took everyone scheduled for medical all the way through Pickett Theater, but we preferred walking straight down on E Parade Road. It took us about fifteen minutes to reach the administration building of 183rd Regiment of Regional Training Institute, Virginia Army National Guard on the southeast side of the main road. The medical building was at the third bus stop across the intersection. We were scheduled for shots at 10:00 am, but the nurses kept telling us that the list provided to us by marines was wrong, so we got the shots at 4:00 pm by which time the children were hungry since they had been waiting for seven hours. We got DTap, Tdap, IPV, MMR second dose, Hib, Hep B, Varicella second dose, Influenza and Hep-A shots.

I had had plantar fasciitis for few months by then, but it started getting worse. It was generally at its worst right after waking up in the morning with the first step but would get better later in the day. Now it was bad 24/7. Wadan Khan and Shamla both got urinary infections, they had to run to the toilets every one - two hours. So, all three of us went to the clinic the next day, I thought it wouldn't be a tiny clinic like the ones in Germany, surely in America, we would meet specialists, but I was disappointed by seeing the big staff at the big tent hospital. All the medical staff except the translators were very friendly and caring, but unfortunately, they were not well-trained doctors. We were interviewed by some paramedics or nurses at the reception in tent 03 and were sent to the acute diseases center in tent 02, where a single doctor tried to treat all of us. This reminded me of some doctors in Afghanistan with their sign boards saying "Orthopedic, Pediatrist, Cardiologist, Neurosurgeon, General Surgeon and medical specialist." The same doctor who had never heard of Plantar fasciitis prescribed six Ibuprofen for me and some PediaSure for Shamla and Wadan Khan. Since I grew up in a medical family where there were five specialists including my parents, two sisters and a brother-in-law, I knew enough about the basic medical issues and their treatment. I tried asking the doctor to at least get Wadan Khan and Shamla's urinary lab tests, he would for sure prescribe them antibiotic then, but he emphasized that they needed Pediasure only. Most of the translators were not only rude and discriminating but also very weak in English fluency. A woman of about fifty with dark make up and blond hair refused to help a patient in translation by telling her, 'Find yourself a Pashtun translator, I don't speak Pakistani.'

I was shocked how big companies had hired her and others like her who don't speak even very basic English, but I soon found out that their fluency test was taken over an audio phone call where of course the friends or family members passed the tests for them, and they were hired with salaries of USD$10,000 - USD$16,000 a month. Similarly, most of the medical staff seemed to be retired or jobless nurses who were hired by the contractor.

Spogmai had given me a haircut two days before we left Germany with the trimmer Capt. Wiener had given us. The trimmer was broken by a friend who had borrowed it the next day, and the only available trimmer was the one Said Ahmad Safi bought me from PX. It was only good enough for short beards, not hair. We had been looking for a trimmer when Mr. Safi saw a board that said, 'Ibrahim Barbering Services,' in front of the next trailer. He gave me the good news and I got seated in the open air, Ibrahim was charging $10 for a haircut. I thought he might had been a barber in one of the SFUs because everyone including the barbers, cooks and cleaners of those units were evacuated. But Ibrahim had never worked anywhere except his own small local hair salon in Juzjan.

"How did you make it to the U.S, man?" I asked.

"Well, it had only been one day since Kabul had collapsed, I was busy doing my job in my shop when a friend who had worked as the cook's helper with a Turkish company in Kabul called and asked me if I wanted to go to Turkey since the Turkish forces were evacuating people to Turkey. I did not even finish the work for the customer whose beard was being trimmed, I told him that I had an emergency and needed to go home. I went home about 10:00 am and asked my wife to get the six children ready we could go to Turkey, my wife was shocked because people like us who hardly make AFN 300-500 (equivalent $3.50-$5.50) a day, can only dream of Turkey. However, I made her, and we left for Kabul with some AFN 3000 in my pocket at about 12:00 am and reached Kabul late night. My friend picked us from the station, and we left directly for the airport, where we were scared of the shooting that went on all night.

"We made it to inside the airport about 5:00 am. I was expecting Turkish forces to take us to Turkey, but all I saw were the English soldiers. We stayed for about three hours in the airport and then got on the plane, we reached to another camp after some seven hours. My friend Mohammedullah and I were very confused and could not ask anyone anything, we were still expecting Turkish soldiers or someone speaking Turkish, but all soldiers there were again the English. We thought that we were taken to an American camp in Turkey. I said to my friend that I didn't know that Turkey was so hot, and he told me that Turkey is not like Afghanistan, it's a very big country, some places are very cold, while some are very hot.

"There were thousands of people, but we were not talking to anyone, we just kept eating the delicious food. After four days in the camp, we were taken to another camp, the flight took all day. The interesting part was that after spending a night, we came to know that we were in Germany and place we had lived in was Qatar not Turkey, and now we are here in America."

"Oh, you are such a lucky man," I said, "Didn't they ask you for any documents?"

"No, they did not ask anything in Kabul, but in Qatar, they asked for our Tazkeras (NICs), which I had only for me and my wife."

"So where are you going in the States?"

"Someone in Germany told me to select North Virginia, so I have chosen the same place," he said.

"Will you be able to afford living in Virginia?"

"Why would I afford anything? America will give me a house, food, education to my children and salaries to all of us for the rest of our lives," he said it very confidently.

I smiled and pretended to agree with him.

"By the way, the soldiers you call English are not English but Americans. English soldiers are different, they are from the country we call England. I left the chair for Mr. Safi.

Three days later, Ibrahim departed for North Virginia.

Fort Pickett was a lot better than the camps in Germany, but we had become like the rose grown in the Arab desert that no soft hand would take us to her face, the illnesses had made their way to our home. I started having a dream that hundreds of wolves keep tearing anything painted with black, red and green. I saw they set fire to a beautiful tall building with an exterior paint of black, red and green. I had to check Ghani Khan's and my clothes to make sure we were not wearing those colors, I then took a deep breath of thanking God that we were not wearing those patterns, yet we keep running. Abruptly, I realized that the wolves led by a big black dog were chasing us, I heard the big black dog asked the wolves in a familiar language to attack the little Ghani Khan because he had got black hair, red cheeks and green eyes. We kept running but felt that they were too close and would attack my Ghani Khan, I scream, and then understood that it was just a bad dream. I was sweating, thanked God that it was a dream and kissed Ghani Kha who has been sharing my bed since he was only six months old.

The next day, I had a migraine, body ache and was vomiting all day, but it did not end there. I kept having the same bad dream every night, and had been upset with headache, fever and an ulcer. Additionally, I started losing my temper, I did not want to give yet more tension to Spogmai, so I did not tell her about my condition, but she noticed a frequent change in my mood. Life had begun to cruise us more around the old Asian schools' examination halls, where the students were expected to pass all tests but were not provided enough blank papers, or a government places emphasis on education and graduates hundreds of thousands of students every year but in the government and private job markets they require years of experience, otherwise home is the best place for them. We were in America, where we were breathing the air free from dust, smoke and chemicals of explosives, where world's best facilities are available especially in the medical sector, so I was not expecting any long-lasting health issues.

Wadan Khan who is sensitive beyond his years started asking me questions to which I did not have answers. For instance, his big concerns were if I would find a fair job with which I can send him and his siblings to a good school, would we live in sound home? Would I be able to make sure his grandparents, uncles and aunts are safe? Would he ever see them again or see his country again?

I realized that my little buddy had understood that his dad was going through a tough time, fighting within himself. So, the innocent soul started getting sicker, his abdominal pain made him vomit even looking at food, I had to massage his belly all night so he could at least sleep for an hour or two, but it wasn't working. His pain made me forget my own condition, I got him in Barlas Khan's stroller and ran towards the clinic on the E Parade Road. It was freezing cold that day and I had him wearing warm jackets, but I myself forgot to wear shoes and had put on shower slippers. On our way to clinic, one broke but I still kept pushing the stroller on the frozen road in my bare feet. Unfortunately, the doctors were not able to diagnose his problem, neither there was an ultrasound machine, which of course was available even in very small private clinics in Kabul. I asked them to at least get him some analgesic since I was sure it wasn't his appendix because he had felt like this since our early days in Germany, and an appendix problem doesn't last for months. They gave him some analgesic, which did work and asked us to see another doctor in the afternoon. After examining Wadan Khan, Dr. Chee diagnosed him with an ulcer, which is normally caused by deep stress at his age. He then asked me to see Capt. Tricia Booker, a mental health counselor. It took four days to find a time to see Capt. Booker.

There were two brown desks facing each other, there was baseball bat with a red rubber chain on the first table on the right, which attracted Wadan Khan, who told me, 'Wow, baba, a baseball bat." Tricia who had just taken a seat on her black rocking chair under the window smiled at Wadan Khan. I understood that she had found him to be a good boy who would not try to attack her with the baseball bat, of course he wouldn't. Wadan Khan took a seat on the other side of the table, while I sat at the head of the table between the two. Before she began, I had found the opportunity to cash in for myself as well. The meeting started with providing a bottle of water for each of us. The meeting which was supposed to last for about thirty minutes only, lasted three hours. I did not expect a therapist to get emotional because their job is to mentally support their patients, but our story made her cry. She was surprised that how people who had been through so much could be so confident and eloquent. At the end of day, Wadan Khan was found to be stressed beyond his age, because looking at me was making him depressed, which caused him to have an ulcer. He was recommended back to Dr. Chee again, who provided us with a six-page questionnaire to fill in for him and prescribed him 25mg sertraline daily for two weeks. In order to lessen his abdominal pain, we were advised to have him drink honey and lemon in warm water.

Our unwanted friendship with the clinic had become like a piece of sweet that gets stuck in the throat which can neither be swallowed nor taken out. Shamla and Ghani Khan started getting scared and screaming in dreams, they also stopped eating and started vomiting. Shamla loudly screamed at about 3:00 am and tried to run while the other bed above her stopped her by hitting her head. I kept hugging her and tried to wake her up, but it took quite a while that she understood that she was in her dad's lap. This page of the painful journey was the hardest one, only a father can feel when his child one after the other starts fighting with severe pains. The evil eye had caught my red Kabuli apples, they begun to lose weight and were pale. I was tired with God's tests; my innocent children did not have stamina to fight with destiny anymore. Even the two-year-old Barlas Khan started asking me when we would go back to our home, the poor baby did not know that a storm had destroyed the gardens he used to play in, the beasts from an unknown planet has swallowed his beautiful home, the clouds had stopped raining and the snakes from the deserts had made their way to the towns where babies like him were being stung by taking their fathers from them.

The trailer with no windows lacked oxygen yet we could not keep the door open as soldiers would be at our door in a minute asking us to keep the door closed so the central heating system would keep working automatically. The only person in the family I was happy about was Spogmai, she about whom I always had been worried due to her anxiety had been doing quite well so far, but she also couldn't keep it up. The weather in Blackstone was just like big powers' politics, it would be freezing cold one day, while very warm the next day. The warm day of November 07 turned to a freezing cold night, at about 3:00 am I was busy reducing Ghani's high fever with a wet towel on his forehead, when raindrops started hitting the trailer. I love rain, so I opened the door halfway. I was sure that no soldier would come and find me with an open door while I stood and tried to enjoy God's blessings. Then a scream pulled me back to Spogmai's bed, she was very scared and breathless. I tried to hug and calm her, while she was crying. She had seen an unknown creature, probably a soul, I tried telling her that it was an anxiety attack, but it is always hard to tell who suffers anxiety and trauma that they have had an attack. She kept emphasizing that she had seen the soul or jinn. It was about one foot tall, wearing white dress, with big black squared eyes and long hands with long nails right next to her feet. Spogmai was very sure that the soul was there to ask her to leave the trailer, she told me that 'it did not want us to live there, it gave us the messages by making me and the children sick, but we did not care or hear the message and finally it appeared. We need to move to another trailer, or she will kill my children'.

Spogmai did not know that the marines had put up a big notice that changing the living section was impossible, I understood that the stress and untold story of her pain had finally filled the glass to the top and now it started flowing out. The stress had attacked her nerves and mind badly. I kept trying to help her, she had moved her bed to the opposite end of the section where Wadan Khan, Ghani Khan and I used to sleep, now we six people had to sleep on three beds, two beds on each side and one mattress on the floor in the middle because except for the two-year-old Barlas Khan they all used to get scared at night. So, I had to keep staying awake all night, because the anxiety had badly affected Spogmai's mind and nerves.

I had found a way of taking care of the children with making them eat, I became their chef by making them sandwiches from the food we were given. The boiled eggs, tomatoes and cucumber, mayonnaise and ketchup were good enough with the milky toasts for delicious sandwiches, and of course grilled beef, chicken legs or wings, and sausage were even better with the mayonnaise, ketchup, salad and dressing for lunch and dinner sandwiches. Unfortunately, this also had to be stopped. My sore throat kicked me to bed like Mohammed Ali Keli' Phantom Punch on Sonny Liston in the ring. Within 24 hours I couldn't swallow even my own spit let alone drink water or eat. I kept going to the clinic every day for six days, but all I was receiving were some candies and 25mg Azithromycin, although, I kept telling the doctors that our antibodies requires at least 500mg antibiotic, because we had been given high doses all our lives. They were doing what they believed to be right. My condition worsened, I could not breath while laying or sleeping straight on my back, I felt that kind a knife was cutting my throat while talking, so I started typing on my cell phone anything I wanted to tell or ask Spogmai. I finally told Spogmai that I was feeling a big piece of flesh on my tongue, which when I lay down falls to the trach tube and makes me unable to breath. She started crying when what she saw inside my mouth, she did not tell me what she was thinking but I understood that she was scared that I could have throat cancer. She made a video of my swollen mouth and throat and tried send it to Mallani and Agha Jan who she thought could easily diagnose it, but our bad luck, that night there was no internet signal even around the clinic where the network used to be very fast always. We spent the night looking at each other with hundreds of questions on our minds. The next morning when I had finally fallen asleep, Spogmai made it to the clinic area, and she got the opportunity to talk to Mallani and Agha Jan, who of course were very worried about me. We never wanted them to know about our issues because they were thousands of miles away and could do nothing but worry. This time, we had no other choice since the doctors at the clinic had no clue what was wrong with me. Fortunately, Mallani and Agha Jan diagnosed the issue as Uvulitis the most painful throat problem, and prescribed a heavy dose IV antibiotic, which was not available at the clinic. Spogmai had also found it on google. When Spogmai showed the video to some doctors at the clinic they got scared as well, and finally Dr. Alia Ibrahim a very sweet doctor listened to us and accepted the prescription but replaced the IV with capsules, which took about ten more days to bring me back to the normal life.

I was going through the worst health condition when Ghani Khan started vomiting and crying of abdominal pain. We were very scared since there wasn't even decent medical facilities on the camp. They would ask everyone for the thorough checkup and treatment at their final destination after resettlement. I took him to tent 03, which was the reception, the first portion of the tent was made the waiting hall with twenty-one chairs and, there were nineteen people waiting on those chairs before us. The translator wrote twenty on the back side of the reference and questionnaire form. After waiting for about one hour, we were called to the second portion of the tent where six nurses three on each table were checking patients' blood pressure, oxygen saturation and asking their issues so they could refer them to the relevant tent. Ghani Khan was referred to pediatrics in tent 04, where there were eight chairs four on each side, and a registration desk with the weighing machine and a thermometer. One of the two nurses took Ghani's form and asked us to go to bed 06, where Dr. Alia Ibrahim who became like a family doctor saw Ghani and called the lab for his blood test. They collected the poor boy's blood sample in four attempts because they could not find his veins. We went to collect Ghani's reports after three days, but the lab had lost his blood sample while his condition had got worse, and he could not even walk but had to give them the blood sample all over again and then wait for another three days to get the result and start treatment. I had already told them that his skin and eyes had turned yellow, and that he had clearly jaundice or hepatitis. I told them he needed glucose until we got the lab result, but they did not do that.

After seeing Ghani, Dr. Alia told me that she wanted to see my other three children too. The next day a medical team of four people led by Sadia Khan from the Public Health department knocked our trailer door. Sadia Khan told me in confidence that nothing would affect our departure. She like all other medical staff including the nurses in the reception was very kind and friendly, but she moved the earth under my feet when she told me that all four of my children should be taken for a panel test, she said that they wanted to see the other three children were well or not.

I kept asking her if everything was okay with Ghani. She did not tell me about his illness, but she tried to make sure that I wasn't worried; she told me there was nothing seriously wrong with him, but as a father how would I not take any tensions? This was the first time during the week that I totally forgot my own severe throat pain. I didn't tell Spogmai about how the negative thoughts had undermined the castle towers of my mind and pulled me by horses on the boiling hot sands where my mind stopped thinking or knowing anything. I told her that since Dr. Alia had been so kind to us, she just wanted to make sure if the other three children are good and eating well, but I could not close my eyes for a second that night. The lab collected the samples from all four of them and asked us to wait for another four days for the result. The four days passed like four decades, Sara Khan with the team came to the trailer again. All four children had tested positive for Hep A, which was fortunately not a very serious issue, she asked to take all four for another panel test of their liver.

As the group leader I started attending daily meetings led by the Pickett village mayors from the third day of our arrivals at the village, but soon I noticed that whoever wanted to be the leader they were made leaders without any prerequisite. There were people who were not even listened to by a single person but started disrupting the meetings with their irrelevant and personal interests and demands. Capt. Wiener and Lieutenant Girlado were professional enough managers, but Pickett meetings and management were different and every meeting would end with no result. Thus, I had to quit attending the daily Pickett village meeting.

On November 19, we were called to attend an important meeting in Pickett Theater. The van picked up eight people including Khan Agha Mumand, Said Ahmad Safi and Obaidullah Bowra. We arrived at the theater at 10:50 am and the meeting was started at 11:00 am by General Richard, the Taskforce commander of Fort Pickett, Col. Sanshin, Capt. George contracting department heads, James Smith from the Logistics Department, David France from the State Department, Mr. Chris from the Federal Coordination, and Danial, Lisa and Karlina, Betsi and John from KBR, USCIS and the Law dept, IRC and IOM respectively. They began the meeting with the answers to the questions they were asked in the first session a week earlier. Most of the answers were about getting better quality food. General Richard started his speech so politely and pledged his and the U.S. army commitment to take care of the Afghan evacuees well.

The second session questions began with a legal and technical question by Khan Agha Mumand.

Mumand, a dark man from Kunar province looked like a typical Peshawar primary schoolteacher. The struggles of life had made forty-year-old Mumand look well over fifty and it did not surprise me to know that Mr. Mumand only graduated from elementary school and then served as a primary school teacher for years. He was from a family that had been tribal elders for decades in Khas Khunar district. His family were respected by everyone including some senior U.S. officers and journalists. Maj. Jems frequently visited their home every time he was in Afghanistan.

Mumand had been working as a security officer at the USIP (United States Institute for Peace) Afghanistan office for years and had been frequently threatened by the insurgents because of his work for the U.S. government, thus he applied for Special Immigration Visa in 2019. He was approved at the U.S. Embassy Kabul so that he and his ten family members could have Special

Immigration Visas in September 2021, but August 15 changed everything. Mr. Mumand, along with his other fifty Afghan colleagues were evacuated by USIP head office Washington D.C on August 22, 2021.

In the meeting Mr. Mumand asked the panel, in particular David France from the State Department and Mr. Chris the Federal coordinator that their status as holders of the Special Immigration visa be upheld. David France looked a little angry with the question, took a while to think and then answered the question,

> "Well, it's our senate and congress who decided that every evacuee shall be treated equally, and I think it was a great decision, you should have been happy with the decision rather than criticizing it."
>
> "Mr. David, it is not equal treatment at all, according to the law and rule of the law, the amended law is only enforced for the future, it shall not negatively affect the past hearings or decisions, unless it's in their favor, which means every past case can be dealt with the amended law only if the law benefits. So, based on this rule and internationally recognized custom, it would be an equal treatment if the refugees, asylum seekers and parolees had been treated with the privileges an SIV applicant receives. I mean, they should have been brought to our level of privileges in terms of benefits, while the case is vice versa, we were brought to their levels of benefits. We don't receive the benefits the law provides to an SIV applicant, we are not only living in the same camps with all others, but also our cases are delayed and others are departing, the benefits we were supposed to receive according to law, are not being given to us now, the State Department has had our background

including issued visas to us after all the background and medical checks and an interview, yet we have been waiting for months just like all other ineligible evacuees and will get the same few months benefits like they do, so again, don't you think the law is openly violated?"

"Well, this is how it is," Mr. David answered.

After the meeting, a friend of mine Mr. Abdul Rahim who was in camp with his two daughters and their families, his son and daughter-in-law and his wife, looked very angry. I knew no one was satisfied with the question answer session but he seemed to be very disappointed. I asked him the reason.

Since Abdul Rahim had been an audit officer all his life. He noted that Mr. David France said that the Afghan evacuees on Fort Pickett cost them about $5 million a day. He also said that one of the biggest reasons in delaying the resettlement process was that the housing rents were increasing fast.

"They spend $5 million a day, which means $150 millions a month, and there are eight domestic installations hosting the Afghan evacuees, which roughly cost about $1.2 billion a month. And, according to the State Department about 90,000 Afghan evacuees have been successfully brought to the U.S. by Operation Allies Welcome, which on average is 11,250 Afghan families. So, if the $1.2 billion which is only one month's cost is divided by 11,250 families, each family receives $106,666.00, which is good enough for at least two-year housing rent, and the other billions of dollars for other months will be totally saved."

Said Ahmad Safi, who had always been a happy man, grabbed Rahim's hand and told him that we Afghans are very bad at mathematics especially when it's about estimating and counting others money, so forget it and enjoy smoking until Mr. Azad goes and comes back.

I had already planned that after the meeting I would knock on the IRC door. There were about twenty people inside the reception waiting for their turn when I opened the door. A tall young translator wearing a mask gave me a warm welcome and called me by my name. I was given the token to wait for my turn. About fifteen minutes later the same translator came and asked me very politely, in Dari, to follow him. He took me to the second last desk on the right where two young gentleman one the IRC employee and the other a translator greeted me; the first translator requested the two gentlemen to fully cooperate since I was a friend of his. There were ten desks in the room with two - three employees on each desk trying to answer the applicants' questions and inquiries.

I requested them to provide me with the information on my case status. It had been one month since I selected Maryland as our desired state. The main requirement to select a state was to provide U.S. tie contact details in that state. I had many U.S. ties in places like North Virginia, California and New York where I actually wanted to go, but these states were already 'full', so I provided Maj. Michael's contact details for Maryland. He had been in contact with local agencies to check on my case and find me a house, but even after a month and completion of the entire process we had not progressed. Now, I changed my preference to Wisconsin.

After changing the preference, I contacted Maj. Michael who requested his Jewish community to find me a local resettlement agency in Wisconsin. Two days later, Maj. Michael gave me good news and put me on a joint call with the branch director of the agency.

The Struggle Of Four Generations

The sicknesses had planted their roots in our family, so I could not check and respond to the messages regularly or promptly. I noticed that Sanga (whose name has been changed for her safety) had tried to contact me multiple times. She was worried about her security and was living in hiding.

Sanga was once the youngest and most popular civil rights activist; she ran for the lower house in 2004, she made it to the house with a majority. The outspoken Sanga became one of the favorite representatives among people and politicians, so that Former President Hamid Karzai kept inviting her to every important meeting. Sanga, after her term in the lower house, was appointed as an Afghan diplomat to various western countries. where she spent few years. This smart Afghan politician had lost her parents when she was just ten years old, but she did not lose hope and kept studying hard while also looking after her younger siblings. She, like all other Afghans, faced awful times during the civil war in the '90s. Her life changed when she graduated with an undergraduate degree in political science from Kabul University and so did her siblings.

A particular international media outlet became very popular during the Cold War, and Sanga was soon a very popular voice on it after the 9/11 attacks. After her successful assignment to western countries for few years, she was appointed on different high positions.

This Afghan woman is one of the bravest Afghan women I have ever met. The majority of the Afghan MPs became millionaires in the very first year of their presence in the lower house, while Sanga who spent five years in the first term of the democratic government, few years as senior diplomat and many years being a high-ranking official did not even have enough money for her abdominal surgery in India three months before the fall of Kabul.

The Taliban knocked Sanga's door on their sixth day in power but fortunately she had already made it to her sister's house. She was worried for her life, and she contacted me when I was in Kaiserslautern Germany. The only thing I could do for her at that time was pass her information to a friend in State Department, who she already worked with in the past, but lost his contact. He was not only a great friend but also a beautiful soul, he was one of those American diplomats who always worked for peace and Afghanistan's development. He had already asked me to put him in touch his old Afghan partners.

My friend recommended her for the Priority 1 visa right after receiving her information. We all were expecting her evacuation in a few weeks, she had already gone to another city ready for the evacuation, but things went slowly. my friend kept doing all he could, he had already got three families out, but the slowness in the State Department's process made many eligible applicants feel hopeless. It reminded me the Afghan proverb, 'When God gives, he doesn't ask whose son you are.' Tens of thousands who were evacuated by the U.S. forces were not eligible at all, but those who should have been evacuated were living in hiding.

Sanga's message made me more upset. She was hiding in the house of a friend in another city, a city where four female activists were killed the day before she sent me messages. The Taliban had reached the house she was hiding, she had to leave that place too. I didn't have anything for her except telling her to be strong and patient.

Similarly, Abdullah (whose name has been changed for his safety), the only clean judge was also at risk. Abdullah had been the high court judge in different provinces for sixteen years where he was offered millions of dollars by different warlords including Atta Mohmmaed Noor, the governor or Balkh province to skip many court hearings which went against his and his people's interest. Abdullah had sent hundreds of murderers, kidnappers, rapists, robbers, and Taliban and ISIS members to prison, and now they were all free and of course trying to find him. Afghanistan had always been on the most corrupt countries' list. Many in Abdullah's position had made themselves millionaires yet Abdullah's family is still living in a rented mud house in Kabul.

I was still thinking of Sanga, Abdullah and others like them. My stress needed to be released, so I went out of the trailer, and pulled out a cigarette and lighter from my blue cotton pajama pocket. A group of military police, marines and intelligence officers caught my attention, this was at about 03:00 am. I tried to smoke my cigarette and avoid knowing what happened, but this kind of situation naturally grabs one's attention. I lit another cigarette and tried to listen in. Soon I heard a man trying to explain the situation in Dari to the translator, while a woman accused him of something. The MPs told the translator that they needed to talk in the office, so the man was taken in the white 2020 Chevrolet car while the woman with three children were taken in a black Ford truck. The two cars were escorted and followed by two other white Chevrolet Home Security Department cars towards the E-Parade Road. I finished smoking. I had planned to use the washroom before the bed but Jamshid and three of his other roommates were cursing the woman. I offered if I could be of any help.

Kazemi began to explain the dispute, which was actually a case of domestic violence. Anisa the young lady of about twenty-five and the mother of three children was smart, she used to help the other women with translation and hygienic matters they needed from the distribution center in Germany. She and her husband, Faheem, and children were also among the evacuees who were not eligible but had been lucky to make it to the U.S. Although domestic violence is a severe crime in both the Afghan penal code and Sharia Law, it has always been on papers, and responding to the husband has often been considered unethical and shameful act in the Afghan culture and customary law which is practiced by ninety percent of the people in the country.

Whilst in camps in Germany no one explained laws to the Afghan refugees, and no one was punished for violence against women. In the U.S this was different: they had a welcome meeting for every new group upon arrival, and in the meeting, they not only explained the rules and regulations at camp Fort Pickett, but also the general and basic federal laws, rights and responsibilities of people living in the U.S., which included a detailed briefing on domestic violence against anyone including wife, children, and husband. Most of the Afghan men and women were shocked with what they were strictly told to do and not to do. Attending the briefing was compulsory for all members of the family arrived on Fort Pickett, the briefing was translated in both Pashtu and Dari so everyone could understand.

There are pros and cons to giving this legal briefing immediately upon arrival in the USA: of course, it is good for people to know the rules but since no one was brought up with these laws they were open to abuse. Most of the children grew up in tribal areas of Afghanistan where they had never seen a school or modern urban life. They could be seen as rude and undisciplined, so the parents, especially the fathers had to be controlling parents. Some children began to enjoy the privileges of US legal protection they received in the briefing and started being even ruder and misbehaving but the poor illiterate fathers could neither explain anything to the authorities on camp nor control the kids in their traditional manner. The case of women was a bit different, the typical tribal Afghan wives would never knock on the door of law enforcement even if they are badly beaten up, insulted or harassed, because the only thing they had been taught the whole life was that below God, there's a husband, they cannot even look into their husbands' eyes, if they do so, it is a sin, and God will deprive them from entering the heaven. More educated Afghan women, who could read and write, started complaining about their husbands even when they just raised their voices to them, which of course is not a good way to speak to your wife but there should be time to understand and adapt to living in a different territory under different rules and laws.

There were four small families living in the first section in our trailer.

"Anisa used to go out without notifying her husband, and Faheem had tried to prevent her going on walk after dinner, but she did not listen. That evening, she went for a walk for about two hours and had left her breastfeeding baby at home. The baby cried for about one hour, and Fahim failed to calm him, so I believe the baby was hungry. When Anisa got back, they started arguing with each other, and Fahim slapped his wife. Not only did she slap him back but then brought the police. She was asking her husband for a divorce, and both were taken by the police now," Kazemi explained.

The next day Anisa with her three kids were separated from her husband, and their case was restarted all over again to make sure that they would be resettled in two different places.

We were somehow disappointed in the IOM and their promise to move us soon, because they had been telling me for about two weeks that we would move soon. On December 06, at about 09:00 am when I was just about to take Ghani Khan to shower, two marine soldiers with a female translator stopped by my door, they asked me to get my family ready right away as we needed to be moved from Pickett village to another camp. It did not surprise me, since they often asked us to do things at the last minute. I, of course, needed at least four to five hours to get everyone ready and pack all the luggage we had been using for months, and then clean the trailer. Yet, we only took two hours to get all the bags and ourselves ready. We were signed out from the village, and three shuttle buses were ready to take the families from village. Prez, a marine soldier asked me to hold the meal card for a while he left to talk with his boss, it took about thirty minutes and when he came back, he told us to leave the luggage there and come back at 03:00 pm because we were late: a van would take us to our destination. They also apologized for telling us at 09:00 am when they were supposed to let us know a night before.

There was no van so we had to get on the bus with other families who were being moved too. No one knew where they were going, but I was shocked when heard a marine soldier asking the bus driver to take us to the 1600 blocks. After waiting for about an hour, the bus left towards its final destination which took about fifteen minutes to reach to the 1600 buildings' main mayor cell office. The bus stopped by the cell on the E Parade down the clinic and biometric office, two E1s led by a 1st Sergeant entered the bus and welcomed everyone. The sergeant started asking every one's Hummingbird number (a special registration card for Afghan evacuees) and the family members. He asked me if we knew that we were going to live separately. We were not told by the Pickett village cell that where we were going but I only heard a marine soldier telling the driver about the location. I told the sergeant that we would not live separately, he was still trying to convince me when the mayor entered the bus and explained the rules and regulations that applied in 1600 buildings. The women, girls and boys under ten had to live in one building while the men and male children above ten had to live in a separate building. They were not allowed to walk around each other's building, and there was no internet in the building so those wanted to use internet needed to walk by the mayor's cell, no one could stay out of their buildings between 10:00 pm and 05:00 am. It directly reminded me Atal's story. All six of us were sick and on medications, Spogmai was taking the anti-stress and spasm medication could not take care of the four kids all alone, she herself needed a caretaker. I explained our conditions to the mayor and provided him the medical documents that I had in my hands, but the answer was no, he was not sending us either back to the Pickett village or to the 2000 buildings where families were living together.

It really surprised me that the same army camp had different rules for three different spots just one or two miles from each other. I was also thinking that how could the most democratic and pro-humanity country could force families to live separately just because a senior army officer thought so. When I noticed that even after explaining our medical conditions and children's attachment to me did not work, I started arguing based on the U.S. Federal law mandates, which clearly states that "Although, laws, policies and procedures vary by state, the U.S. Federal law mandates that no one has the right to separate or terminate the parental rights but an authorized court." Our discussion and arguing took about one and half hours, and then the very polite and well-mannered officer the 1st Sergeant John Tey, supported my words, he emphasized that I needed to live with my family. He then contacted the Pickett Village office and told them about our return to our original trailer. Sergeant Tey and his two soldiers took our luggage off the truck, and we waited outside in the bitter cold for about one hour. Sergeant Tey and I smoked together, we were still talking about the tragedy that the van arrived and took us back to our trailer. One other family on the bus also disagreed with the rule and asked to be allowed to live together, but they were taken to 1600 buildings anyway.

The next morning, I went to see Maj. Chapman the Pickett Village mayor, to whom I had already explained our medical conditions, he very nicely apologized for what had happened last night and pledged that the rest villagers would go to the 2000 buildings where families remained together. On December 09, at 12:00 pm, we were signed out again, the bus drove all the way on W Parade to building T2439 opposite the IRC building. In this two-story block, the ground floor was already occupied, so we and six other families were taken to the first floor, which had two rooms and a hall. The rooms are already taken by other families, so we and six other families started building the privacy walls with the available tall lockers and beds. The building was much better than all other places we had lived so far, it was very clean with three modern toilets and five showers, we had windows and we could at least sit, unlike the trailers with triple bunkbeds where we could only sleep. We built our privacy walls but the bad thing about the building was the noise the children were making all the time, because the seven families live in the same hall. Similarly, Pickett Theater was on our left where they play children's movies at 06:00 pm every day. Wadan Khan and Shamla enjoyed this very much because they had not watched TV for four months. Furthermore, IRC's office was there next to the theater, and the office for IOM was just two blocks down. The area had a small but beautiful library in building 2638; we were often the only family in there. It did not shock me because Afghans can be said to be either illiterate or no book lovers. Wadan Khan loved the library,

284

where he read the Lion King series, King for a Day, Ninjago, Starla and Zeg, and Paw Patrol on the first day. Additionally, the portion of the same building was used as a tea house, where women were taught handicrafts, cutting, stitching, embroidery, tapestry, and knitting. The third section of the building was day care center for the children, where they were provided with toys and activities.

Most of the entertaining and educational services were provided by Samaritan's Purse International Relief. They also provided three tea houses for men, where they served tea, cookies, and candies, and had cards, carrom boards, chess and American Jenga for entertainment. Brand new jackets, headwear, mittens and shoes for all ages were also donated by SPIR. It did not shock me seeing thousands of people wearing SPIR donated caps from which they had removed the logo, but it did make me ponder how Afghanistan had been a warzone for five decades, why it became the battlefield for the super powers to compete, why Charlie Wilson and Mikhail Gorbachev tried their bull horning there, and why countries like Saudi Arabia, Iran and Pakistan all practiced their version of Islam on my soil. It struck me that while crowds of girls in Jeddah were dancing to Justin Bieber, the Islam Saudi Arabia and Pakistan imposed on Afghans has made them think they need to remove the SPIR logo from their caps, otherwise they will commit a sin, because they believed that the logo looks like a cross which is the symbol of Christianity.

Spogmai had gone to the tea house where she was teaching Afghan women design and embroidery skills. I was speaking live with VOA in a roundtable talk show when Ghani Khan and Barlas Khan emptied fifteen bottles of water in the room. Spogmai and I both entered the room at the same time; we had neither a floor wiper nor a mop, so Spogmai was mopping the floor with a towel, which reminded her the rain in LSA5 when we spent a night removing water from our space.

She said, "Azad, you know what? The anxiety of being here for two months is sometimes relieved when remembering Germany, oh, thank God we are not in Germany anymore, it was terrible, so I am happy to be mopping this water here."

"Ah, Germany, it's so beautiful and Emma lives there," I said.

"Emma? Who is Emma?"

Although, I knew that she would not mind, because who knows me better than her, but I was also sure that she would not like this story either. Nonetheless, I had to tell her. Her response surprised me, and I could say nothing but had to give her a smile.

"I wish you had brought her to the tent so I could have told her that I could not own this man in ten years so could you hope to?"

"You don't own me, what you mean?" I asked her.

"Yes, I don't, the only thing that has ever been on your mind and in your heart was our country. I have never felt a room in your heart for me, you have not only given mine but also your children's ten years to the country. You never saw us during the day, we would be sleeping when you had to leave, and you would return home after we had fallen asleep. So how could I be scared of Emma, you cannot cheat on me, so I am lucky in that case," Spogmai said.

Her big green eyes filled with tears, and she restarted mopping the floor.

"But I have returned all at once, I have been with you guys 24/7 for almost four months now," I grabbed her hand and passed her smile.

The big drops in her gorgeous eyes changed into red blood and fell on my hand like a drop of lava this time.

"No, Azad! I never wanted you this way, not at such a big price, not with a price that takes Afghanistan from me. If I get a chance to live thousands lives, I will only choose and love you, but I never wanted your time at this price. My soil is also my love, I might sometimes have been frustrated at what you were doing. It wasn't about Afghanistan but the politics or work you were doing for people who didn't understand. I wish it didn't happen, Azad! Please say it's not true, it was a nightmare, our country... our county..."

She kept hugging me like an orphan kid who loses her beloved parents. That day, Spogmai cried hard and if God owned a country, I am sure he would have cried too.

Spogmai's sobs took me back to the very first day I ever started thinking about and understanding life. It was a beautiful spring Wednesday afternoon; I was wearing grey shorts with a half sleeve azure blue shirt, and I had a black school bag. I saw the drab olive UAZ 496s jeep at the gate. I was surprised that Agha Jan had come directly home since he always used to leave hospital at 3:00 pm and go directly to his private clinic in Chehalsatoon bazaar where he would see his patients for about four hours and make it home after 8:00 pm. After greeting the driver, I felt kind a strange silence at home. Agha Jan used to water and take care of the fruit trees and flowers when he was at home during the day, but now I did not see him in his gorgeous garden. I entered the house and without putting my school bag down, I went upstairs. I was shocked when for the first time I saw Agha Jan was weeping, I gave him a big a tight hug and tried to find out what happened. Moraka, who was crying too kissed and told me that Lala (my paternal grandpa) had passed away in Lucky Marwat. Agha Jan hadn't seen his father for a few years at this point.

The world was bigger in those days, Agha Jan would barely receive a letter from his father or siblings more than once a year.

The so-called Cold War for the world's two biggest powers had always been the hottest war for Afghans. Millions of Afghans, including Lala, my uncles and aunts had to leave some of their loved ones, homes and properties and live in refugee camps where aid donated to the refugees by international communities was regularly swallowed by the Pakistani and Irani governments.

Agha Jan wiped away his tears and told me, "Everyone has to leave the world one day, but I wish Lala were here in his own home while taking his last breaths. I am one of those millions of unlucky people who could not even see the grave of their parents and loved ones."

The USSR invasion and the two big bull races had made millions of people go door to door, life in Pakistan had never been less than a prison; no Afghan had the right to open a bank account, enroll in public high schools and universities, they were not even allowed to get a sim-card issued in their names, let alone buy cars and other property.

In only thirty-five years, I have seen the four generations of migration in my family, first my grandparents, then my father, me, and now my children had no option but to leave everything back at home in order to protect their lives. I can never forget how Moraka cried for months when she found out that Adey Moraka had passed away destitute during the first era of the Taliban in Kabul. She did not even have enough money to buy a prescription of medication. During the civil war in 1990s, Shah Wali mama had no choice but to flee the country and illegally enter Moscow where he was jailed for about decade. Adey Moraka, who lost her husband when she was only twenty-seven with her youngest son Gull mama, just one month old, brought up the three sons and two daughters alone. She supported the family by washing peoples' clothes and dishes not to make her children rich but make them the best citizens that she could. She was pretty successful; two military officers and two doctors she gifted to the community. Happiness did not last long, and the so-called Cold War took her young and talented doctor son's life by a roadside mine while he was on his way to the hospital to take care of others in Tarinkot Rozgan.

The wounds were not healed when Moraka (her daughter and best friend) and the second son left the country. Adey Moraka had waited her entire remaining life to find out the whereabouts of her son. He was jailed in Moscow, but nobody knew at that time. Ahamd Shah (Shah Wali's son) was her reason to keep living, the child whose father left when he was only one year old. After Adey Moraka's death, Shah Wali's wife had been bringing up her children, earning a living by sewing clothes for thirty years. A seventeen-year-old young wife turned into a fully white-haired woman but did not smile for a single day.

The difference between death and a refugee life in Pakistan was that we were not dead yet. The host country had always behaved like a stepmother. Afghanistan was the victim and paid a heavy price for the Cold War, yet life, civilization and modernism loving people were not even a step behind developed countries. The Kabul university was one of the best universities in the region, the professors, lecturers and instructors had to have a doctorate and master's degrees respectively. All institutions including those for security and defense were full of highly educated women. Miniskirts and shoulder length haircuts was the fashion in Kabul and Paris at the same time. National Radio Television beside the news of ongoing war in the country was providing the best entertainment and educational programs. Thursday nights were made enjoyable with Bollywood and Hollywood Pashtu and Dari dubbed movies; the Pamir, Park, Aryoub, Behzad, Ariana, Barikot and Baharistan were the most prominent cinemas in Kabul that one had to book a ticket a day or two before going to watch a movie especially on Fridays. Charlie Chaplin's "The Kid" was one of the best entertaining silent comedy-drama film among many other Haji Kamran's stage shows comedies and cartoons. Where there were bullets, rockets and blasts, there was also life, civilization, modernism, education and smiles on peoples' faces. This ended in 1992 when the Mujahideen took. The sky changed its color, the smiles were replaced by everlasting cries, screams and grief. The street food stalls and carts started carrying torn and bleeding bodies instead of fresh and dried fruits.

The Taliban era erased this difference by making all women look the same, the blue burqa made it difficult for one to know if it was his wife or sister walking with him unless they spoke. Similarly, most of the men wearing the same black or white turbans, long beard and the same dress also looked the same. The Van Dyke beard changed into untouched hair on men's faces, the blue burqas had replaced the modern and catwalk dresses, the schoolboys' shorts and half sleeve bow shirts, and tie neck puff sleeve shirts of schoolgirls started getting old in bags. 'The Kid' the silent comedy drama film was replaced by the silence across the country, Televisions and radios became safe havens for rats and mice. The five years of drought, poverty, illiteracy and hostage had marred the entire country like woodworm.

I could not stop missing my classmates and friends of Chehalsatoon, yet I made new ones in Qala-e-Wakeel that did not last longer either, as we soon migrated to Pakistan and when I returned, I found nobody left: some had died, and others had left the country. It was half hour before sunset when I entered the Pol-e-Charkhi area, the Kabul I had left a decade ago was totally changed, there was no single building or home that was not hit by rocket, the destroyed roads and buildings told the stories of massacres, tyrannies, murders and tortures of Afghans by non-Afghans and their brokers and top dogs. I thought that the iron birds landing in our country would wipe away the three decades sorrow and grief, and the country once again tried to stand on its own feet; the construction, rehabilitation, education and business got on with it but unfortunately the same iron birds of peace once again brought the old wolves and dogs to protect the flocks of lambs.

Mothers and wives once again started giving tight hugs to their children and husbands before sending them for school and work in the fear of they may not see them again. Hundreds of children and wives became orphans and widows everyday across the country. Schools became more graveyard than educational institutions. Fraud and corruption became the culture, while the iron birds and their ponies in power used to cheer every evening. Afghanistan experienced 9/11 not every day but every hour. Yet, the only nation of such long misfortune did not lose hope, not even the worst war could frighten them; yes, the most beautiful city was being wounded every day, but still, the wide roads, the tall buildings, the shopping malls, the restaurants, the cafeterias, the schools, the universities, the parks, gardens and the millions of students were making Kabul look like the most beautiful city in the world.

On December 17, 2021, at about 5:00 pm Ghani Khan and Shamla entered the trailer with pale faces, they were scared and wanted me to protect them. I asked them if something very bad had happened to them? They could not talk for about five minutes but later told me that they had seen a helicopter flying overhead for the first time in Fort Pickett, all they knew about helicopters was war, killing and wounds. Indeed, this is the story of every single child in Afghanistan. I don't agree with the proverb, 'Children of the east and west smile and laugh the same way,' children in other countries know only toys, cartoons, films, dramas, books, pens and Santa Claus, while children in

Afghanistan know to ask if it was a suicide or a motor bomber, if it was a rocket or RDX and many other unacceptable wartime realities.

Wadan Khan, Shamla and Ghani Khan have made it to a developed country where there are no blasts, no war and no torture, but will they see their friends and classmates ever again or they will be as unlucky as my generation? I was still drowning in my thoughts of what Spogmai's sob had taken me to that she passed me a glass of water. I, as usual, felt like smoking and went outside.

Does it always happen at this point, or I just feel it this way? I asked myself and sadly trashed the last empty packet of the red Marlboro.

The only entertainment I had in the camps was a little time playing cards with Safi, Mumand and Bawra. We used to play cards for few hours at night in tent 01 in the beginning, but ROB soon turned into a cooling machine while we did not have any heating system in tent 01 so Safi arranged a tiny but colorful room in the corner of our tent because the families living at that corner had already left.

Fort Pickett had nice and big open areas including the soccer field behind our trailers, so we used to play cards there but of course, during the day because there was no light at night. This did not last long as nature's seasons changed the green soccer field into brown. The cold and rainy Pickett Village had worn a warm furred plain robe of red and brown, and asked us to get locked down by lying in the triple bunkbeds in the trailers. Of course, there was no place to play cards at night, so we could only entertain ourselves by meeting in the DFAC for about half hour after dinner and take the hot milk tea made by Safi in the electric kettle he bought. Our only entertainment and stress relieving gatherings began once again after we were moved to the 2000 buildings. The other two families living with Safi, Mumand and Bawra departed the camp, and building 2442 remained for the three gentlemen's extended families, a small curtained-off room left by one family was changed to a teahouse; the hot milk tea started warming our chests once again, and the "peace out" calls brought smiles to our faces once again. A friend of Safi used to check and take the photos of the pre-departure list on the notice board every day and share them with all of us via a WhatsApp group. One day when Safi and Mumand had badly been defeated by Bawra and me, we took a tea break and Safi showed us the pre-departure list containing my name. Ah, human nature, nothing makes him happy at all, all of us had been waiting to leave the camp, yet the news of my departure brought a strange silence to the gathering. Not only my friends, but I also got sad at the news. We looked at each other and understood that time had come to separate us. Mumand put the cards in the corner and asked us to go for a walk. PX had been closed for four days during the new year holidays, and all of us had run out of cigarettes.

"I have no idea, why this always happens to me when I badly need it," I said.

"I hope they open the store tomorrow so I can get you some cigarettes tomorrow before you leave, you won't be able to find some right after you move to your new home," said Safi.

The next day after the pre-departure meeting held by IOM in the Pickett theater, Spogmai and I started packing. It was hard to accept that I was once again leaving our chosen extended family; we had only known each other for about four months, but our relationship and attachment was as if we had known each other since childhood. Yes, 'friends in need are friends indeed,' we really needed each other during those hard days to heal each other's stress, trauma and depression. We cried together when we discussed what and who we had left behind. I was not able to help Spogmai with packing, so I just made it to Building 2442 where my mates were waiting for me. We played a single game in order to make the promise that we would play it together soon. Unfortunately, PX did not open on January 04th either, but Mumand had somehow found four cigarettes for me. I did not sleep the entire night and woke Spogmai and the children up at 3:00 am. The ice-frozen road made all of us to hold each other's hands so I could escort them to the bus station in front of the theater. I kept commuting between the building and bus station to take the luggage. The third and last round assured me that I was leaving the golden leaves, the tall trees. the white Christmas snow, and all those people who had helped us: Dr. Alia Ibrahim, 1st Sargent John Tey and many others who had helped us, but yes, I was taking the memories with me. The hardest time was saying goodbye to Said Ahmad Safi, Khan Agha Mumand and Obaidullah Bawra. Fort Pickett had become kind a home, but we had to leave it one day, I reached the bus station with the last bag, Spogmai and the children were already on the bus, and I left Fort Pickett with the last puff of my last cigarette mixed with my breath vapor in the freezing cold air of Fort Pickett. Before I got on the bus, I looked back for the last time, that last puff of freezing breath hung in the air and seemed to wish me well, telling me that the journey did not end there, but was just beginning. I was still reading the message of nature when my cell phone screen blinked with a WhatsApp message from a German number saying "Azad! It's me."

Acknowledgements

First, I would like to express my sincere gratitude to Spogmai, my dearest love and wife for her continuous support while writing this book. This book would never have existed if she did not support and push me to release my anxiety and depression by writing everything down. She knew it would not only give me a release but that it would stand as a source of research and history for the next generations. Indeed, Spogmai is the person who first in 2013 insisted and turned me into a writer. She did not only support me writing this book, but unlike majority of other Afghan female evacuees, she stood by my side and kept telling me that this hard time would end.

Besides my wife, I would like to thank my dearest parents, who lived the hardest lives just to get my siblings and me educated. We were the few ones in hundreds of thousands of Afghan refugees in Abbottabad, Pakistan who got all possible higher education, and that was of course just because of our parents.

My sincere thanks also go to Shakir Azizi, my dearest buddy, without whom this book would never have been possible. He did what a true friend does. Furthermore, I cannot thank Jan enough. My buddy and brother Jan K Staab has always been there when I needed him. He is a man of dignity and honor. Jan always puts his friends ahead of his own needs. The world looks better because people like Jan still live there.

How could I forget William Selber, my American buddy from Kabul? Will and his wife, Charity have always supported me at every point during the journey of pain and hope. Moreover, Dr.

Shaima Sule, a woman who has been elder sister to Spogmai and me, a grandma to my children, and a genuine motivation to all of us during the journey of pain and hope.

Last but not least, I sincerely thank my younger siblings and my children who stood beside me in all the hard times we have been through.

Moreover, I would like to express that any income from this book will be donated to needy families.

References

Amin Saikal, Kirill Nourzhanov, Raven Farhadi. (2006). *Modern Afghanistan: A History of Struggle and Survival*. London: I. B. Tauris.

architecture, O. (2017, February 14). *Asia Historical Architecture*. Retrieved from orientalarchitecture: www.orientalarchitecture. com

Dalrymple, W. (2013). Return of a King. In W. Dalrymple, *The Battle for Afghanistan* (pp. 355-356, 378). New York: Alfred A. Knopf.

Dupree, N. H. (1981). Revolutionary Rhetoric and Afghan Women. *Revolutionary Rhetoric and Afghan Women*, 8.

Ebtikar, M. (2021, August 14). *Long Form*. Retrieved from Ajam Media Collective: https://ajammc.com/2021/08/16/ rabia-balkhi-afghanistan-poet/

Ghubar, M. G. (1997). *The History of Afghanistan*. Kabul: Nuhzat Publisher.

GPSMYCITY. (2014, July 12). *Shah-Do Shamshira Mosque, Kabul*. Retrieved from GPSMYCITY: www.gpsmycity.com

Guard, V. N. (2022, January 14). *History of Army National Guard Maneuver Training Center Fort Pickett*. Retrieved from Virginia National Guard: The Commonwealth's Guardian: www.va.ng.mil

History, M. (2013, November 04). *Malalai of Miawand*. Retrieved from Military History: www.military-history.fandom.com

Ketabkhana.com. (2916, October 12). *Ayesha Durrani Afghanistan*. Retrieved from rumibalkhi: www.rumibalkhi.com/category/ayesha-durani/

Marsden, P. (1998). War, religion and new order in Afghanistan. In P. Marsden, *The Taliban* (pp. 88-101). London: Zed Books Ltd.

Mayanaam. (2019, February 07). *'Words By Me' By Ayesha Durrani*. Retrieved from Mayanam.wordpress: www.mayanaam.wordpress.com

Military. (2014, April 06). *Bala_Hissar*. Retrieved from Military History: www.military-history.fandom.com

Paliwal, A. (2017, October 29). *Murder of a President*. Retrieved from Quartz India: www.qz.com

Salomon, R. (1998). A guied to the study of inscriptions in Sanskrit, Prakrit and other Indo-Aryan languages. In R. Salomon, *Indian Epigraphy* (p. 153). New York: Oxford University Press.

Security, G. (2022, January 07). *Afghanistan - Kabul*. Retrieved from Global Security: www.globalsecuirty.org

Security, G. (2022, January 07). *Camp Phoenix*. Retrieved from Global Security : www.globalseurity.org

Security, G. (2022, January 07). *Rhein Ordnance Barraks, Germany*. Retrieved from Global Security: www.globalsecurity.com

UNESCO, P. D. (2019, February 11). *Afghanistan, Bagh-e-Babur*. Retrieved from UNESCO: www.whc.unesco.org

Vogelsang, W. (2001). The Afghans. In W. Vogelsang, *The Afghans* (p. 186). New Jersey: John Wiley and Sons Ltd.

Wueschner, D. S. (2012, March 16). *The History of Ramstein Air Base*. Retrieved from Kaiserslautern American: www.kaiserslauternamerican.com

About the author

Najib Azad is one of the many Afghan evacuees recently resettled in the United States. He lives with his wife and four young children.

Azad is a well-known face to those following Afghanistan in the news: he was the spokesman for Mohammed Ashraf Ghani, the former Afghan president, and a senior political and legal advisor to NAMSA/NATO in Afghanistan. He has also been a political, legal and social analyst, commentator and expert for various news organizations including VOA, BBC, Al-Jazeera, DW, India Times, WION, DW, Radio Liberty, and others.

He holds a BBA, LL. B-LAW (J.D), MBA, and MA degrees and is the author of the upcoming book Treason: The Engineered Collapse of the Republic of Afghanistan, a documentary of key logistical factors that accounted for the takeover by the Taliban in 2021. Azad has written hundreds of political, legal, cultural, and historical columns and articles and was a founding member of the humanitarian organization, Focus Welfare Organization, which provides food, clothes, and shelter to thousands of Afghans in need.

To sign up for his mailing list and receive updates including notes on current events, and upcoming book releases, please go to www.najibazad.com

Made in United States
North Haven, CT
24 July 2023

39467768R00165